Two week loan

Please return on or before the last date stamped below.
Charges are made for late return.

ECONOMY TERRITORY IDENTITY

Politics of West European Peripheries

Stein Rokkan
Derek W Urwin

Sponsored by the European Consortium for Political Research/ECPR

SAGE Publications London Beverly Hills New Delhi

SAGE Publications Ltd
28 Banner Street
London EC1Y 8QE

SAGE Publications Inc
275 South Beverly Drive
Beverly Hills, California 90212

SAGE Publications India Pvt Ltd
C-236 Defence Colony
New Delhi 110 024

British Library Cataloguing in Publication Data
Rokkan, Stein
Economy, territory, identity.
1. Ethnic groups — Political activity
2. Ethnology — Europe
I. Title II. Urwin, Derek W.
302'.2'094 JF1061

ISBN 0-8039-9760-4
ISBN 0-8039-9761-2 PBK

Library of Congress Catalog Card Number 83-042837

First Printing

Printed in Great Britain by J.W. Arrowsmith Ltd, Bristol

Contents

Preface i

1. Peripheries and Centres:
   Some Preliminary Considerations 1

2. The Territorial Structuring of Western Europe 19

3. The Survival of Distinctiveness:
   Sources of Peripheral Identity 66

4. The Politicization of Peripheral Predicaments 118

5. The Central Response:
   Policies of Accommodation 166

Notes 193

References 201

Subject Index 211

About the Authors 218

SAGE Modern Politics Series
sponsored by the ECPR

1
Interorganizational Policy Making
Limits to Coordination and Central Control
edited by Kenneth Hanf and Fritz W Scharpf (1978)

2
Democracy, Consensus and Social Contract
edited by Pierre Birnbaum, Jack Lively
and Geraint Parry (1978)

3
Power, Capabilities, Interdependence
Problems in the Study of International Influence
edited by Kjell Goldmann and Gunnar Sjöstedt (1979)

4
Models of Political Economy
edited by Paul Whiteley (1980)

5
Policy Analysis and Policy Innovation
Patterns, Problems and Potentials
edited by Peter R Baehr and Björn Wittrock (1981)

6
The Withering Away of the State?
Party and State under Communism
edited by Leslie Holmes (1981)

7
Patterns of Corporatist Policy-Making
edited by Gerhard Lehmbruch and Philippe Schmitter (1982)

other books sponsored by the ECPR

Challenge to Governance
Studies in Overloaded Polities
edited by Richard Rose (1980)

Balancing the Books
Financial Problems of Local Government
in West Europe
by Kenneth Newton (1980)

The Local Fiscal Crisis in Western Europe
Myths and Realities
edited by L J Sharpe (1981)

The Impact of Parties
Politics and Policies in Democratic Capitalist States
edited by Francis G Castles (1982)

The Politics of Territorial Identity
Studies in European Regionalism
edited by Stein Rokkan and Derek W Urwin (1982)

Preface

This is a report on the politics of the peripheries of Western Europe. It represents the final product of a research project initiated by the late Stein Rokkan. The project was sponsored by the European Consortium for Political Research, and generously funded by the Volkswagen Foundation and the Norwegian Research Council for Science and the Humanities, to whom we are deeply grateful. It also includes the last work written by Stein Rokkan before his untimely death in 1979. As far as is possible, I have attempted to remain faithful to Stein Rokkan's conceptions and to retain his preliminary drafts: hopefully, the final result is not too far removed from them.

While the volume throughout bears the hallmark of his ideas, it is very much a collaborative production. Three people in particular must be singled out for acknowledgement. Frank Aarebrot of the University of Bergen worked on the project throughout as both collaborator and critic; in particular, the section in Chapter 4 on the aims and strategies of peripheral parties is based upon his work. Pamela Malerba of Yale University served as a highly competent senior and coordinating research assistant; she also assembled the economic data in Chapter 2 and collaborated with Stein Rokkan in writing the section on geoeconomic core-periphery contrasts. Riccardo Petrella of the Commission of the European Community prepared a lengthy manuscript on economic policies towards peripheries, and the relevant analysis in Chapter 5 is based upon his work.

We would also like to acknowledge the written contributions, advice and criticism of all those who participated in the research project: Risto Alapuro, Erik Allardt, Denis Balsom, Jack Brand, Jim Bulpitt, David Campbell, Jan Ulrich Clauss, César Díaz López, Wanda Dressler-Holohan, Jørgen Elklit, André Frognier, Tom Garvin, Christian Gras, Solange Gras, Olafur Grimsson, Hervé Guillorel, Christian Haerpfer, David Handley, Marianne Heiberg, Martin Heisler, James Kellas, Adrian Lee, Jeanine Lothe, Ian McAllister, Tom Mackie, Peter Madgwick, Karl-Johan Miemois, Kerstin Nystrom, Thore Olaussen, Edward Page, Michel Quevit, Colin Rallings, Marie Stenbock, Henry Valen, Jon Wagtskjold. We would also like to thank the many graduate students at the University of Bergen who worked on the project, collecting and cataloguing information. Finally, we would like to thank Astrid Blom and Gillian Chiles for their valuable and necessary secretarial assistance.

Derek W. Urwin
University of Warwick
Coventry, England

1

Peripheries and Centres: Some Preliminary Considerations

A territorial approach to politics, which seemed to disappear from the academic lexicon after 1945 with the seeming discrediting of political geography, acquired a new respectability in academic studies after 1960. Within the space of a decade, the twin concepts of centre and periphery became part of the common vocabulary of political science. However, problems still surround their usage, since neither is a precise technical term. To read the literature is to become quickly aware of the fact that centre and periphery have been employed to refer to both territories and population groups. Moreover, people have used very different criteria in classifying territories or populations as peripheral or central, and there is often disagreement on rank-orderings from one pole of the centre-periphery continuum to the other. Yet despite these difficulties, there does seem to be an underlying dimension that cuts across all the variations in usage. The objective of this chapter is, first, to identify this common element through a review of the meaning of both peripherality and centrality; we shall then attempt to build this discussion into a formal model of territorial politics, which will be employed in subsequent chapters to analyze the territorial structure of Western Europe and its related political activity.

The meaning of peripherality

In geographical terms a 'periphery' may be formally defined as one element in a spatial archetype in which the periphery is subordinate to the authority of the centre. Within this archetype the centre represents the seat of authority, and the periphery those geographical locations at the furthest distance from the centre, but still within the territory controlled from the latter.

Such a definition implicitly attributes specific characteristics to a periphery. More concretely, we can say that a periphery is dependent, with little control over its fate and possessing minimal resources for the defence of its distinctiveness against outside pressures. It is often a conquered territory, as it were a kind of colony, administered by officials who are responsive less to the desires of the periphery than to instructions from a geographically remote centre. It will also tend to have a poorly developed economy, at the extreme either a subsistence economy standing outside the territorial network of economic exchanges and trade, or one that is dependent upon a single commodity that is sold in distant markets, and thus is more easily prey to frequent fluctuations in both demand and prices, over which the periphery itself will have little or no control. Finally, the periphery will also tend to have a marginal culture: without unified and distinctive institutions of its own, its culture will be fragmented and parochial. Though not fully integrated into the overall system of communication and identity that is dominant across the politically defined territory, its ability to resist absorption by the latter remains weak and precarious. These are obviously ideal-type characteristics which may not apply in all particular cases. They do, however, draw attention to the fact that peripherality can exist in three distinctive domains of social life: in politics, in economics, and in culture. But whatever the domain, the essential point is that the periphery depends upon one or more centres, and its situation, its predicament, cannot be understood apart from the latter.

If, however, we consider a periphery only in geographical terms, as an outlying area within the territory controlled by a centre (itself defined as a concrete location in space), then we are referring only to a *horizontal* dimension of peripherality. In other words, we are simply contrasting one area and its total population against another and its population. We may, however, think of this spatial archetype as being determined primarily by people, rather than by territory and distance. In this sense we can define space as the totality of a system of interaction, within which the centre consists of a set of key decision-makers, while the periphery is composed of those sets of participants in this interaction system who have the least influence upon the central group and upon the making of decisions. We may describe this alternative view of space as *vertical peripherality,* where it is possible to compare groups of actors both across and within both centre and periphery. Both horizontal and vertical peripherality must be incorporated in any analysis of centre-periphery structures. We cannot study territorial differences without considering differences within the population of each area, nor can we study elites or decision-makers without looking at their territorial ties.

While it might be possible to avoid at least some terminological confusion by reserving the application of the concepts of centre and periphery to describe only territories, this would not be entirely satisfactory. What is important is the interaction between the two dimensions of peripherality. When we say that one area is peripheral to another, this is not just an abstract matter of geographical location: the peripherality will be expressed concretely in the daily life of the inhabitants of the area, and in the nature of their links with groups in the centre. In short, a physically defined periphery is not an isolated one without a character of its own. It consists of a set of populated sites which offer a variety of opportunities to, and impose a number of constraints upon, their inhabitants. In this sense, a periphery can also be described as an *opportunity structure,* that is, as a space offering several possibilities of action to those people living and working within it. However, the range and the attractiveness of these possibilities are also heavily influenced by factors external to the periphery. The most important of these external factors emanate from the centre; and in their interactions with the latter, some inhabitants of the periphery take a more active part than others.

The key characteristics of peripheries, then, are distance, difference and dependence. A periphery is located at some distance from the dominant centre or centres, and its transactions with the latter are fraught with costs. A periphery is also different from the central areas on one or more scores: while the degree of distinctiveness will vary, being to some extent a function of distances and dependence, there will invariably be some minimum level and sense of separate identity. Finally, a periphery is dependent upon one or more centres in at least one of the three domains of behaviour mentioned earlier: in political decision-making, in cultural standardization, and in economic life. Together, the three characteristics of a periphery can interact to generate uncertainty, ambivalence and division within its population. These people are part of a system, yet are marginal to it. They possess some sense of separate identity, but this is constantly threatened by central agencies. Their awareness of spatial distinctiveness is counteracted by the lack or weakness of established procedures for the defence and control of the boundaries separating them from the outside world.

The degree to which the political, economic and cultural boundaries of a periphery can be penetrated has important consequences for the internal structuring of the peripheral population. Boundaries towards the remainder of the territory controlled from the centre are easily penetrated by at least some of the agencies of the central authorities, while the question of control over those boundaries that are still of some importance may generate conflict within both the elites and the masses of the periphery. We can distinguish three primary types of transactions across boundaries, corresponding to the three domains identified earlier: (1) economic (imports/exports of goods, services, labour, credits, investments, subsidies); (2) cultural (transfers of messages, norms, life styles, ideologies, myths, ritual systems); and (3) political (conflicts over territorial rights, wars, invasions, blockades, alliances and accommodations between elite groups). These three types of transactions constitute the major dimensions of centre-periphery relationships. For each of them we can ask questions about the strength and the distinctiveness of the boundary between periphery and central territory. To ask such questions, in fact, is to probe the meaning of peripherality. We want to know how dependent each sector of the periphery is upon the centre. We want to identify cases of direct dependence. And we want to single out those sectors and groups that offer the most persistent resistance to the removal of the boundaries, and hence to a more thorough integration of the periphery within the territorial system controlled from the centre.

In any such inquiry we have to distinguish between boundary-opening and boundary-strengthening groups or agencies within the periphery. To illustrate what we mean by this distinction, we can refer to the classic study by Daniel Lerner (1958) of village life in

Turkey. Lerner compared the attitudes of the grocer and the chief towards the boundaries of the village. The grocer depended for his living upon an opening up of the boundaries towards the urban centres and the outside world. By contrast, the chief stood for the traditional values of the village, and feared the changes that could result from increased trade and monetarization. The grocer wanted to keep the outward boundaries as open as possible; the chief, to strengthen them. This conflict over boundary control reflected a profound difference in economic stakes. If he lost the contest the grocer, who had exportable skills, could always move to another location, another village, without suffering too much in economic terms. By contrast, the chief, tied to his land and rooted in the local networks of alliances and rights, was bound to the village: he simply could not conceive of moving.

We could construct similar oppositions throughout the peripheries of Europe. Since, however, this is a major theme of subsequent chapters, we can for the moment simply illustrate the point further by considering the case of France. The French Revolution had pitted the landowning nobility and clergy against agents of a variety of territory-wide institutions. In one form or another, this conflict has persisted in France through to the present day. After 1870 the opposition in the Third Republic between the Droite (Right) and the Radical Republicans reflected a conflict over boundary control between the periphery and the central territories: the former asserted local particularism, but the latter monopolized the channels of communication towards the centre. Later still, in the more recent debates in France over decentralization and regionalization, much attention was focused on the power of the peripheral 'notables', who depend so strongly on support within the local networks that there can be little doubt about their loyalty towards the periphery. At the same time, they have acquired a considerable degree of control of the channels of interaction with the central agencies. The notables then, have used their power to preserve their control of the boundaries between centre and periphery.[1] More precisely, they have not necessarily opposed the opening up of economic boundaries as long as they can maintain some control of the cultural and political transactions with the centre. By contrast, the 'fonctionnaire' and the 'cadre' represent an alternative strategy in the control of boundaries: increasing centre-periphery integration through the spread of public and private bureaucracies. Their primary stakes are in the continued expansion of the territory-wide systems that offer opportunities for promotion and other benefits. Finally, there is a third group in France which has advocated an increasing closure of boundaries. These are typically teachers, journalists and publicists who have invested much time and energy in acquiring a fuller command of the artefacts and symbols of the periphery's cultural heritage, and who wish both to maximize distinctiveness and to profit from it.

This cursory glance at France suggests the persistence over time of problems associated with peripheral boundaries. Since these are themes to which we shall return in later chapters, it will suffice for the moment to conclude that, while peripheries have poorly defined boundaries, the degree to which these can be penetrated will vary according to circumstances and according to the character of the transaction involved. Our suggestion that there are three major types of transaction — political, economic and cultural — implies that we might also fruitfully distinguish between economically, culturally and politically distinctive peripheries. In each case the decisive criterion would be the penetrability of the boundary. Since, however, peripheries depend upon centres, we must also review the meaning of centrality before we can consider how we might construct a typology of centre-periphery structures.

Centres and centrality

Harold Innis (1951: 92-131) once described centre-building as temporal imperialism: you privilege one site over others by investing so much effort in just this one location that it becomes progressively more difficult to conceive of an alternative contender. The reasons for the original choice may have been utterly arbitrary, but once a number of arenas have been established and monuments built in the one site, the costs of founding another prove too high. Centres, then, can be minimally defined as privileged locations within a territory.

A few simple questions can set us on the road towards identification. Where within the territory do the holders of key resources most frequently meet for negotiations and decision-making? Where do they convene for ceremonies that affirm the integral nature of the territory and the distinctive identity of its population? Where have they built monuments that symbolize this identity? The location of major military-administrative, economic and cultural institutions gives the first and most obvious clue to the identification of territorial centres. A high concentration of such institutions in all three arenas in one small area identifies what can be described as a *monocephalic* structure: all resource-holders within a territory tend to congregate within short distances of each other, and consequently to share a variety of facilities. By contrast, a marked geographical dispersion of the different types of arenas across a very wide area indicates a *polycephalic* structure — a spatial segmentation of different types of resource-holders, and a chain of distinctive centres, each with its own profile of elite groups.

Centres, however, can also be identified by checking what people do, locality by locality: how they make their living, and the networks of cooperative activity in which they participate. We have already suggested that a centre is one element in a spatial system of authority and subordination. In terms of human activity, an essential part of the control implied in this definition is the ability to tell others what to do. In this respect a centre can also be defined as that location within a territorial system that possesses the largest concentration of the economically active population who are engaged in the processing and communication of information and instructions over long distances. Another way of saying the same thing is that the centre controls a disproportionately greater share of the total communication flow in the system than any alternative location.

What we are saying, in other words, is that a significant proportion of the centre's population would be employed in the tertiary sector of the economy. In fact, this traditional threefold classification of economic sectors does express an underlying rank-ordering of the territorial reach of different types of economic activity. The products of the primary sector are often consumed within short distances of their origin. Where they are not, where the primary sector engages in long-distance trade, it helps to increase the size of the tertiary sector: one necessary consequence is an increase in the number of middlemen in the distribution and transportation networks. Similarly with the secondary sector. As soon as the commodities manufactured by the secondary sector begin to travel greater distances, this increase in scale tends to stimulate the growth of the tertiary sector, for exactly the same reasons as with the primary sector. However, it is important to note that the growth of the various sectors need not occur within the same location. We find again and again that secondary sector activities can be spatially separated from centres of tertiary activity. There can, moreover, be important variations across territorial systems in the degree of overlap between the two sectors, and the indicators of such overlap are important in the comparative study of the overall structure of territories.[2]

Clearly, however, severe problems can arise with such crude groupings, especially with regard to the tertiary sector. While official employment statistics lend themselves easily to a classification by these three sectors, for the study of centre profiles the tertiary is clearly too heterogeneous. It covers highly privatized activities and services as well as those promoting pronouncedly long-distance communication; and the former do not form any necessary component of centrality. It is for this reason that Gottman (1971) proposed that the tertiary sector should be disaggregated in order to identify centres by the proportion of the economically active population engaged in the processing of information over long distances. Such a 'new' quaternary sector, covering all the agencies responsible for the registration, handling and diffusion of decisions, orders, instructions and information across a wide territory, is a more cogent indicator of centrality. Within Western Europe France, for example, is illustrative of a high degree of concentration, with an extraordinary clustering of such agencies and activities in Paris and the Île de France (Noin, 1976; Pumain and Saint Julien, 1976). By contrast, there is a much more territorially differentiated pattern of distribution in West Germany and Switzerland between typically industrial cities and typically tertiary-quaternary ones (Juillard and Nonn, 1976; Urwin, 1982a).

Where there is a concentration of both secondary and tertiary-quaternary activities in one location, this will tend to be reflected in a greater gap in population size between that location and the next site in rank within the territory. The size of cities, in other words, can be used as a simple indicator of the degree of centralization. While we are not able to review here all the measures that are available for utilizing size in this way, we ought to refer to at least one easily calculated method for measuring the degree of centralization of a territorial structure. This is the rank-size step, a method that is widely employed by geographers. The most satisfactory technique for using the rank-size step is the log-normal model (Zipf, 1949; also Gibbs, 1961; Berry and Horton, 1970). This model requires that in any collective series the descending population size of the units conforms to the sequence 1, $\frac{1}{2}$, $\frac{1}{3}$, $\frac{1}{4}$, etc. In this approach it is customary to use city size as the indicator of centralization. We can use the French case as an example. Figure

FIGURE 1.1
Rank-size relations for the French conurbations in 1801 and 1968

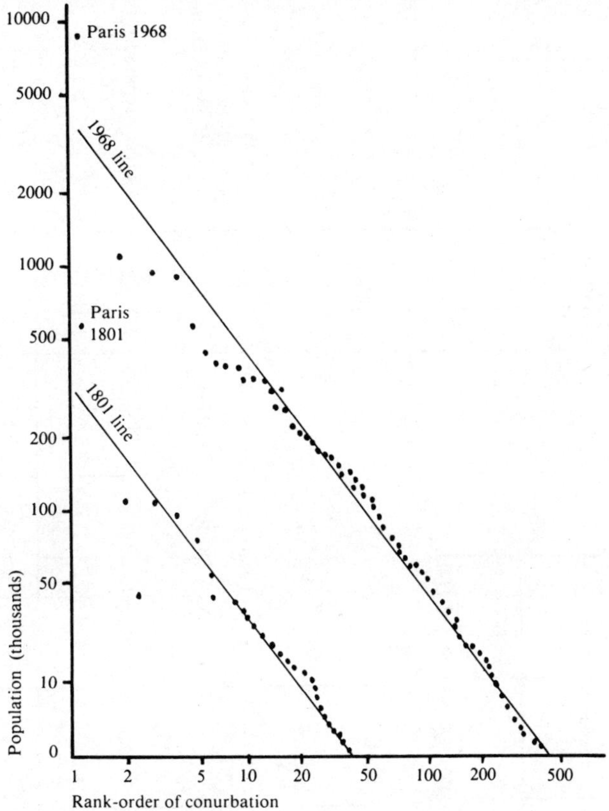

Straight lines indicate log-normal distributions.
Source: Noin (1976: 33).

1.1 shows that Paris was clearly above the log-normal line (the diagonal) in both 1801 and 1968. The diagram, in illustrating the predominance of Paris, demonstrates that France represents a clear case of first-city dominance. Even so, it is worth noting the remarkable extent to which the lower-ranked French cities tend to approximate Zipf's log-normal line. Similar diagrams could be constructed for other European countries. Many of these, for example for the United Kingdom and, most noticeably, Iceland, would also indicate cases of clear first-city predominance: in others, most particularly West Germany, the reverse would be true, with the largest city falling well below the log-normal line.

FIGURE 1.2
Primacy scores for selected territories, 1800-1970

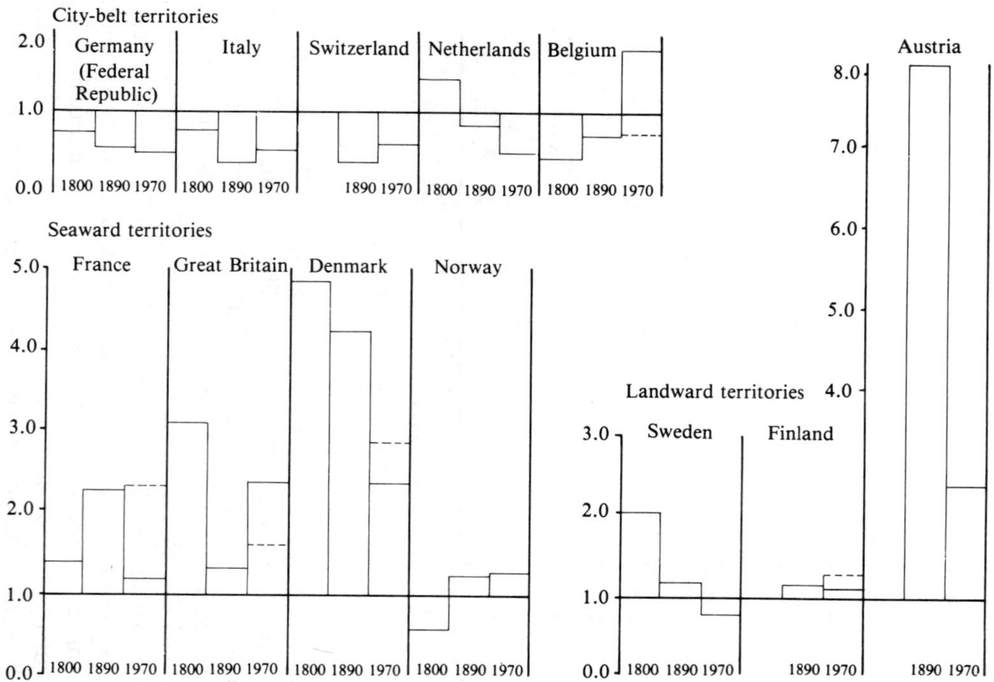

Note: broken lines indicate score based on size of conurbations.

Source: Prepared by Pål Bakka.

A quicker method, and one that can easily illustrate the pattern of changes over time, is simply to compare the population size of the largest city with the summed total of the population of the next three or four largest cities. If the first-city size is larger than that sum, we have a case of primacy; if it is smaller, the distribution is more polycephalic. An illustration of this approach is given in Figure 1.2, where for selected European countries, at various time points since 1800, the population of the largest city is compared with the sum of the next largest four. These graphs of primacy scores confirm that there do exist important differences in territorial structure across Europe. Those for West Germany, Italy and Switzerland indicate the presence of a polycephalic pattern, while France, Britain and Denmark are cases of undisputed first-city dominance.[3] Similarly, Figure 1.2 shows that some of these structures have changed over time. The development of new industries or the rerouting of transport flows can lead to either an increase in primacy or, as perhaps with Sweden and the Netherlands, a decline. By contrast, the heightening of first-city dominance in Belgium and Norway reflects the achievement of independence and the consequent rise of central administrative machineries.

The essential point about these exercises is that they reinforce the argument that territorial centres as sites for the provision of services, the processing of information and the control of transactions over long distances cannot be analyzed in isolation. To study hierarchies of centres is to look at the characteristics of the overall linking networks of communication. In other words, centres must be analyzed at two levels: the centrality of the single site, and the degree of centralization within the network of which this site is part. In Western Europe these networks were historically influenced by economic factors: the historic distribution of central cities was affected by the successive changes in dominant trade routes. The Mediterranean helped originally to orient trade along an east-west axis until the downfall of the Roman Empire and the conquests of Islam. In the next phase, in the early medieval period, the decisive trade routes turned northwards from Italy across the Alps to the North Sea and Baltic, producing a closely-knit string of cities along their whole length. Around the end of the fifteenth century the Alpine routes declined in importance with the rise of sea routes along the western littoral of the continent and across the world oceans. The next three centuries saw the continuous strengthening of dominant centres within territories on either side of the medieval Alpine trade route: London, Paris and Madrid to the west; Vienna, Munich, Berlin and Stockholm to the east. These centres controlled much larger territories and could build up greater military-administrative strength, resources that counted heavily in the next round of network building — the construction of national railway grids after the 1830s. The investments made in the development of rail networks reaffirmed temporal imperialism: the new communication grids strengthened the established structure of centres, freezing it for more than a century.

Take the French case. Figure 1.1 showed the clear primacy of Paris within the French system of cities in 1801. When Baptiste Legrand drew up the first plan for a railway system for France, he proposed a star-shaped network centre upon Paris, with no transversal lines linking other cities independently of the capital.[4] The network generated enormous benefits for Paris. The centre was not only assured privileged access to all other points within the territory: travellers crossing the latter from one province to another were almost invariably obliged to stop over in the capital. Even though several transversal routes were built during the nineteenth century, the radial lines from Paris were privileged, almost without exception, by faster services (Gravier, 1972: 28-9). By contrast, the railway network built in Germany over the same period produced many more cross-connections among middle-level cities (Urwin, 1982a). Prussia was anxious to link the Ruhr and North Sea harbours with Berlin and the eastern provinces, while the Rhineland areas and Bavaria pushed for north-south connections. The result, particularly in western Germany, was a grid much closer to maximal connectivity; only in 'old' Prussia, east of the Elbe, did there emerge a star-shaped pattern similar to that in France. From a political perspective, while this network-building effort in Germany constituted an important element in the overall process of consolidation that led up to the unification of the Second Reich, it also served to restrict the degree of centralization upon Berlin.

Contrasts such as that between France and Germany were further accentuated in the twentieth century during the next phase of infrastructure construction. For example, all French motorways begin in Paris, with no fast connections between any pair of cities that do not cross the capital. By contrast, the West German and, to some extent, the Italian motorway systems come much closer to a complete integration of centres: hardly any pair of cities with a population of over 100,000 is not directly connected (Juillard and Nonn, 1976). Similarly with the development of air traffic: we can, for example, contrast the hegemonic place of London and Paris in the air networks of their respective countries with the situation in West Germany, where Frankfurt, the largest airport, handles only about one-third of the volume of commercial passenger traffic.

Obviously, the cost of such infrastructure building will vary with topographical conditions: historically, at least, we cannot ignore the possible impact of barriers such as mountain ranges or fjords. But political and administrative considerations also count. For example, one noticeable gap in the European system of heavy freight waterways is a Rhône-Rhine canal (Juillard and Nonn, 1976). This has been a much discussed problem case for much of the twentieth century. While the canal would constitute an attractive alternative to the railways over the Alps, its construction has not occurred, not because of topographical or economic drawbacks, but because of political objections. The authorities in Paris have for long been reluctant to invest in a transport system that would move eastern France closer to the Rhineland axis and allow Paris to be bypassed. The differences, apparent in so many ways, between Paris and Alsace (Gras, 1982) have no doubt been a contributory factor, but this reluctance is simply another consequence of the over-centralization so characteristic of French territory-building since Richelieu and Louis XIV.

By contrast, in the coastal and mountainous territories of Europe, topography and the costs of infrastructure development produced a concentration of networks along a few privileged routes around a single centre. In Switzerland we find a concentration of centres along three historically important trade routes across the Alps (Rokkan et al., 1983: Ch. 6). In Norway there emerged both a coastal chain of cities and an inner belt running from Christiana (Oslo) to Trondheim. With the coming of the railways, the position of the Norwegian capital was strengthened. All the main lines began in Oslo, and no two coastal cities of the west were connected by transversals independently of this star-shaped system. In this sense the Norwegian capital was as central as Paris: the difference was that the coastal cities continued to be linked to each other and to the rest of the world by well established sea routes.

These examples have been introduced, somewhat ahead of the substantive analysis, to illustrate the complexity that can arise when the concept of centrality is applied to concrete situations: both centrality itself and the degree of centralization will vary according to the several possible combinations of geographical location, economic developments and political decisions. They serve, moreover, to emphasize the importance both of the control of the communication flow and of the concept of temporal imperialism for the building of infrastructures: the legacy of the past can significantly affect the direction and content of subsequent efforts.

Towards a simple model of centre-periphery relationships

We can now summarize our discussion of peripherality and centrality. The key concepts for centre structures are the endowment of resources, distances, and channels of communication. Typically, a centre controls the bulk of the transactions among the holders of resources across a territory; it tends to be closer than any alternative site to the resource-rich areas within the territory; and it is able to dominate the communication flow through the territorial diffusion of a standard language and through its control of a set of institutions for consultation and direction. By contrast, a periphery controls at best its own resources, tends to be isolated from other regions, and contributes little to the total communication flow within the territory. Let us now take each of these components and attempt to combine them in a possible model of centre-periphery relationships.

Our starting point is illustrated by Figure 1.3, which offers a 'base-line' model for the processes of integration and resistance within large-scale territorial systems of control. The diagram is intended to illustrate the relationship of a periphery (peripheral community) with the three distinct elements of central system-building emphasized earlier: military-administrative, economic and cultural. For each aspect of system-building, the diagram suggests the probable infrastructure base in terms of resources and method of territorial penetration: for example, churches, schools, language and the diffusion of information in the case of cultural system-building. However, the centre-periphery relationship in each element is reciprocal. For each process of centralization there is a corresponding effort of boundary accentuation, of attempting to preserve peripheral distinctiveness: juxtaposing the process of cultural standardization, for instance, is the peripheral concern for maintaining a separate identity.

FIGURE 1.3
An abstract model of processes of interaction and resistance within large-scale territorial systems

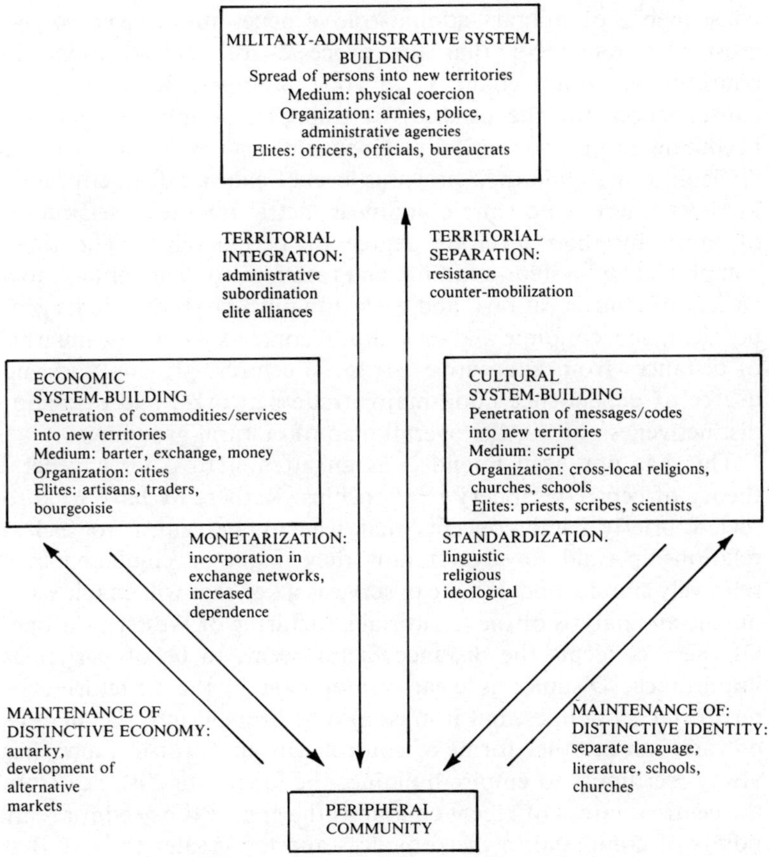

Figure 1.3 might seem unduly complicated, but it is necessary to stress the multidimensionality of the centre-periphery relationship. What is important is that the three sets of relationships (military-administrative, economic and cultural) do not necessarily form a single cluster. A conquered periphery may nevertheless have been able to escape economic dependence on the political centre. Alternatively, cultural standardization may not be an inevitable consequence of military-administrative penetration. Even so, we must also remember that the processes of centralization are continuous, that changes in one component may have consequences for the others: for example, peripheries that are becoming more economically dependent may well find it more difficult to maintain their previous level of cultural distinctiveness. In short, there is no simple unilinear metric for the classification of areas by their level or degree of peripherality. The three components of system-building, and reactions to them, enter into a variety of configurations, and each case must be studied in its geopolitical, geoeconomic and geocultural contexts — that is, in terms of distances from alternative territorial centres, proximity to and degree of dependence upon major trade networks, and degree of distinctiveness within the overall map of cultural groupings.

This has not been intended as an attempt to offer a general theory of centre-periphery relationships. Rather, we have tried to review briefly some concepts that seem to be central to such a relationship, and to suggest how they might be combined in a relatively simple model that can serve as a key that will enable us to pursue an analysis of the territorial structuring of Western Europe. Of these concepts the distance factor seems to be of particular importance. Distance is clearly significant in the structuring of territorial economies, but it must also be brought into the analysis of variation in other forms of control. Distance, for instance, has always set limits to empire-building: the longer the distance from the centre to areas of recent conquest, the greater the need for relay points of command in the provinces and the greater the risk that these will become the nuclei of independent centre formation. Similarly for systems of cultural communication via script, the greater the distance between the core area and the outlying mission field, the greater the likelihood of 'noise' and distortion in the message flow.[5] Distances, therefore, count not only within politically defined territories: they are equally important across territories as indicators of the potential influence of alternative external centres. To link up these different centre-periphery levels, we can use the simple notation employed by Galtung (1971): *C* v. *P* for continent-level polarities, and *c* v. *p* for within-territory polarities.

The distinction is of no little importance when combining geo-economic and geopolitical perspectives within an overall typology of sources of variation across territories. This is the major theme of the following chapter, which seeks first to construct a multi-dimensional grid within which we can plot the variations in the structure of the Western European territories, and then to suggest a possible typology of peripheral predicaments. Such a typology of necessity leads on to questions about the sources of differences in the distinctiveness of peripheral cultures and institutions. Chapter 3 reviews both cases of peripheral success and those that still struggle against processes of centralization: while both cultural and economic factors are incorporated in the analysis, the chapter concentrates upon the history of linguistic standardization within each periphery. A discussion of the conditions for the defence of distinctiveness leads naturally to a comparison of the political expressions of peripheral protest. Chapter 4 takes up the theme of the politicization of peripheral predicaments: the resource potential for mobilization, the catalysts that set it in motion, its relative success or failure, and the alliances and alignments that have been attempted. However, we cannot understand such developments without studying the reactions of the central authorities and organizations to peripheral challenges. The final chapter will review trends in the development of policies of economic aid to peripheral areas as well as the cultural and political options that are available to governments. We shall conclude with a consideration of how the historical roots of the differences between the federalizing and the unitary territories of Western Europe may affect the costs and benefits of changes in decision-making structures, before offering some speculative thoughts about the future of territorial government and about the pros and cons of different solutions.

Clearly, this is a vast task, and one that might be regarded as overly ambitious. However, it was not our intention to present either an all-embracing theory of centre-periphery relationships or a detailed and systematic comparison of cases.[6] Rather, our objective was to adopt an eclectic approach and a simplified analysis that combines three distinctive routes towards the comparison of political systems: the historical political geography of centre-building and boundary demarcation; the political economy of territorial integration or fragmentation; and the political sociology of identity maintenance and mobilization. The extent to which this satellite perspective provides a true picture of the territorial structure of Western European politics will have to wait upon the results of more rigorous single-case or comparative studies.

2

The Territorial Structuring of Western Europe

During the past two decades there has appeared a substantial body of literature that has sought to employ geopolitical and geo-economic perspectives in a plotting of the history of European states. We shall first briefly review this literature and suggest how its perspectives may be utilized within the framework of the model outlined in Chapter 1 in an analysis of European developments. We shall then outline those features of European history that seem to be most salient for the territorial structuring of the continent before combining them in a multidimensional grid of European variations.

Much of the recent macro-historical theorizing about the structure of Europe and the development of the European state system has focused on broad east-west and north-south gradients. A west-east gradient, for example, is inherent in the classic study by Barrington Moore (1966) of the conditions for the development of liberal-democratic or authoritarian regimes. There is an equally strong emphasis on the west-east contrast in the interpretation of the rise of absolutism by Perry Anderson (1974a, 1974b). By contrast, the more economic-oriented studies by Immanuel Wallerstein (1974) and William McNeill (1974) supplement this gradient with a north-south axis. Equally important is the fact that all these efforts at a continent-level mapping of structural contrasts begin at some point in the Middle Ages and focus on the differences that manifested themselves most markedly in the first phase of dynamic commercial capitalism in the sixteenth century.

For the west-east gradient we owe a set of powerful formulations to Perry Anderson. To him the great dividing line north of the Alps followed roughly the course of the River Elbe. Anderson argues that the significant development to the west of this line was a progressive fusion of the communal mode of agricultural production of the Germanic tribes with the urban, slave-oriented economy of the Roman world. By contrast, to the east there was no fusion of distinctive historical forms of economic system, but a protracted conflict between the agricultural economy of the Slavs and the pastoral nomadism of successive waves of invaders from the steppes of inner Asia (Anderson, 1974a: 218). McNeill (1974) develops this perspective in greater depth: the west built up strong networks of cities and was saved from the worst ravages of Asian nomadism; the east developed only weak bourgeoisies, and was exposed for at least a millenium to Asian invasion. McNeill's vision of history, moreover, has a strong technological undertone: he shows how changes in the material possibilities of generating economic surpluses produced changes in the balance between political systems, how innovations in the technology of warfare produced one structure in the west and another in the east, and how changes in the fuel base of the European economies brought about a decisive decline in the Mediterranean centres after 1600 and accentuated the hegemony of a core area of oceanic capitalism in north-western Europe (McNeill, 1974: 96).

These notions are taken a step further by Wallerstein (1974) in his attempt to map the emergence in the sixteenth century of a world economy. Wallerstein combines this north-south axis with the west-east gradient to produce three distinctive regions of Europe: an innovative and increasingly dominant core in the north-west, a stagnating 'semi-periphery' in the south, and a dependent agricultural periphery in the east. This model assigns primacy to the economic developments brought about by the rise of the north-western core: all else — the rise of the bureaucratic nation-state, the Reformation — is analyzed as sets of reactions to the decisive changes in the world economy with the opening up of the oceans during the sixteenth century. However, this focus on the core means that little space is devoted to trying to explain the development of strong military centres, for example Prussia, in the agrarian east. These are accounted for by Anderson (1974b; also Brenner, 1977), who asserts the primacy of the state and its military-administrative apparatus. To Anderson long-distance trade was not so important in the sixteenth century; what really counted was the consolidation of systems of political control across conquered hinterlands.

This cursory summary of several panoramic analyses and their (at times) conflicting conclusions has been introduced for several reasons. In particular, it brings us back to the utility of our model presented in Figure 1.3. The stress there on the multidimensionality of the centre-periphery relationship helps to place the different interpretations by Wallerstein and Anderson in perspective: each of these authors tends to give primacy to a single element of the system-building process. Taken together they suggest that developments in the sixteenth century tended to bring about a freezing of military and, to some extent, cultural boundaries, but an opening of the boundaries that had hindered long-distance trade. The structure of modern Europe was influenced by how these policies of boundary control varied from territory to territory, and also by how they changed over time as external developments impinged on the balance of alliances among resource-holders in each territorial system.

This macro-historical theorizing, moreover, suggests how our model might be applied to a study of European developments. In the first instance, these approaches stress the value and necessity of considering developments (*c* v. *p*) in any one territory in the context of a polarity between centre and periphery at the continent level (*C* v. *P*). Furthermore, the stress on a north-south and an east-west gradient enables the model to be deployed within a geographically determined grid linked to distance: topography, as it were, can be married to typology. Finally, these studies, in stressing the impact of the dawn of capitalism upon structures developed during the Middle Ages, offer us an appropriate time perspective. However, these medieval structures did not arise in a vacuum. Two earlier features of European history ought also to be reviewed. One is the legacy of Rome, the influence of which, as Anderson (1974a) suggests, was extremely deep, not only in the bequeathing of Latin as an elite language for centuries, but also because the structuring of medieval western Europe arose partly out of the disintegration of the western Roman Empire. The other feature is the complex ethnic configurations produced by successive 'Völkerwanderungen'. The disintegration of the Roman Empire and the subsequent attempts at territory-building were obviously affected by these large-scale migrations of ethnically distinctive populations who differed not only in language and custom, but also in ideas of governance, styles of centre-building, and resistance to centralization. We shall begin the discussion of sources of differentiation within Western Europe with a very brief review of this geocultural variable.

The peopling of western Europe

A multitude of waves of migration, conquest and occupation has layered the European landscape since the Early Iron Age. At a minimum we can identify seven important waves: (1) the Celtic expansion; (2) the long series of Roman conquests; (3) the multiple invasions of Germanic tribes into the crumbling western Roman Empire during the fourth and fifth centuries; (4) the eighth-century wave of Arab conquests; (5) the succession of Viking raids and conquests; (6) the westward drift of the Slavs and Finno-Ugric peoples into the territories to the landward side of the Germanic tribes; (7) finally, from the twelfth century, the return expansion eastwards of the Germans, part of the great drive to Christianize the rest of Europe, but accompanied by well-planned efforts to colonize and improve poorly used agricultural land.

These successive waves of conquest and occupation, penetration and retrenchment produced a complex distribution of ethnic and linguistic groupings across western Europe. Using the two topographical gradients discussed earlier, and simplifying in the extreme, we can accommodate this complexity within a rather crude geoethnic map of western Europe. Figure 2.1 distinguishes an east-west gradient of four sets of ethnic groupings: (1) an Atlantic periphery made up of the Celtic and Basque lands and, after the collapse of the Norwegian North Sea empire, also of a Norse fringe; (2) the western coastal plains, the heartland of the early seaward kingdoms of Europe; (3) the central plains, lying between the Meuse-Rhône line and the Elbe, which formed the heartland of the German-Roman Empire; and (4) the periphery extending towards the Asian plains. Each of these segments can in turn be divided into three distinctive layers from north to south: (1) the lands that remained beyond the reach of the Roman Empire;

FIGURE 2.1
A crude geoethnic map of Europe before the high Middle Ages

	Atlantic periphery	Coastal plains	Central plains and alpine territories	Landward marchlands
Beyond the reach of the Roman Empire	Icelanders Faeroese West Norse Celts: Scotland Ireland	East Norse Danes	Swedes	Finns Balts Prussians Poles Lithuanians Moravians Czechs
Territory of the Northern Empire	Celts: Wales Cornwall Brittany	Angles Saxons Frisians Jutes West Franks/Gallo-Romans Normans	Burgundians Saxons Alemannians East Franks Thuringians Bavarians Rhaetians	Hungarians Bavarian settlers Tyroleans
Mediterranean territories	Basques	Occitans Catalans Corsicans Portuguese Castillians	Lombards Italians Sardinians Sicilians	Slovenes Croats Serbs

(2) the imperial territories north of the Alps; and (3) the Mediterranean territories that were most heavily imprinted by Latin institutions and least influenced by Germanic invaders.

While this classification is necesarily tentative and, because it utilizes other, and sometimes later, historical events as criteria for categorization, somewhat unsatisfactory, it does nevertheless serve a useful purpose. What is important is that these territorial distributions of settlement patterns provided the basic ethnic and linguistic infrastructures upon which were built the crucial institutional developments of the Middle Ages — the first steps towards the consolidation of centralized monarchies, the early city leagues, the first consociational structures. Later still, the distributions of ethnic identities and affinities affected both the character and the costs within each political unit of the processes of linguistic standardization which were accelerated by the invention of printing and the consequences of the Reformation.

Roman collapse and the formation of new centres

At its height the Roman Empire maximized the extent and control of communications in all three dimensions of system-building that were identified in Figure 1.3.[1] It controlled a vast network of cities and a trading system around the Mediterranean, and it built up a strong centre for the conquest of more distant areas still at a low level of economic development. Equally important, the Empire became the essential vehicle for the penetration across Europe of a major script religion, Christianity. For a while the three processes reinforced each other, but, significantly, generated separate organizational structures, each with resources of their own. While the western Empire collapsed as a military-administrative structure in the fifth century, the city network survived, as did the Roman church with its tradition of long-distance communication via an alphabetic script, Latin. In other words, while the Empire broke up as a political system of territorial control, much of the economic and cultural infrastructures for long-distance communication remained intact; indeed, they were strengthened after the several centuries of conflict with Islam, the other empire-building religion in the Mediterranean.

The system of states that emerged in Europe between the twelfth and the twentieth centuries can only be understood against the backdrop of the Roman inheritance and the reduction in the range and scope of cross-territorial communications that occurred in the wake of the fall of Rome. Three processes that were a consequence of Roman fragmentation proved to be important. First, military-administrative unity gave way to a process of feudalization, a territorial dispersal of political and economic control. Second, cultural variations were strengthened by a process of vernacularization. And, finally, there was the emergence of new centres at the fringes of the fallen Empire. What proved crucial in the western European case was that these three processes of imperial disintegration moved out of phase with each other. Most importantly, the eventual emergence of a new city network in the heartlands of Europe stopped the process of feudal fragmentation and produced a new and powerful thrust towards establishing an effective long-distance communication flow that could transcend territorial boundaries. By contrast, the strengthening of vernacular cultures and the emergence of strong territorial centres at the edges of the old Empire accelerated the break-up of the latter, consolidating new sets of boundaries and setting the stage for the development of a range of highly distinctive political systems. The disjunction between these processes continued in later centuries: the breakthrough towards merchant capitalism produced a world network of economic transactions and undermined political and cultural boundaries, while on the other hand the emergence of strong states tended to mark off clear boundaries and to accentuate territorial identity and citizenship. This is the great paradox of western European developments, and it is towards the elaboration of this trend and its consequences that much of this chapter is directed.

The rise of feudal structures is a much-discussed theme in comparative history. Within our simple paradigm, however, what matters is the rise of intermediary power-holders who control resources in the primary economy. While a parochialization of economic and political power was widespread in the territories of the old Empire, it was far from being geographically uniform. There were few signs of it in the territories to the north of the old Roman border, as well as considerable variations in the level of agricultural development and in the degree to which areas were exposed to the onslaughts of nomadic raiders and armies. Two factors proved important in the later development of territorial units: differences in the resources that were generated within these agrarian structures, and the strategies adopted by the owners and controllers of land in their dealings with the urban bourgeoisie and the military-bureaucratic agencies of state-building.[2]

Developments were much slower on the cultural front. The Roman Church established itself as the central spiritual authority across the whole of western Europe, and for centuries proved able to maintain its two languages — Greek and Latin — as the dominant standards of elite communication across cultural boundaries. As Goody (1977) has shown in his penetrating analysis of the social consequences of script, there is a fundamental difference between systems of cross-cultural communication based on ideographs and those using an alphabet. In China it was possible to keep the literati and gentry integrated across a vast territory which contained a multitude of vernaculars: the ideographs had no direct relation to speech, and could be pronounced in a variety of ways, even though conveying the same message. By contrast, while Greek and Latin for long survived as vehicles of elite communication, the alphabetic script opened up possibilities for the direct expression of vernacular languages. While the latter did flourish in the Middle Ages, the decisive breakthrough came with the invention of printing and the Reformation, which set the stage for the establishment of a variety of linguistic standards in an increasingly fragmented Europe. In permitting the mass reproduction of messages *within* vernacular boundaries, Gutenberg created an essential technology for the building of nations. The Reformation reinforced this process in northern Europe, where the break with Rome meant more than matters of theological doctrine. Protestantism strengthened the distinctiveness of each territorial culture by integrating the priesthood into the administrative machinery of the state within the confines of the local language. In terms of the paradigm suggested by Hirschman (1970), the Reformation raised a wall against cultural 'exits' into other territories. This barrier was not only an important strategy in legitimizing the territorial state; in the long run it was also a crucial step forward in preparing people for the use of 'voice' within their system.

Again, however, this process was not uniform. The strongest and most durable territorial systems emerged at the periphery of the old Empire: the heartlands remained fragmented until the nineteenth century. To reach some understanding of this contrast, we have to reason in several steps. The core of the old western Empire was studded with cities linked together in a broad trade route belt from the Mediterranean over the Alps to the Rhine and the Danube. This city belt was also the stronghold of the Roman Church, with a high density of cathedrals, monasteries and ecclesiastical principalities. This density of established centres made it very difficult for any one to emerge as superior to the others: there was no clear geographical core area for the development of a strong territorial system, and there was little space for expansion. By contrast, it proved much easier to establish large territorial systems at the edges of the city-studded territories of the old Empire. Here, emerging centres faced less severe competition, and could more easily achieve control of large areas that lay beyond the reach of the cities of the central trade belt. Such centres and territorial systems emerged first on the coastal plains to the west and north of the imperial heartlands, in France, England, Scandinavia and Spain. A second wave occurred later on the landward side: the Habsburgs with their core in Austria, Sweden and, finally and decisively, Prussia.

The fragmented middle belt of Europe saw endless struggles and efforts of reorganization during the long centuries from the death of Charlemagne, which brought to an end the most important attempt at unification, to the triumph of Bismarck. Its economic strength, moreover, was gradually eroded. While the cities' economic prominence persisted through to the initial stirrings of capitalism, their more limited hinterlands came more and more to be a restriction upon their ability to compete with the greater natural and demographic resources of the larger territorial states once capitalist modes of production became generalized (Habermas, 1976: 258). First, with the failure of the Burgundian effort to build in Lotharingia (the middle territory of the Frankish Empire) a strong state between the French kingdom and the imperial heartlands, the French monarchs gradually took over this buffer zone, which extended from Provence to Flanders. Second, the key cities to the north of the Alpine passes managed to establish a defensive coalition against all-comers, and gradually built up the Swiss Confederation.[3] The Habsburgs made several unsuccessful encroachments into the central city belt: however, their short-lived control of the crucial territories at the mouth of the Rhine did in fact trigger the next successful effort of territorial consolidation, the United Netherlands. Finally, in the wake of the French Revolution, Napoleon moved across the city belt, setting in motion a series of efforts of unification which culminated in the successes of Piedmont and Prussia.

The geopolitical location of peripheries

The great efforts of state-building that took place at the borders of the collapsed Roman Empire most obviously produced a number of subject peripheries at the furthest edge of the continent: these are classified in Figure 2.1 as belonging to the Celtic-Atlantic west and to the landward marchlands. However, they also generated a number of marginal territories lying between the state-building cores. We can call these 'interface peripheries', caught in the crossfire between two or more dominant centres, and never fully integrated by any of them.

First, starting from the North Sea, we can identify several interface peripheries between the French core and the territory of the old Empire: (1) Flanders and Wallonia, straddling the age-old boundary between the Romance and Germanic languages; (2) Luxembourg, a border territory both politically and linguistically, which ultimately survived as an independent territorial system; (3) Lorraine and Alsace, heavily Germanic-speaking but strongly oriented towards French culture and political tradition; (4) the French-speaking Bernese Jura, which passed in 1815 from the control of the Prince-Bishop of Basle to that of the Germanic-speaking canton of Berne; (5) Savoy, once a duchy within the Holy Roman Empire, later the original territory of the dynasty that was to unify Italy, but ceded to France in 1860 as the price for its consent to the formation of an Italian state; (6) the Val d'Aosta, a French-speaking enclave within Italian territory; (7) Nice, a city with strong Italian affinities, but also ceded to France in 1860 by the House of Savoy.

We have not included Occitania, the region of the 'langue d'Oc' language, in this list, since to classify this as an interface periphery would be to stretch that concept beyond recognition. The failure of the state-builders in Toulouse was not parallel to that in Burgundy: Occitania had been part of the western empire from the outset, and only briefly was there an alternative centre challenging for effective control of the territory. Along with other cases — for example, Scotland, Catalonia and Bavaria — Occitania might more appropriately be classified as a 'failed-centre periphery', that is, as a territory that tried to build up its own core structures, but fell victim to more effective drives of incorporation launched by other centres.

An examination of the imperial heartlands enables us to identify a further type of periphery. At their height these included large areas of Italy and the Germanic lands. The standard literary language in the latter was Hochdeutsch; that south of the Alps was, increasingly, the Florentine variant of Italian. But there remained great variations in dialect, and even a few distinctive languages. The most important of these linguistic isolates were the Rhaeto-Roman populations in the Swiss Grisons (Graubünden) and in Friulia on the border between Italy and Yugoslavia. These are better described as 'enclave peripheries', since they are distinct from a single culture that dominates the encircling territory.

Enclaves are therefore quite distinct from interface peripheries, which are under cross-pressure between two major centres. Such is the case of the Alto Adige (South Tyrol), Habsburg territory which lay south of the Alps. The areas with clear Italian majorities had been brought into the new state in 1859 and 1866. The South Tyrol, with an important Italian-speaking minority, was promised to Italy in the negotiations that led to its entry into World War I on the western side in 1915. With the peace treaty, Italy succeeded in imposing a strategic boundary along the Alpine crest, but this did not correspond to the cultural boundary. There remained a considerable German-speaking population in the South Tyrol, leading to a protracted conflict that was not resolved until the 1970s.

The other interface peripheries to the east of the old imperial area all confront Italians or Germans with Slavs or Hungarians. The major areas of tension have been in Carinthia and Burgenland in Austria, the Czech Sudetenland, and along the extensive German-Polish interface, once pushed far to the east, but since World War II placed on the Oder-Neisse line.[4] To the north we can identify two major interfaces: the German-Danish in Schleswig, and the Frisian, straddling the Netherlands and Lower Saxony. The Danish kings were active in imperial politics for centuries, and held important fiefs south of the linguistic border: while these were ultimately conquered by Prussia, the question of the exact tracing of the political boundary remained an intractable issue until at least 1920. By contrast, there were no corresponding conflicts on the German-Dutch border: the Frisians adjusted peacefully to their predicament.

We can look even further north to identify interface peripheries within the extensive territories that had remained well beyond the reach of imperial expansion. Two cases deserve particular mention:

the Danish-Swedish interface in Scania, Halland and Blekinge; and the Swedish-Finnish interface in south-west Finland. In the former case, Sweden conquered the Danish lands to the east of the Kattegat in 1645 and 1658, and was able to integrate them remarkably quickly. This territory has remained firmly in Swedish hands ever since, with no trace of serious irredentism. By contrast, the Swedish presence in Finland remained a difficult political issue until quite recently. Finland was an early target of conquest for the Swedish kings, and its elite remained predominantly Swedish-speaking until well into the nineteenth century. The rapid mobilization of Finnish identity after 1850 generated protracted conflicts, but these were gradually settled through a policy of central equalization of, and local majority rule for, the two language groups (Allardt and Miemois, 1982; Alapuro, 1982).

With the Swedish-Finnish case we have, in fact, moved into the analysis of a fourth category of peripheries. These are the 'external peripheries', geographically remote at the edges of western Europe and exposed to the influence of only one centre. Their predicament is more obvious than that of interface peripheries, and so does not perhaps require any further elaboration at this point. The most important cases of external peripherality have already been listed in the two extreme columns of Figure 2.1.

A conceptual map of Europe

These long sequences of migration, centre-building, cultural standardization and the imposition of boundaries, which we have only been able to sketch with a broad brush, produced an extraordinary tangle of territorial structures in Europe, with great variations in terms of size and degree of centralization. It is our contention, however, that it was the alphabet and the city that ultimately decided the fate of European territories. The emergence and consolidation of vernacular standards of communication prepared the ground for the later stages of nation-building at the mass level: because of the impact of the Reformation, this development can be considered in terms of a north-south axis. On the other hand, the geography of trade routes and the consequent patterns of urbanization made for differences in the resources available for state-building along an east-west gradient.

The essentials of these differences in the conditions for polity building can be set out in a conceptual map, a simple two-dimensional typology which, by utilizing the two geographical

FIGURE 2.2

A conceptual map of Western Europe, 1500-1800

THE STATE-ECONOMY DIMENSION: WEST-EAST AXIS

Centre formation City network		Weak Weak Seaward peripheries	Strong Strong Seaward empire-nations		Weak Strong City-state Europe			Strong Weak Landward empire-nations		Weak Weak Landward buffers
			Distant	Close	Integrated into larger Systems	Con-sociational Formation	Fragmented until 19th Century	Close	Distant	
THE STATE-CULTURE DIMENSION: SOUTH-NORTH AXIS	Protestant state church	Iceland Norway (SCOT.) Wales	ENGLAND	DENMARK			Hansa Germany	PRUSSIA	SWEDEN	Finland
	Mixed territories					NETH. SWITZ.	Rhineland			Baltic territories Bohemia
	National Catholic	Ireland Brittany		FRANCE	'Lotharingia' Burgundy Arelatum			BAVARIA		POLAND
	Counter-Reformation			SPAIN PORTUGAL	Catalonia	Belgium	Italy	AUSTRIA		(HUNGARY)

Note: Territories recognized as sovereign during the period from 1648 to 1789 are in capital letters.

gradients, can be structured so as to reflect the overall topology of Europe.[5] In Figure 2.2 the east-west axis differentiates the economic resource bases of the state-building centres, contrasting surpluses derived from a monetarized economy in the west with surpluses from agricultural labour in the east. The axis is built upon variations in strength of dominant centres and in degree of urbanization. The north-south axis is meant to measure the conditions for rapid cultural integration: it juxtaposes the early closing of cultural borders in the Protestant north against the continuing supra-territoriality of the Church in the Catholic south.

At the centre of the grid lies city-state Europe, the dominant urban network of the politically fragmented medieval trade belt. Here, early centre formation was weak: the only successes were the consociational constructions of the Netherlands and Switzerland. Other territories, apart perhaps from the German and Italian lands, can more appropriately be regarded as either failed-centre or interface peripheries. On either side of city-state Europe the two columns represent the major state-building efforts: in turn these empire-nations are subdivided into two groups according to their proximity to the central trade belt. A comparison of the eastern and western state-building efforts demonstrates the fundamental asymmetry of the geopolitical structure of Europe. The crucial difference, which helped to fashion the overall economic structure of the continent stressed by Wallerstein (1974), was the strength of cities in the territories consolidated to the seaward side of the central trade belt: urbanization remained limited in the territories brought together under the strong military centres of the eastern marchlands. Finally, the two outermost columns, containing territories at the fringes of the content, are where we would expect to find the 'classic' cases of external peripherality. We should also point out that our conceptual map is firmly time-specified. We have limited it to the period between the sixteenth and eighteenth centuries, since it was during this time that there occurred the first and, in terms of affecting the future structure of the continent, the most decisive thrusts of state-building.[6]

Let us spell out the consequences of the grid in more detail. As we have said, the west-east axis is essentially a contrast in the levels of monetarization reached at the time of the decisive consolidation of territorial centres.[7] In the west the greater surge of commercial activity made it possible for centre-builders to extract resources in easily convertible currency. In the east, by contrast, the cities were much weaker, and could not offer an adequate resource base for the building of the military machineries that accompanied the drive for territorial acquisition and incorporation in the eastern marchlands. Here, the only alternative partners were the owners of land, and the only resources that they could offer were food and manpower. This contrast in the economic resource bases for political consolidation goes far towards explaining the differences between the western and eastern systems both in their internal structure and in the character of the later transition to mass politics. Clearly, however, it cannot explain all the cases, nor can it pinpoint the sources of variation on either side: these can be understood only through an analysis of the other dimensions of the polities.

The north-south axis of the conceptual map differentiates the conditions of nation-building. We have interpreted the Reformation as the first major step towards the definition of territorial nations. Lutherans and Calvinists broke with the supra-territoriality of the Roman Church, and merged the ecclesiastical bureaucracies with the secular territorial establishments. This led to a closing of exit options, and an accentuation of the cultural significance of borders. The Reformation occurred only a few decades after Gutenberg, and the state churches of the Protestant north became major agencies for the standardization of national languages and for the socialization of the masses into unified national cultures. In Catholic Europe the Church remained fundamentally supra-territorial in orientation, and did not to the same extent prove to be an agency of nation-building. True, the Catholic Church played a major role in the emergence of peripheral nationalisms in some of the territories of Counter-Reformation Europe, but these were much later developments. They occurred in the aftermath of the French Revolution, and took the form of alliances between the Church and nationalist leaders against the central authorities, whether these be Protestant (the cases of Belgium and Ireland), Orthodox (Poland, Lithuania), or simply secularizing (the Carlist wars in Spain). Overall, however, even in the most loyal Counter-Reformation states the Church remained supra-territorial in outlook, and never became a central agency of nation-building in the same way as the Protestant churches did.

Whether Protestant or Catholic, the churches had to work with populations varying widely in their openness to efforts of standardization. The Völkerwanderungen and the struggles of the Middle

Ages had produced very different conditions for linguistic unification in the various territories. The result was a variety of conflicts between claims of territorial control and claims of cultural identity. While nowhere was there a complete fit between state and nation, the conflicts between the two were particularly violent in trade belt and Catholic Europe. In the north the processes of state- and nation-building could progress pari passu, but even here claims for territorial control often clashed with those for separate identities.

Trade-belt Europe inherited strong linguistic standards from the ancient empires, but there was no corresponding development at the political level: national identity came first, political unification only much later. In the Burgundian buffer zone between the German Reich and the French monarchy, linguistic borders hardly ever followed territorial frontiers. The Swiss cantons had several exoglossic language standards and never became a 'linguistic nation'. Alsace-Lorraine maintained a German dialect, but tended to identify politically more with France. Luxembourg also kept its dialect, but veered between Germany and France. Belgium was split between a Flemish north and a Walloon south. While there were dominant languages at the territorial centres in the rest of Catholic Europe, these were challenged by strong movements of cultural resistance in the peripheries. France went furthest in linguistic standardization, but still had to persist in 'building the nation' throughout the nineteenth century in such peripheries as Brittany and Occitania: the 'levée en masse' and the nationalization of public education were the decisive vehicles of cultural unification (Weber, 1976). Castille was never able to construct a unified national culture in Spain, where the Basque country and Catalonia remained strongholds of regional resistance. Austria tried for centuries to make German the dominant language of south-east Europe, but without success. With the rise of nationalist ideologies this vast empire fell apart into several territorial fragments, but even these were torn by cultural conflicts. While Austria extended the domain of its state apparatus far beyond the borders of the Germanic language community, Prussia, which originally had expanded on the eastern marches, in the end turned westwards into the ancient core areas of the German nation. The Catholic power stuck to the supra-territorial ideal; the Protestant power endeavoured to acquire control over the one linguistic community. The struggle for Germany between Prussia and Austria, between 'kleindeutsche' and 'grossdeutsche' strategies of consolidation was a struggle over conceptions of state and nation between a political and a cultural conception of territorial community.

Monocephalic and polycephalic Europe

In the discussion so far, we have identified three fundamental dimensions in the tangled histories of the territories of western Europe: the strength of the city network, the strength of the state-building core areas, and the resistance to cultural unification and standardization. The conceptual map and the subsequent brief review of particular cases was intended to illustrate how we might structure the production by these three dimensions of the extraordinary diversity of political systems in territories that had been under the sway of a single empire. We can now consider in greater depth how these historical developments were influential in shaping the map of contemporary Europe. Figure 2.3, which is derived from the conceptual map in Figure 2.2, suggests how these variations — not only in size, but also in the urban structure and cultural balance within each territory — may be combined in a tentative typology of the states of twentieth-century Europe.

The city structure of each territory in Figure 2.3 reflects the distances between the core areas and the dominant trade routes: the greater the distance, the greater the dominance of the territorial centre (capital city) in terms of both demographic size and territorial functions of control. Most importantly, territories immediately to the west and east of the central trade belt are largely monocephalic, built up around strong core areas that did not face serious competition from cities closer to the old south-north trade routes. There is, however, an intriguing exception at the Mediterranean pole of the trade belt. Along the Mediterranean littoral there was a much older tradition of east-west trade: interrupted by the Moslem conquests, it remained of vital importance after the Crusades. For the Mediterranean territories in the city-state belt, this affects the fit between typology and topology: the greater strength of the city-state tradition in the south made it more difficult to build up dominant core areas. Instead, the result was polycephality, but of a more polarized kind than that further north. Let us contrast territorial developments in the two southern corners of the grid, in the Iberian peninsula in the west and in the

FIGURE 2.3
A typology of the political systems of twentieth-century Western Europe

SYSTEM CHARACTERISTICS			SEAWARD PERIPHERIES: sovereign after 1814	SEAWARD NATION-STATES: retrenched empires	CITY-STATE EUROPE: early consociations or late unification	LANDWARD NATION-STATES: retrenched empires	LANDWARD BUFFERS: sovereign after 1918
Size	City structure	Linguistic structure					
Larger	Monocephalic	Integrated		France		(German Democratic Republic)	
		Endoglossic peripheries		United Kingdom			
	Polycephalic	Integrated			German Federal Republic Italy		
		Endoglossic peripheries		Spain			
Smaller	Monocephalic	Integrated	Iceland	Denmark	Luxembourg	Sweden Austria	
		Divided	Norway Ireland				Finland
	Polycephalic	Integrated		Portugal	Netherlands		
		Divided			Belgium Switzerland		(Yugoslavia)

Habsburg territories in the east. Both Spain and Austria built up their core strength as crusading frontier empires through a mobilization of military and administrative resources. However, Spain was much closer to the Mediterranean trade belt. While Madrid became the dominant political centre, it proved unable to compete economically with Barcelona, which remained an integral part of a broader economic network. Vienna arose in the eastern marchlands: it was too far from the Mediterranean and the trade belt, and became completely dominant within its territory.

This contrast emerges also in a comparison with two other Mediterranean states, France and Yugoslavia. Like Spain, France had absorbed parts of the trade-route belt, in this instance Burgundy and Provence. But the Île de France core proved able to dominate these economically strong peripheries much more effectively than Castille could Catalonia. While this contrast reflected differences in the balance of resources within each system, there were also differences in the cultural thrust of nation-building. French energies centred upon the domestic territory, while those of Spain were dissipated largely in empire-building and missionary activities in the Americas. There is a similar contrast between a markedly monocephalic Austria and a Yugoslavian federation deeply divided both economically and culturally. The parallels between Yugoslavia and Spain are striking: both experienced a build-up of a military-administrative centre in a fight against foreign dominance, as well as conflicts between this centre and economically stronger cities which lay closer to the major trade routes.[8] In all these cases, the economic strength of the peripheral cities reinforced the cultural distinctiveness of their regions: in other words, claims for economy autonomy paralleled claims for cultural recognition.

Such a polarization between economic and administrative centres was much less marked in city-belt Europe, where polycephalic city structures developed in all the territories. Here, however, the territorial distribution of functions tended to be more diffuse. Italy, for example, was unified from a mountain state, Piedmont, which led economically as well as politically, and which retained a good deal of control even after the transfer of the capital to Rome. By contrast, Switzerland and the Netherlands developed remarkably balanced city structures, standing out as the two European polities with the most distinctly consociational structure (Daalder, 1973).[9] The basic prop was the league of cities, an open contractual organization for the protection of trading privileges and the control of markets. There was also a profusion of such leagues in Germany, but these proved to be much less viable. This large area of independent cities and petty states could be unified only from outside. The Habsburgs, indeed, had tried in vain to do so for centuries. The final push towards unification came in three stages: the build-up of the Prussian state on the eastern marchlands; the reorganization of German territory under Napoleon and the emergence of a strong nationalist ideology; and, finally, Prussian military victory and the establishment of a German Reich. The resulting territorial structure of the German state was markedly polycephalic: Berlin had to compete with the strong economic centres that had survived in western Germany. One consequence of the defeat of the Reich in 1945 was that the Prussian core was again separated from the western city belt: the highly polycephalic Bonn Republic inherited the traditions of the old leagues, while the monocephalic Democratic Republic conserved several traits of the old centralized Prussian monarchy (Urwin, 1982a).

The Napoleonic wars and the subsequent peace settlement of 1815 created vast upheavals throughout the continent. Changes important for future developments included the granting to Prussia of important possessions on the Rhine, the transference of Norway from Denmark to Sweden, the handing over of Belgium to the Netherlands, and the transference of Finland from Sweden to Russia. Yet, overall, the basic structure of western Europe remained much as it had been before the French Revolution: a polycephalic fragmented city belt in the centre, with more monocephalic states to its east and west, and beyond the latter the Atlantic and eastern buffer peripheries.

However, the French Revolution and the Napoleonic wars did leave a time bomb behind them: the idea of the nation-state and the ideal of popular sovereignty. While the 1815 Congress of Vienna had restored the traditional authority of crown and altar, the radical ideologies of the French Revolution spread continuously in the nineteenth century to produce a number of changes in the status of peripheral territories. The process began again in earnest with the second French revolution of 1830, bringing independence to Belgium. The repercussions of the next French revolution were even greater: 1848 marked the opening of the decisive struggle for unity within the city belt — the Italian Risorgimento and the

Prussian drive for leadership in the North German Federation. At the same time, there were intensified nationalist struggles in the east. The Hungarian uprisings marked the beginning of the dissolution of the multi-ethnic Habsburg Empire, which eventually disintegrated into several sovereign states in 1918.

These developments on the political front might have been much slower if the spread of the political and cultural ideas of the French Revolution had not been paralleled by an equally profound transformation of the world economy. While the French revolutions did generate a variety of peripheral independence movements, their appeal was deeply affected by the changes wrought by the diffusion of the Industrial Revolution outwards from England. The development of an economy based on coal and steel triggered important changes in the equilibrium between core and periphery in western Europe. The Industrial Revolution strengthened the economic dominance of the territories centred upon the North Sea, and at the same time increased the dependence of the traditional peripheries on these core economies. Equally important, within each territorial system these economic changes tended to consolidate its monocephality or polycephality that had emerged in earlier centuries.

We can now turn our attention to a more detailed consideration of how the contemporary structure of Western Europe can be understood in terms of our model and interpretation of history. First, we can consider the question of primacy, already reviewed in Chapter 1. Estimates of city sizes were not very reliable before the era of national censues.[10] However, adequate statistics for the sizes of administratively defined cities are available from around 1800. Such data have already been used in Figure 1.2, which showed how city rank-size steps could be studied historically. This diagram is based on a simple primacy score, which takes the size of the largest city as a ratio of the sum of the next four largest. Three sets of primacy scores — for 1800, 1890 and 1970 — were used for the current territories of western Europe; and to allow for easier testing of our model, these states have been divided into three broad categories along a west-east axis: the seaward states, the central city belt, and the landward states. The distribution of the primacy scores, lowest in the city belt and higher in the unitary polities, does confirm the model, albeit roughly. More importantly, as we suggested earlier, the scores also reveal significant changes over time. One interesting contrast, for example, is that between the Netherlands and Belgium, where Amsterdam declined relatively despite nationhood, whereas Brussels gained in importance because of nationhood. Amsterdam was clearly a dominant centre within the former in 1800, but during the nineteenth century the other cities gained rapidly in size, resulting in a marked polycephalization. By contrast, the future Belgium was highly polycephalic in 1800, but Brussels grew faster than the other cities to be central within the Belgian structure by 1900: the picture in 1970 was one of unambiguous monocephality. Changes over time, such as those in this contrast, can be informative about the consequences for the structuring of territorial networks of the timing both of state-building efforts and of major spurts in economic growth. There is, for example, a parallel between Belgium and Norway, both new states in the nineteenth century, and both moving from initial polycephality to an increasing concentration of resources in the capital.

The rank-size approach, however, is necessarily a gross measure. One major difficulty is that similar overall scores can conceal very different network structures. While we can, if one city is markedly larger than the next in rank, assume a high geographical concentration of personnel and resources for territorial control, the totals do not help to determine whether concentrations for the other cities have a strong administrative, financial, industrial or cultural component.[11]

Two other approaches appear to hold much greater promise. We can inquire into the degree of geographical concentration of decision-making personnel, or we can check the location of major political, economic and cultural institutions which are designed to serve the whole territory. There are several examples of single-country analyses of localization structures (e.g. Prost, 1965), but we know of only one comparative synchronic analysis. This is the study by Ahnström (1973) of the location of the headquarters of financial and industrial corporations in Western European countries around 1960. Ahnström measured the degree of centrality by the percentage of sales or income controlled from the dominant headquarters city. The results (Table 2.1) confirm the monocephality-polycephality model: the degree of congruence between the political organization of each territory and the level of economic concentration shows that the polycephalic countries are characterized by a clear-cut dissociation of the political from the economic centres, most especially in West Germany (cf. also Urwin, 1982a). The one surprising result, perhaps, is the classification of Belgium as monocephalic. But this merely confirms our

TABLE 2.1
Concentration coefficients for different sectors of the economy

	Industrial (sales)	*Commercial (sales)*	*Banks (deposits) or loans)*	*Insurance (income)*
Monocephalic countries				
France	0.92	0.82	0.88	0.91
United Kingdom	0.74	0.77	0.86	0.68
Belgium	—	—	0.94	0.82
Austria	0.92	—	0.96	0.97
Denmark	—	—	0.94	1.00
Intermediary countries				
Sweden	0.42	0.69	0.69	0.90
Norway	0.61	0.80	0.66	0.67
Finland	—	—	0.99	0.83
Polycephalic countries				
West Germany	0.13	0.22	0.21	0.26
Italy	0.42	—	0.34	0.35
Netherlands	—	—	0.50	0.30
Switzerland	—	—	0.47	0.66

Source: Derived from Ahnström (1973).

analysis of primacy scores. It reflects the rise of Brussels after independence to a position of dominance (Frognier, Quevit and Stenbock, 1982), and perhaps also makes sense within our overall model of Europe. Belgium, a territory originally defined by the Burgundian attempt to create a military polity at the edge of the city belt, can be regarded as part of a 'transition zone' between that belt and the successful unitary states to the west. The extent to which there exists a disjunction between political and economic centrality, to which a country is monocephalic or polycephalic, can affect the nature of centre-periphery contrasts in each territorial system. Before discussing this question, however, it would be more appropriate first to complete our review of the influence of the past upon the territorial structuring of Europe with a consideration of continuity at a continent level in terms of the European core that emerged in the sixteenth century.

Geoeconomic core-periphery contrasts

The geographical contrasts that emerged as part of the new world economy in the sixteenth century were accentuated during the next phase of economic development. The Industrial Revolution was based on coal, and a new industrial civilization spread along the belts of coal deposits. At first, this transformation of the energy base of the world economy simply reinforced the old core of commercial capitalism. The one decisive change brought about in the core-periphery structure of Europe was in the Rhine valley and its adjacent areas. Once part of the thriving north-south trade route, this region had lost out in the sixteenth century: the Industrial Revolution brought it back into the core of the world economy, as well as creating the economic prerequisites for the building of the new German Reich.

While there were also isolated developments around sources of mineral wealth (for example, in Asturias, Silesia and Northern Sweden), only in the north-western core was there a continuous fusion of commercial and industrial capitalism in a compact network of enterprises that extended across political boundaries. Improvements in hygiene and nutritional standards brought huge increases in population and, ultimately, a persistent rural exodus into the new industrial areas. Finally, the opening up of the grain markets to overseas competition also weakened the economic position of the primary-producing peripheries, which were no longer able to trade food for industrial goods on tolerable terms (Urwin, 1980). The Industrial Revolution not only increased the gap between the countryside and the urban centres; by doing little to change the geography of production and trade, it accentuated the contrasts between the northwestern core and the rest of Europe.[12]

To pinpoint these historical continuities, let us look at two maps of Europe produced 50 years apart (Figure 2.4). That by Delaisi (1929) gives the contours of the European core at the time of the great economic crisis of 1929. Seers (1979) offers a parallel mapping for the year after the dramatic oil crisis of 1973. The two maps are remarkably similar. Despite some differences, the basic message is that the geoeconomic structure of Europe has remained roughly constant during 50 years of dramatic change. The 1979 map differs from the earlier in only two respects. Delaisi traces the eastern boundary of his core along a line running south from

FIGURE 2.4
The boundary of the European core in the 1920s and 1970s

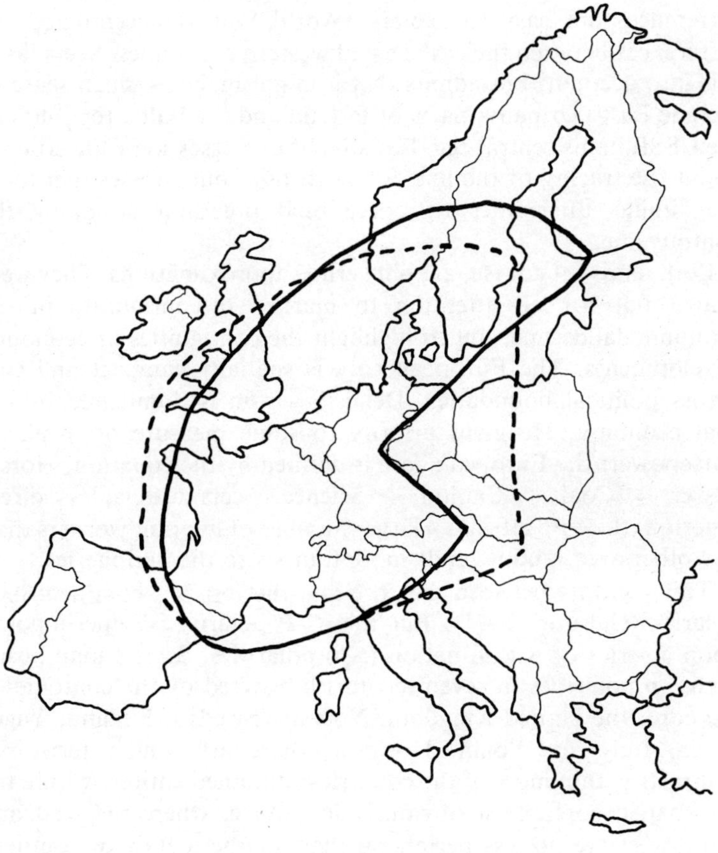

Notes: _ _ _ after Delaisi (1929)
——— after Seers (1979)
The state boundaries shown on the map are those of post-1945 Europe.

Sweden to northern Yugoslavia, while Seers incorporates south-western Finland and omits East Germany and western Poland. Similarly, Delaisi includes much of the United Kingdom in the core, while Seers, who characterizes Britain as a semi-periphery, includes only the south-east in his egg-shaped core. These differences are easy to explain. World War II accentuated the differences between the eastern and western economies. Seers takes this into account, but admits that it might make as much sense to include East Germany, parts of Poland and the Baltic republics of the USSR in his central egg. Equally, he expresses some uncertainty about the tracing of the line across Britain, but stresses that there are similar difficulties of operational precision all along the contour line.

Both maps, of course, are only crude approximations. They were drawn not to call attention to marked discontinuities in the economic landscape, but to highlight the contiguities of economic developments. The European core is spatially compact and cuts across political boundaries. Delaisi's vision is dominated by the coal economy. He gives priority to some measure of available horsepower: the European core is defined by the equation, Horsepower = Coal + Capital + Science. Seers uses a less direct criterion: the core attracts a larger number of migrant workers than any other area, and it sends more tourists to the peripheries.

This contrast between the core and the rest is a continent-level polarity (Galtung, 1971). But this *C-P* polarity is superimposed upon a series of within-nation (*c-p*) polarities. Seers's map posits such *c-p* polarities in seven territories bisected by the contours of the core: the United Kingdom, Norway, Sweden, Finland, Yugoslavia, Italy and Spain. However, there are similar territorial contrasts within most of the countries contained entirely within the egg-shaped core, most obviously in France, where the west and south-west are no less peripheral than southern Italy or southern Spain. Nevertheless, while the area covered by Seers's egg may be far from being evenly developed, it does help to bring out the interconnectedness of the most dynamic centres of the European economy. It could be assumed that, because of this structure, the extent of variance within the core is significantly smaller than that between the core as a whole and the areas outside it. However, to test such a hypothesis we would require not just more data, but also a more differentiated model of spatial structure with a level of sophistication that is beyond the scope of this chapter. Instead, we merely propose to examine the results of two well-known comparisons of interregional variations across several countries.

The classic comparison of regional differences in development by Williamson (1965) offers a first basis for a test of the variances across the demarcation line of the core. Williamson's data cover three countries wholly within the core and seven at its edge. To test for differences in internal structure, Williamson established for each country a coefficient of variation weighted for the size of the regional units.[13] There are obvious problems with the definitions of income in this comparison, but the results (Table 2.2) do show some differences between core and edge. Two core countries, West Germany and the Netherlands, show consistently low coefficients, at least since 1945. At the edge, Norway and Sweden had very high

TABLE 2.2
Selected coefficients of variation in core and edge countries: declared or assessed income per capita

	Prewar Data		*Postwar Data*			
			Earliest		*Latest*	
	Year	*Coefficient*	*Year*	*Coefficient*	*Year*	*Coefficient*
Core						
France	(1864)	(0.260)	1951	0.289	1958	0.299
West	1930	0.160	1950	0.221	1960	0.191
Germany	1934	0.116	1950	0.218		
Netherlands	1938	0.302	1946	0.151	1958	0.178
Edge						
United						
Kingdom	1937	0.116	1949/50	0.074	1959/60	0.071
Sweden	1920	0.440	1944	0.311	1961	0.192
	1930	0.530	1950	0.229		
Finland	(not available)				1950-58	0.331
Norway	1939	0.424	1946	0.151	1958	0.128
Italy	1928	0.313	1951	0.363	1960	0.372
	1938	0.345	1952	0.384		
Spain	(not available)				1955-57	0.415
Yugoslavia	(not available)				1956-60	0.340

Source: Williamson (1965).

coefficients in the prewar period, with a marked decline afterwards, while those for Finland, Italy, Spain and Yugoslavia were still fairly high around 1960. The results for France deviate from those for other countries placed entirely within the core by Seers: this simply confirms the broad consensus of opinion on the strength of the *c-p* polarity in France. More difficult to interpret are the figures for the United Kingdom: their indication of a very low level of interregional variations does not strongly support the characterization of the United Kingdom as a semi-periphery. However, Williamson does show that interregional differences increased with initial industrialization, to decline once the national economy reached some level of maturity. On the other hand, he does not consider what happens during protracted periods of stagnation, and his analysis does not help us find out which types of peripheries are most vulnerable and which less so.

An alternative approach established measures of variation across 97 regions of the original six-member EEC in order to look at the overall decline in disparities from 1960 to 1969, and at the importance of the geographical distance from the core of the

TABLE 2.3
Changes in regional disparities within the old EEC 1960–69: gross internal product

	Weighted coefficients of variation		
	1960	*1969*	*Difference*
97 regions of EEC Six	35.20	32.84	–2.36
Core			
Belgium	18.52	17.98	–0.54
West Germany	18.83	20.00	+1.13
France	19.49	19.44	–0.05
Netherlands	11.20	12.07	+0.87
Edge			
Italy	37.80	30.99	–6.81

Source: Biehl, Hussman and Schnyder (1971: Tables 1, 3). The coefficients cited are those based on population weights for the same year as the gross internal product data. The authors also give estimates for a number of alternative assumptions: population, prices, currency parities.

continental economy for the size of the gross internal product for each region (Biehl, Hussman and Schnyder, 1972). The weighted coefficients of variation (Table 2.3) confirm Williamson's findings for core and edge countries. The disparities are lower within the core, but seem to have reached the same plateau. Italy stands out as the country with the greatest disparities, though the coefficients did decline from 1960 to 1969. However, the main geoeconomic thrust of this analysis shows how regional products vary with distance from the core of the European economy (Figure 2.5). The German

FIGURE 2.5
The dependence of regional gross product on distance from the EEC core

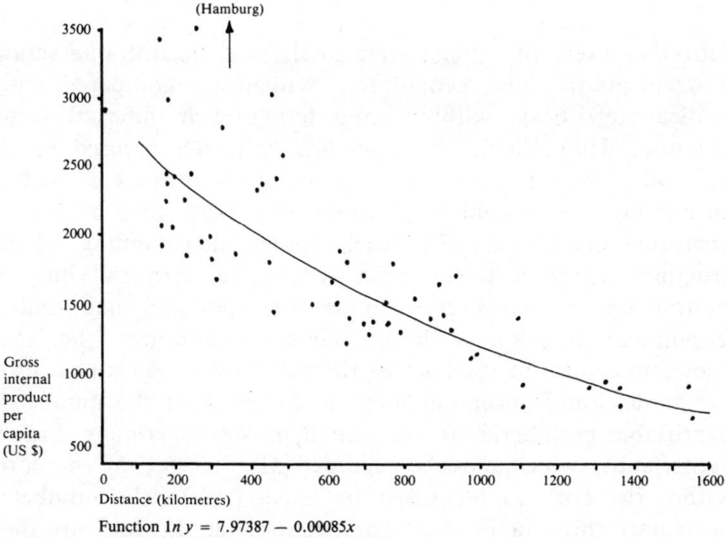

Function $\ln y = 7.97387 - 0.00085x$
Source: Biehl, Hussman and Schnyder (1971).

'Land' of North Rhine-Westphalia was selected as the core region, and the direct distance by air from the centre of this region to each of the other regions of the EEC was measured.[14] The fit in Figure 2.5 is quite close for the more distant regions. The greatest deviations were found closer to the European centre, but these — regions such as Brussels, Bremen and Hamburg — would seem to reflect differences in levels of urbanization; and indeed, the correlation did improve when population density was brought into the equation.[15] The major conclusion (Biehl, Hussman and Schnyder, 1972: 76) is that the European economy is structured around one nodal region, the space of the lower Rhine. From this core, income gradients can be established in all directions. Only where there are national capitals and other major urban centres, with a concentration of resources, are these continental income gradients disturbed.

Centre-periphery economic variations

Both these sets of comparative analyses disregard interactions between politics and economics. Williamson compared entire political territories without considering their internal centre structure, while Biehl, Hussman and Schnyder focused on the economic consequences of core-periphery distances without considering the possible distortions that may be produced by territorial boundaries. To reach some understanding of the structural differences that exist across the territorial units of Western Europe, however, we must use typologies that combine geopolitical location with geoeconomic distance: the same algorithm cannot be used across the entire range of regions. From our model and conceptual map, it is clear that the number of identifiable peripheries is very small in West Germany and the Netherlands, which may be regarded as 'the core of the core'. Within the core as identified by Seers (1979), the number is particularly high in France. The countries at the edge are more varied in their structure. Again, it is clear that there are important differences in the categorization of peripheries. In the United Kingdom, for example, most are external peripheries; in the continental states they are invariably a mix of external and interface. To compare these historically distinctive peripheries, which are identified in our previous discussion, with other regions,

FIGURE 2.6
Centre-periphery gaps in West Germany

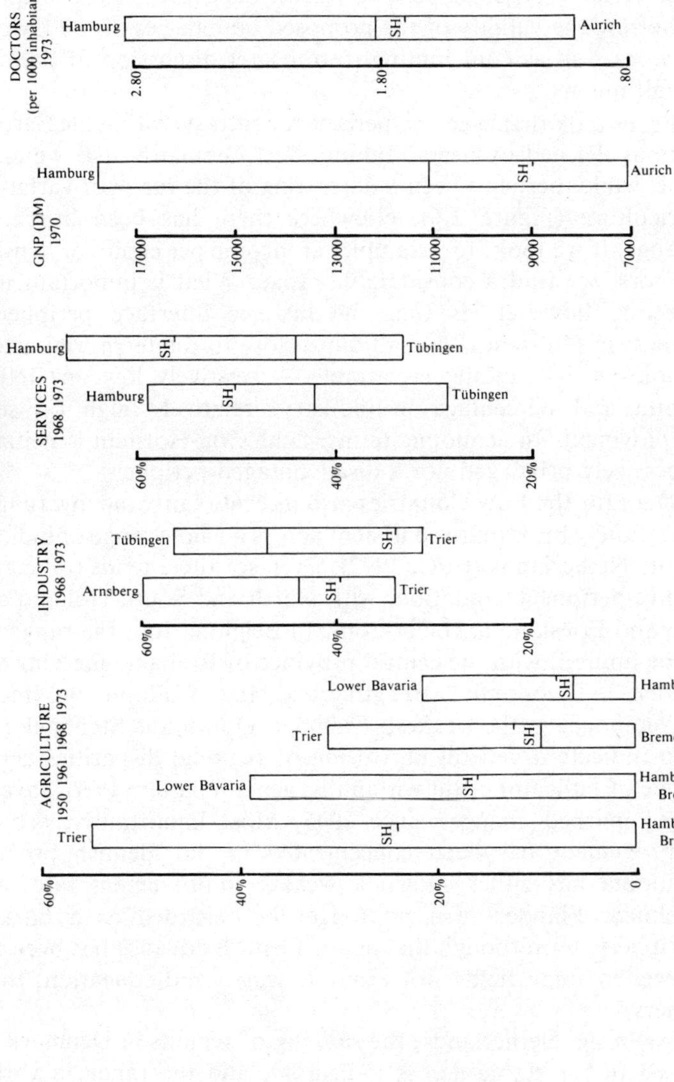

Note: SH = Schleswig-Holstein.

and to fit them into both the contrasts between polycephality and monocephality and the concept of a European core, we propose to indulge in a simple analysis, using available data, to display variations above and below the territorial average for each state.[16] In this way we may be able to indicate the consistency of differences not only between central and peripheral regions, but also between types of peripheries. In turn, this should help us in reviewing the validity of the proposed boundaries of the European core, as well as contributing to our later discussion of peripheral predicaments.

Let us look first at centre-periphery contrasts within the European core as defined by Seers. Taking West Germany first, we can see that, while there has been a narrowing of the range of variation in agriculture (Figure 2.6), elsewhere there has been little or no change: if we look, for example, at income per capita or density of doctors, we find a considerable range. What is important in our context, however, is that the historic interface periphery of Schleswig-Holstein is overall quite close to the territorial average: moreover, its ranking is variable — relatively low on GNP per capita and percentage in industry, relatively high on service employment. In economic terms, Schleswig-Holstein is neither an excessively privileged nor a disadvantaged periphery.

Data for the Low Countries also indicate fairly narrow ranges of variation. This is quite consistent across a whole range of indicators in the Netherlands (EEC, 1972). Even so, there tends to be a clear centre-periphery gradation, with North and South Holland at the top and Friesland at the bottom. In Belgium, too, the range tends to be limited, with the central province of Brabant emerging as the leader in economic strength, and the Walloon province of Luxembourg as the weakest. Frognier, Quevit and Stenbock (1982) also indicate a general narrowing of regional disparities across a range of indicators. But within this general pattern there have been some marked changes since 1945. Most importantly, economic improvement has been concentrated in the Flemish provinces: Wallonia has either shown a weaker improvement rate or has declined. Flanders can no longer be regarded as a backward periphery, even though the rate of Flemish advance has been much slower in some fields, for example wages and education, than in others.

As in the Netherlands, the ranking of regions in Denmark tends to be rather stable across indicators, and the range in variation rather narrow (*Statistik Årbog,* 1976; Nordrefo, 1978; Larsen, Rasmussen and Villadsen, 1976; Søfelde, 1977; Andersen, Jensen, Plum and Villadsen, 1974). The Copenhagen region is the most central, while western and northern Jutland are the most peripheral. The historic interface of southern Jutland (North Schleswig) is closer than the latter to the national average. Elklit (1980) concludes that this is consistent with viewing Denmark as a sector of a circle (which represents the old Danish empire), with Copenhagen at the centre and the North Sea coast at the periphery. Within this segment, the disadvantageous location of southern Jutland has been offset by its closer proximity to the Kiel-Hamburg economic axis in Germany. This has given it an interface status economically as well as politically and culturally, whereas northern and western Jutland are more purely external economic peripheries.

Of the core countries, we find much greater variation in Switzerland and France. The Swiss variations (Figure 2.7) and their rate of decrease reflect perhaps differences in topography. This was also true of an analysis of income variations (Gaudard, Derron and Repond, 1978). While it is the mountain cantons (some of which geographically are at the core of the historic confederation) that show a lesser degree of economic strength, their ranking across the indicators is rather variable: the Grisons enclave, for example, while holding the minimum figure for industry, is close to the national average in the service sector.

The French variations (Figure 2.8), which are considerable, reflect historical differences of long standing. The internal economic periphery of Limousin has consistently scored highest on agricultural employment, with the external periphery of Brittany close behind. The interface peripheries tend to show much lower percentages in agriculture: only Languedoc-Roussillon scores higher than the national average. Similarly, for data on internal product per capita we find a marked difference between external and interface peripheries: Brittany lowest, but Alsace-Lorraine close to the territorial average. Languedoc-Rousillon again deviates from the pattern: this interface has a very low average product, but distinguishes itself by scoring well above the territorial average on the density of doctors.[17] Overall, the general conclusion is clear: the west and south-west of France constitute a large area of economic peripherality. We might in fact trace a line roughly from Caen in Normandy to Marseilles on the Mediterranean as a boundary separating 'les deux Frances': to the west of this line we find

FIGURE 2.7
Centre-periphery gaps in Switzerland

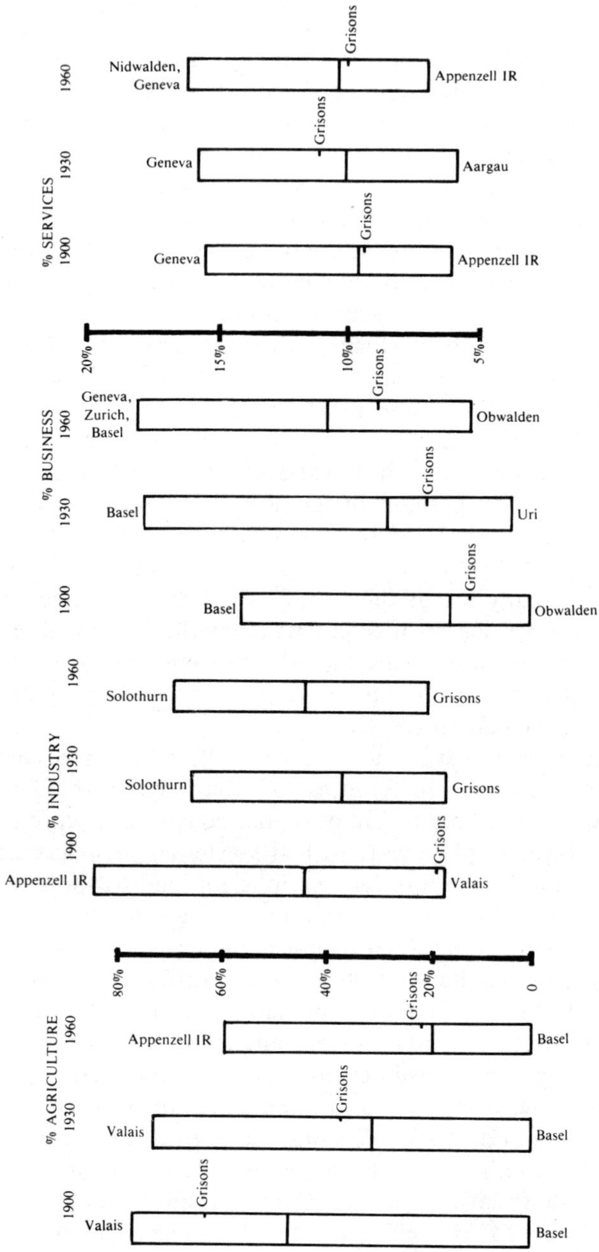

FIGURE 2.8
Centre-periphery gaps in France

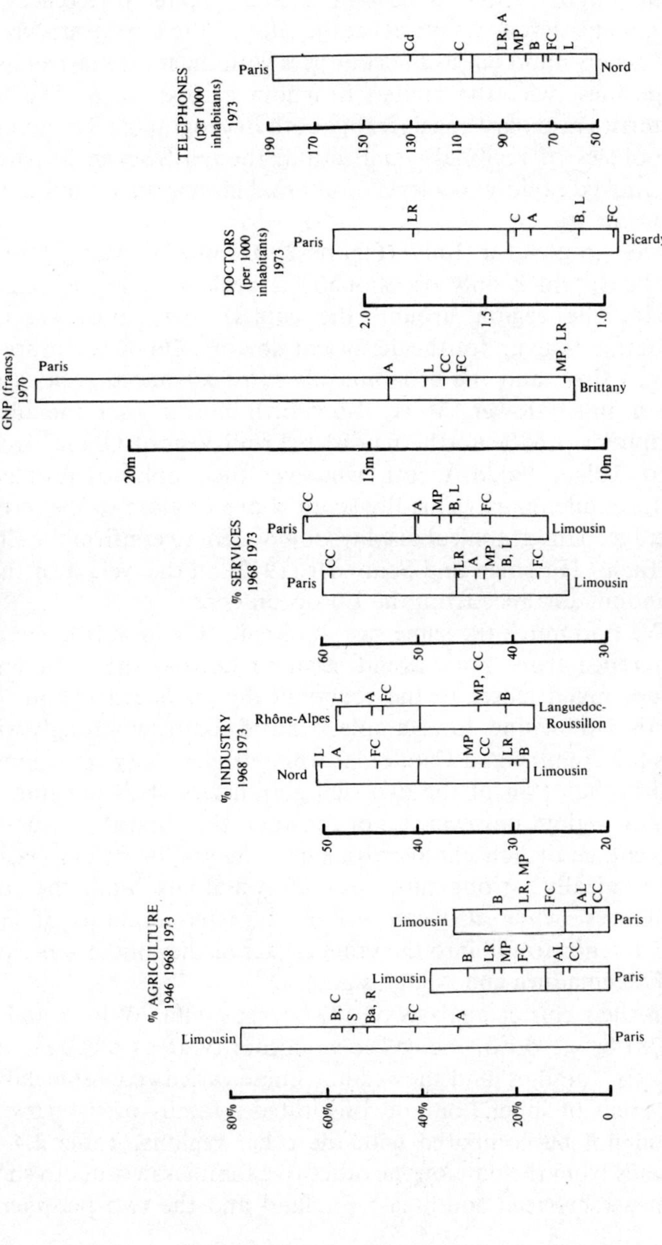

Note: B = Brittany; C = Corsica; S = Savoy; Ba = Basque; R = Roussillon; FC = Franche Comté; A = Alsace; LR = Languedoc-Roussillon; MP = Midi-Pyrenees; AL = Alsace-Lorraine; CC = Corsica-Côte d'Azur; L = Lorraine; Cd = Côte d'Azur.

consistently high percentages in agriculture and low per capita product, while the reverse is true to the east of the line.[18]

We might expect to encounter even greater differences, both within and across countries, at the edge of the European core. Italy and Spain stand out as the countries with the most marked internal disparities, with the United Kingdom a close third. The Nordic countries also vary considerably both in geographical structure and in policies of regional equalization, though Sweden in particular has moved rapidly to a level of internal homogeneity similar to that of Denmark.

The graphs for Italy (Figure 2.9) show a clear north-south gradient, which only occasionally is broken by higher scores for Lazio, the region around the capital. The most spectacular deviation is again for the density of doctors. On this measure Lazio comes first, and the economically most advanced regions of the north much lower. It is also worth noting that the interface peripheries on the northern border (Friuli-Venezia Giulia, Trentino-Alto Adige, Val d'Aosta), whatever their political problems or cultural dilemmas, generally score above or close to the territorial average. This graphical display would seem to confirm the findings by Biehl, Hussman and Schnyder (1972) on the weight of the geo-economic distance from the European core.

We find much the same story in Spain (Figure 2.10). The major difference from Italy would seem to be that the capital region comes much closer to the economically advanced regions of the north. On income, for example, Madrid competes strongly with the Basque country and Catalonia, while its electricity consumption is higher than that of the two rich peripheries. This position of the capital region, however, is not constant: the opposite is true for the percentage of households with cars. The graphs do emphasize the economically strong position of Catalonia and the Basque provinces, while also confirming the external status of Galicia, which tends to fall into the same cluster as the southern peripheries of Extremadura and Andalusia.

In their cluster analysis of 1971 census data, Webber and Craig (1978) broke down the 457 local authority areas of Great Britain into six 'families' and showed how these varied geographically. The ten areas of inner London constituted a family of their own, and could not be compared with the other regions. Table 2.4 extrapolates from the data on the other five families in order to show the contrast between south-east England and the two peripheries of

FIGURE 2.9
Centre-periphery gaps in Italy

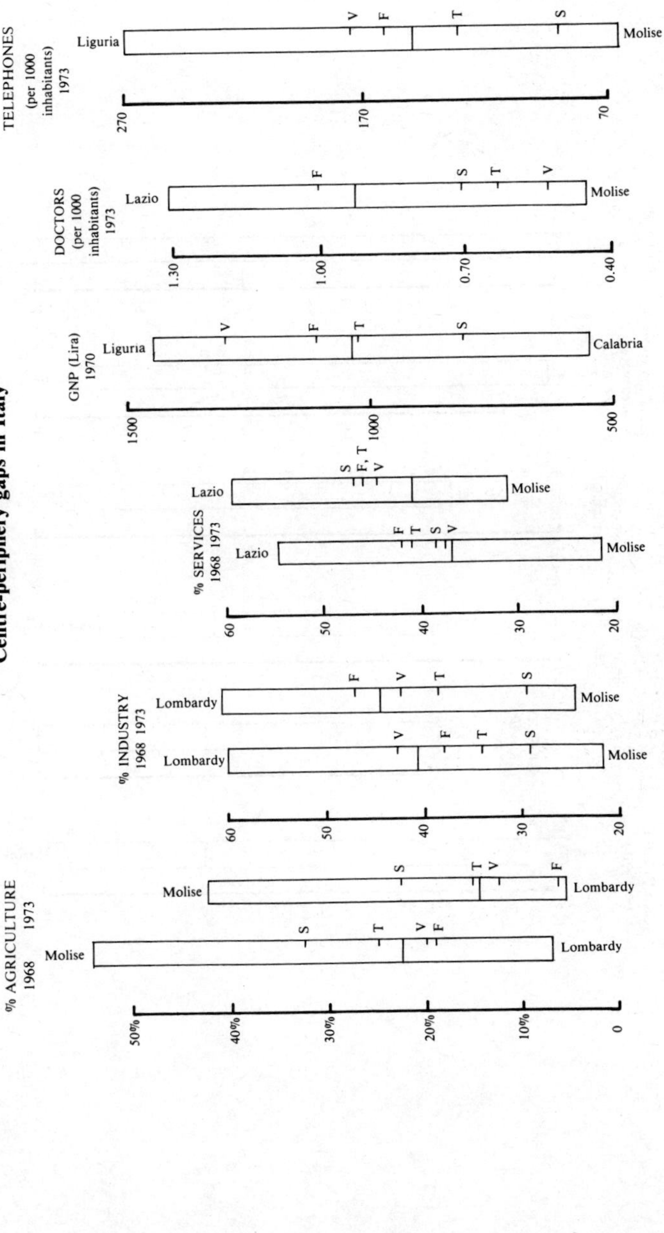

Note: F = Friuli-Venezia Giulio; S = Sardinia; T = Trentino-Alto Adige; V = Val d'Aosta

FIGURE 2.10
Centre-periphery gaps in Spain

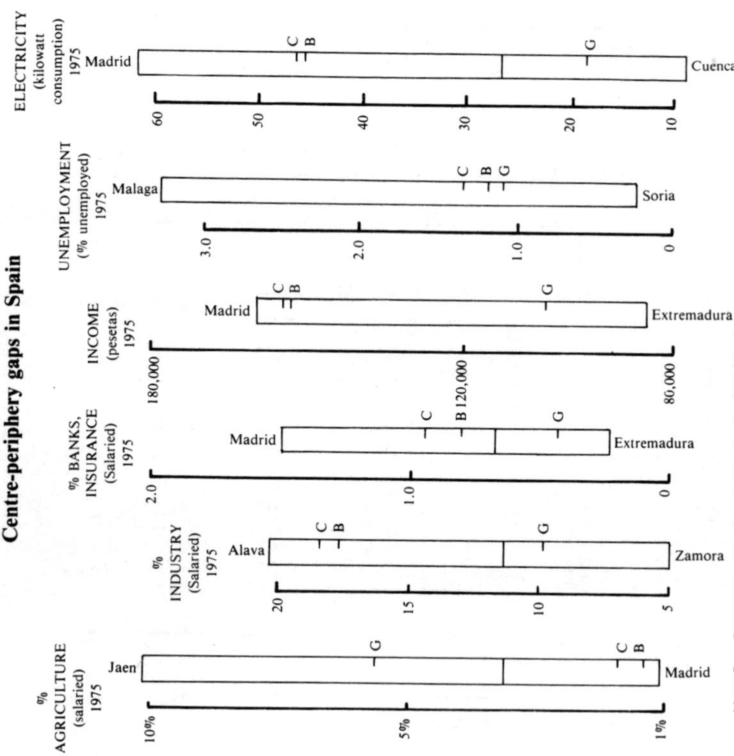

Note: B = Basque country; C = Catalonia; G = Galicia.

Wales and Scotland. In the former there is a strong concentration of the suburban growth family, while Wales and Scotland are largely divided between the resort/rural family and those poorer districts labelled as either 'traditional industries' or 'council housing'. The contrast between the central region and these two peripheries emerges with even greater clarity in Table 2.5, where the figures represent population-weighted scores, with the national mean being set at zero and the mean deviance from this mean being

TABLE 2.4
Distribution of local authority 'families' between centre and periphery in Great Britain

	FAMILY					
	(1) *Suburban growth*	(2) *Rural/ resort*	(3) *Tradition-al industry*	(4) *Service centres*	(5) *Council housing*	*Total*
South-east England (excl. inner London)	76	26	8	11	4	123
Wales	2	16	15	4	—	37
Scotland	2	24	—	9	21	56

Source: Webber and Craig (1978: Table 2).

equal to one. However, these centre-periphery gaps have narrowed over time. The regional data compiled by McAllister, Parry and Rowe (1979; also Urwin, 1982b), covering conventional indicators of socio-economic wellbeing, suggest a not overly large degree of difference between the four constituent countries of the United Kingdom, and one that has progressively narrowed since 1951. Even so, the cumulative effect is that of a territorial gradient, with England and Northern Ireland at the two poles. While Scotland and Wales, which differ very little from each other, consistently lag behind England, they are nevertheless closer to the latter than to Northern Ireland, a pattern that confirms the distinctive position of the Ulster rump within the British state.

TABLE 2.5
Centre-periphery populations in Great Britain: weighted standardized scores

	Family 1/ cluster 6: outer London	*Family 3/ cluster 14: upland industries, mainly Wales*	*Family 5/ cluster 24: Scottish industrial areas*
% professional/managerial household heads	0.719	−1.007	−0.754
% with no inside WC	−0.902	1.813	−1.067
% households with cars	0.662	−0.726	−0.805
% unemployed	−0.904	0.089	0.993
% sick among economically active	−0.942	1.369	0.689

Source: Webber and Craig (1978).

Finally, the three Nordic countries at the edge of the European core have also been marked historically by a clear north-south economic gradient (cf. Aarebrot, 1982; Alapuro, 1982); this, however, has been reduced considerably in recent years through government intervention in the economy. The process of territorial equalization has gone furthest in Sweden, while in Norway and Finland those regional units that lie outside the core still lag in economic strength behind those within (Nordrefo, 1978; Hagström, 1978). Table 2.6 provides some further details on Sweden. It shows that two of the southern peripheries have a lower per capita base than most of the northern counties lying outside their core. In the Norwegian case Table 2.7 suggests that the county of South Trøndelag (centred round the city of Trondheim) could justifiably be incorporated into the European core; its overall performance across the indicators is closer to that of the central region than the two counties listed in the table as being part of the western and the northern peripheries.

This sketchy and rather unsystematic country-by-country review of centre-periphery contrasts across Western Europe can be only suggestive. Nevertheless, it does indicate that the economic core areas of the continent are not at all uniform. There are important

TABLE 2.6
Differences between central and peripheral countries (Län) in Sweden, 1970

	Urbanization %	*Employed in large corporations* %	*Index for tax base per capita*
Central counties			
Stockholm	96.5	36.1	135.1
Göteborg & Bohus	90.3	35.1	104.8
Malmöhus	87.1	31.9	101.1
Southern periphery			
Kronoberg	69.1	18.6	80.3
Kalmar	77.7	14.5	75.6
Gotland	51.7	3.4	68.1
Northern periphery (outside core)			
Västernorrland	73.2	28.3	82.3
Jämtland	55.8	5.3	74.8
Västerbotten	65.6	5.7	80.8
Norrbotten	76.0	15.1	87.1

Source: Hagström (1978: 60).

differences within each country, and in some cases (especially France) good arguments can be made for redrawing the boundaries. Peripheralization, moreover, is an ongoing process: data from the late 1970s and 1980s might well indicate major dents or perforations in the core, for instance at the interfaces between France, West Germany and Belgium, where the problems affecting heavy industry simply stress how vulnerable peripheral economies are to changes in technology and to competition from low-wage industries in developing countries: being inside the core does not necessarily constitute an effective shield against such vulnerability. But whatever its exact boundaries — and these, no doubt, will always be disputed — there *is* a European core, whose geoeconomic origins lie in the emergence of commercial capitalism, and which overall has changed very little since.

TABLE 2.7
Centre-periphery differences in Norway, by county

	Access to secondary schools[a] %	*Access to medical services*[b] *Doctor* %	*Dentist* %	***Income per taxpayer***[c] %	*Higher education*[d] %	*Living accommodation*[e] %
Centre						
Akershus	80	96	94	37	58	91
Northern centre						
South Trøndelag	65	80	78	23	53	103
Western periphery						
Sogn and Fjordane	20	67	60	18	55	111
Northern periphery						
Finnmark	39	69	63	19	35	185

[a] % of 15-19 age group within 45 minutes travel from 'gymnas'.
[b] % of population within 45 minutes travel of medical services.
[c] % over N.Kr. 40,000 in 1973.
[d] % of 15-19 age group in non-obligatory education, 1970.
[e] index of households with more than one person per room, 1970: 100 = national average.

Source: Statistisk Sentralbyra (1977); Asheim (1978).

This review has also indicated the existence of economic heterogeneity within countries. While economic development and change has produced some purely economic peripheries in Western Europe, our major interest lies in those peripheries that had previously experienced some cultural or political distinctiveness, and it is clear that these vary considerably in economic status. Whether a periphery is inside the core or at its edge, its economic resources should still be considered vis-à-vis those of the centre of the political territory. Three simple relationships might be postulated: in relation to the economic standing of the centre, the peripheral economy can be regarded as being backward, similar or superior. A temporal perspective may be incorporated by considering whether, over time, the peripheral economic performance has declined or improved relative to that of the centre.

FIGURE 2.11
The economic status of peripheral regions in Western Europe

<table>
<tr><th>UNDER-
DEVELOPED</th><th>MODEST
DEVELOPMENT</th><th>DECLINING
INDUSTRIAL
AREAS</th><th>SUPERIOR
ECONOMIC
GROWTH</th></tr>
<tr><td>N. Scandinavia</td><td>Brittany</td><td>Scottish Lowlands</td><td>Flanders</td></tr>
<tr><td>N. Ireland</td><td>Friesland</td><td>S.E. Wales</td><td>Catalonia</td></tr>
<tr><td>Scottish Highlands</td><td>Jura</td><td>Wallonia</td><td>Basque country</td></tr>
<tr><td>N.W. Wales</td><td>Roussillon</td><td>Alsace</td><td></td></tr>
<tr><td colspan="2">Occitania</td><td></td><td></td></tr>
<tr><td>Galicia</td><td>Savoy</td><td></td><td></td></tr>
<tr><td>S. Spain</td><td>Val d'Aosta</td><td></td><td></td></tr>
<tr><td>Corsica</td><td>Alto Adige</td><td></td><td></td></tr>
<tr><td>Sardinia</td><td>Friuli</td><td></td><td></td></tr>
<tr><td>S. Italy</td><td></td><td></td><td></td></tr>
</table>

These basic relationships can be simplified into a fourfold classification (Figure 2.11), which serves as a crude guide to the relative economic strength of peripheries. This classification may then be linked later to our review of political and cultural distinctiveness when we come to consider peripheral political mobilization.

A typology of peripheral predicaments

We suggested earlier a simple set of classifications of peripheral predicaments. We distinguished political, cultural and economic peripheries, adding further complexity by introducing a set of geo-ethnic distinctions between external, interface, failed centre and enclave peripheries. Let us return to these distinctions and see how far it is possible to fit them together in a grid that will link up with our overall model.

Figure 2.12 highlights the location of peripheries within our conceptual map of Europe. Each of the territories has been placed in the most appropriate cell within that topological chart. The typology posits seven types of peripheralized territories from west to east, and combines this axis with an Arctic-Mediterranean

FIGURE 2.12
Location of peripheries within the overall structure of Western Europe

	Seaward peripheries		Coastal plains		Central plains/Alps			Germanic marchland		Landward peripheries	
	1	2	S	3	C	F	4	L	5	6	7
	No or only incipient medieval state formation	Distinctive medieval state, but dis-continuity	Continuous state formation since the Middle Ages	Western interface territories	Continuous state formation since 14th-16th centuries	Early state formation, later absorbed within larger systems	Internal interface territories	Continuous state formation since 13th-17th centuries	Eastern interface territories	Distinctive medieval state, but dis-continuity	No or only incipient medieval state formation
Arctic periphery	Greenland Faeroes Orkney Shetland	Iceland N. Norway		Jämtland				Norrbotn			Lappland
Protestant territory		Norway Scotland Wales	Denmark England	Bohuslän Scania Halland Blekinge Schleswig		Hansa Germany	Friesland	Sweden Brandenburg-Prussia	Ostrobothnia Åland E. Prussia		Finland Baltic Territories
Mixed/national Catholic territories	Ireland	Brittany	France	Alsace-Lorraine Burgundy Jura Savoy Provence Occitania Corsica Belgium	Netherlands Switzerland	Rhineland Germany Piedmont Sardinia	Bohemia-Moravia Bavaria Grisons		Sudetenland	Lithuania Poland Serbia	Slovakia
Counter-Reformation territories		Galicia Navarre Basque provinces	Spain Portugal	Catalonia		Lombardy Papal territories	Tyrol/Alto Adige Venetia/Friulia	Austria	Burgenland	Hungary	Slovenia
Mediterranean territories			Andalusia	Balearic islands		Naples/Sicily				Croatia Dalmatia	Bosnia Albania

gradient. At each extreme of the west-east gradient we have distinguished 'pure' from failed-centre peripheries: the former category covers territories not unified within any distinctive governmental organization during the Middle Ages, while failed centres are those territories that did possess a clear state structure at some point in time, but which were later absorbed into larger formations. Such dichotomies obviously do violence to complex realities, but they are simply meant to point to a possible gradation to be established against a set of precise criteria. Whatever the exact gradations, the distinction is theoretically of some importance. There is a great deal of evidence that suggests that the style and structure of peripheral protest politics varies markedly between territories without any history of distinctive centre-building in the past, and those with a legacy and memory of independent institutional structures at some phase in their earlier history.[19]

The chart locates the most important peripheries within a grid based upon three key columns: one for the continuously built-up nation-states on the seaward side of the historic trade-route belt (S); one for consociational formations (C) and fragmented territories (F) in the old imperial city belt; and one for the continously developed state formations to the landward side of the trade routes (L). It also identifies two sets of peripheries to the west (columns 1 and 2) and to the east (columns 6 and 7) of these three key columns: in both these cases there is a further distinction between territories once unified under a distinctive independent centre and those only poorly unified during the Middle Ages. Finally, the grid contains three sets of interface peripheries: one to the west of the old empire (column 3), another between the major territories within the city belt (column 4), and a third in the eastern marchlands (column 5).

The details of this crude scheme would obviously have to be tested against precise statistical data. There are, for example, several intermediary cases, and the locations given in the grid are sometimes arbitrary. The Basque country, for instance, may be regarded as both an interface and an external periphery. The decisive criteria of externality are linguistic distance from the dominant culture, and subjection by only one dominant centre. The Basque country qualifies as an external periphery on the first count, but was caught in a double subjection by both France and Castille. Geoethnically, it makes sense to group the Basque lands with the seaward external peripheries, but geopolitically and geo-economically they have more in common with the interface peripheries: their position at an important political frontier constitutes a very different kind of context from that characterizing such distinctly external peripheries as Galicia.

While this external-interface distinction should perhaps be developed in further depth, our crude grid is essentially a heuristic device, which offers possibilities for the generation of hypotheses about sources of difference not only in cultural development, but also in economic growth and styles of political accommodation. We have, for example, already indicated that interface peripheries have tended to possess stronger economies than external ones. The reasons suggested by our typologies are simple enough. The former are generally closer to dynamic urban networks, and have some degree of choice between alternative centres in their strategies of growth. External peripheries, by contrast, tend to be more remote from the active urban networks, and have less leeway in bargaining for trading advantages and subsidies. Similar analyses could clearly be pursued at several levels, and the potential variations that may exist are only poorly reflected in the grid. However, to construct an over-ornate latticework would, at least in the first instance, probably be self-defeating: it is partly for this reason that we have chosen to review the economic scene separately. Nevertheless, it is only through statistical analyses of community characteristics that we will acquire firm evidence of marked differences between the various types of peripheries. While these should be pursued systematically across all the territories of Western Europe, that task lies beyond the scope of this volume.[20]

For the moment, the grid is designed merely to emphasize our basic message. There is a great variety of peripheries in Western Europe, a diversity that is the result of complex interactions of ethnic, religious, economic and political forces over long stretches of history. In addition, there is no one-to-one fit between economic backwardness, cultural distinctiveness and political marginality: we find varieties of all possible combinations. As a consequence, it is difficult to see how there could be a simple once-and-for-all solution to problems of territorial inequality. Conditions vary too much for any one policy to be uniformly and universally effective: there is no all-purpose panacea.

Finally, it is worth reiterating that peripheralization is an ongoing process. Just as the consequences of the Industrial Revolution served to modify and restructure the original centre-periphery distinctions that began to crystallize in the Middle Ages, so more recent events and trends have made their contribution, refining our charts of conceptual Europe and grids of peripheries. However, while there is no simple fit between the dimensions of culture, economy and politics, the possibilities for dramatic change have shrunk. There has been a progressive freezing of the boundary lines in all three dimensions. The construction of centre infrastructures has progressively increased over time so as virtually to eliminate the possibility of alternative contenders. Dramatic change, when it has occurred, has come about primarily as a result of cross-territorial war and of the decisions imposed upon an area by external victors, as for example with Austria-Hungary in 1919, and in 1945 with the dismemberment of the German Reich and the subsequent removal of West Berlin to become a periphery of the Federal Republic. Overall, however, economic change and ever more efficient forms of communication have strengthened the arsenal of centres and their capacity for seeking political and cultural dominance over their peripheries. At the same time, the general process of secularization has tended to expose peripheries more to pressures of conformity. While change is continuous, it has perhaps been more a matter of degree. The kinds of peripheries that we have identified have basically remained in the same categories over time. In all three dimensions, the freezing process occurred in the past; and current peripheral political protest must be considered not only as a reaction to contemporary economic problems and to cultural and political trends, but also against the backdrop of the geomorphic heritage of the continent. The first stage must be to look in more detail at the sources of the survival of peripheral distinctiveness.

3

The Survival of Distinctiveness: Sources of Peripheral Identity

While both cultural and economic sources of distinctiveness are important, we shall give priority to the former. There are economic peripheries in Europe, but no territorial identity on the continent can be defined solely in terms of a distinctive economy.[1] Similarly, no territorial identity can be distinguished only on the basis of its class character: where identity clashes did have a class basis, as between landlord and rural proletariat in Ireland and along the eastern Baltic littoral, they also were grounded in religious, ethnic or linguistic differences. It may well be that class can provide an issue around which identity conflicts can be generated, but it is perhaps less probable for it to provide the essence of community feeling.[2] More generally, Weber pointed out that objective class or economic differences may not coincide with an awareness of their existence among those they affect: by contrast, status groups invariably possess self-awareness (Gerth and Mills, 1948: 180-94).

Identity is much more part of the cultural dimension. In order to satisfy himself on the issue of 'who, what, and where am I', the individual tends to look no further than his own accumulation of attitudes and prejudices, which themselves are determined by and are part of his own cultural environment. These patterns of orientation provide the individual with an identity and offer him a standard by which he may interpret the world and to which he may adjust his reactions. Collectively, they impose upon a society a set of cultural contours that are enduring configurations. It is in this sense that we can talk of the cultural myth and that ritual practice that ensures the survival of the myth for at least one further generation.

Identity can be broken down into at least four component parts: myth, symbol, history, and institutional. The mythical aspects of identity may be defined as a set of beliefs that creates an instrumental pattern for behaviour in the sense that these beliefs provide aims for their followers. While several sets of beliefs may feed into the cultural myth, our review of centres and peripheries suggests that the most significant myth historically has been religion. Since the nineteenth century, nationalism as a myth can be regarded almost as a civil religion. The symbolic element represents the enduring expressive aspect of culture, transmitting its values from individual to individual, and from generation to generation: language is the supreme expressive component of identity. The history of any given territory has a significance in itself for the indigenous population independent of any scholarly historiographical standards. The object of interest in this lore of the land

FIGURE 3.1
Aspects of the lore of the land

	Macro ←		→ Micro
	FATEFUL EVENTS	SYMBOLIC CEREMONIES	SOCIALIZATION
Centre	France: commemoration of the storming of the Bastille	Annual celebrations (national saints days; USA — Declaration of Independence)	Official history books in schools
Periphery	Ulster: Protestant commemoration of the Battle of the Boyne	Basque 'fueros'	Folklorization: festivals, costumes, dances, songs

can range from commemorations of fateful past events and decisions through the celebration of ritual acts to micro-level socialization into an ideology congruent with the objectives of state- and nation-builders. What actually happened in the past is usually of minor importance in this lore. Figure 3.1 offers some possible examples in a juxtaposition of the content of the collective memory with the centre-periphery dichotomy. Finally, the institutional network of agencies that implement aspects of identity are important for both centre and periphery. For example, the establishment of the Academie Français and the stress on the language in the school system indicate that standardization and penetration of the central language has been an important element in French culture. Similarly, the survival of institutional life from the past can be vital for peripheries. The possession of distinctive laws, privileges, education and taxation systems implies and underwrites some degree of self-consciousness, and, since these often also imply some organizational framework, can heighten the awareness of separateness and contribute towards its survival.

Here we shall concentrate upon language as a focal point of identity, but not to the exclusion of everything else. While language is only one of several expressions of identity, it is the most pervasive and obvious stigma of distinctiveness. Moreover, it is not only a matter of private and individual preference: the ability to speak a language is of little value if there is no way in which the individual can use it. It is also a question of public recognition, of the legitimization of standards: the use of a language is a collective act in which everyone in a territory must share, and it becomes politicized when a set of elite groups establish a standard of written communication and lodge claims for its recognition in public life. Such claims can create conflicts in two directions: internally, between the defenders of distinctive dialect traditions, and externally, in the interaction with central officials and agencies. In what follows we are less interested in the actual behaviours of peripheral populations: our main concern is with the fate and status of the standards, how early and how easily they were established, what kind of recognition they were able to achieve, and how much conflict occurred over these measures of recognition. While the daily behaviour of citizens is important per se, this behaviour takes place within opportunity structures, set through political conflicts and economic transactions. It makes a great deal of difference whether the public media are locally dominated by one or another language, whether there is one or more languages of instruction in the local schools, how much linguistic ability is necessary to secure a public sector job.

A four-step model

To answer questions about sources of variation in the fate and status of peripheral languages, we have to return to the processes of interaction between politics, economy and culture. Territorial consolidation increased the opportunities for elite encounters over long distances. In turn, these increased the chances of acceptance of joint standards for ceremonial languages and for those of administrative and juridical communication. In western Europe these processes of standardization advanced between the eighth and twelfth centuries. The alphabetization of vernaculars in the monasteries and church schools tended to stabilize standards and to prepare the ground for the unification of national languages. The first standard languages owe much to Gutenberg and the early printers: their decisions on orthography, arbitrary and historically questionable, tended to freeze standards. At least in the Protestant countries, the introduction of compulsory mass education later increased the pressures of standardization. These developments in the cultural infrastructure paralleled changes in the economy. The commercial revolution increased the demand for competent communicators, and the growth of both administrative-juridical and military establishments created a territory-wide market for professionals skilled in the arts of reading and writing: the universities, once important agents responsible for the maintenance of Greek and Latin, also began to produce professionals in the vernacular languages. In the next round, the Industrial Revolution generated a demand for workers able to read instructions and manuals, and to learn new skills and techniques through literacy. These changes in the economy produced increasingly open markets for personnel across the entire territory of political systems and across a wide variety of occupations, and moved large numbers of people out of their peripheral or marginal conditions and into increasing contact with a territory-wide culture based upon written communication.

These developments strengthened enormously the weight of established linguistic standards and weakened the inherited 'parlers', patois and dialects of the peripheries. As a general rule, we might say that the chances of survival of a peripheral language were severely reduced if it had not been standardized and had not become a medium of mass communication before the take-off in industrial development. Once a territory-wide labour market had been created, the resources for resistance against the central standard were drastically curtailed. In short, the changes in the economy created a new set of opportunity structures, and the choices made by ordinary people in these situations tended to seal the fates of the peripheral languages.

We can spell out this scheme of explanation in a four-step model (Figure 3.2), where the dependent variable is to be found in Cell C IV. The preceding cultural developments are those reviewed above — early/late alphabetization, early/late standardization, and the timing of mass education — each of which is matched by parallel economic and territorial developments. We can formulate a number of approximate rules for the generation of variations in the dependent variable through the combinatorics of the antecedent conditions in each territory: (1) the successful centres, cases of continuing strengthening of the one central territorial language; (2) the multilingual structures, cases of federalizing accommodation between two or more languages within the same politically defined

FIGURE 3.2
A four-step model of economic, political and linguistic change

	ECONOMY (E)	TERRITORY (T)	CULTURE (C)
I	Medieval geoeconomic position	Early v. late unification	Early v. late alphabetization
II	Commercial expansion, early urbanization	Degree of administrative penetration	Early v. late standardization, timing of printing
III	Timing of Industrial Revolution	Timing of suffrage extensions, formation of national party systems	Timing of mass education in dominant v. peripheral language
IV	Changes in peripheral economy produced by technological innovations, changes in trade routes	Increased politicization on ethnic-linguistic-territorial lines	Strength of peripheral language: official recognition; number of speakers; position in mass media; role in mass education

territory; (3) the victorious peripheries, cases of success in the establishment or maintenance of a distinctive standard language for the periphery; (4) peripheries with weak standards but some level of autonomy, cases where a periphery proved unable to establish or maintain an effective standard of its own, but did achieve some level of political autonomy or independence; (5) marginal peripheries, cases with neither an effective standard nor any significant level of autonomy; and (6) solutions at the interfaces, cases of strong cross-pressures between major language communities. These six categories can be generated by combining two dimensions: the status of each language, and the linguistic system of the territory where it is used. The cross-classification of these criteria almost inevitably leaves some intermediary cases. However, to account for the way in which we have grouped our cases, we can present a two-dimensional chart of variations in linguistic conditions across Western Europe (Figure 3.3). The chart, it must be stressed, is merely suggestive, and the classification of some languages is difficult and dubious. Nevertheless, it may serve as a focal point for our discussion of language as a central factor in the survival of distinctiveness.[3]

The successful centres

These cases of early standardization and successful development of the territorial language were of two kinds: territories consolidated around one centre before the Thirty Years' War, or multi-centred territories strongly marked by the imperial heritage. In the former the standard language tended to develop from the dialect of the core area; in the latter there tended to be a greater distance between the accepted written standard and the local elite languages. The eight languages in this category can be grouped as follows: early territorial consolidation and largely homogeneous populations (Portugal, Denmark, Sweden, the Netherlands); early territorial consolidation with markedly differentiated populations (England, France); imperial heritage with continued fragmentation and multiple centres, but with homogeneity of populations within the core territories (Germany, Italy).

The Portuguese state developed in isolation at the south-western extreme of the European land mass. Its early structure, built up in the fight against the Muslims and the reconquest of the Algarve,

FIGURE 3.3
A scheme for the classification of language in Western Europe

STATUS OF LANGUAGE

LINGUISTIC SYSTEM	Central standard	Peripheral language: established official standard	Peripheral language: ineffective standard but some autonomy/ independence	Peripheral language: marginal status
Unitary: one dominant language	Portuguese (I)			
	French (I) →			Alsatian (VI) Breton (V) Occitan (V) Corsican (V) Franco-Provençal (VI) Catalan (Roussillon) (VI)
	English (I) →	Welsh (III) →	Lallans (IV) → Irish (IV)	Gaelic (V)
	Danish (I) →	Icelandic (III) → Faeroese (III)		German (N. Schleswig) (VI)
	Swedish (I) →			Lappish (V)
	Dutch (I) →	Frisian (III)		
	German (I) →			Danish (S. Schleswig) (VI)
	Italian (I) →		Sardinian (IV) → Valdotain (VI) German (Alto Adige) (VI)	Friulian (V) Ladin (V)
Multi-lingual (minorities more than 5%) 1. endoglossic standards	Castillian (II) →	Catalan (II) →	Basque (IV) Galician (IV)	
		Norwegian (bokmål, nynorsk) (III) →		Lappish
	Swedish (Finland) (III) →	Finnish (III) →		Lappish
2. exoglossic standards only	French (Belgium) (II) →	Flemish (III)		
	Alemannic Hoch-deutsch (Switzerland) (II) →	French (Jura) (III) →	Rhaeto-Romansch	
		Letzeburgisch (III)		

Note: The Roman numerals (I-VI) refer to the categories discussed in the text.

proved strong enough to resist amalgamation into the wider Iberian alliance headed by Castille.[4] Outside its borders, only to the north in Galicia was there a similar dialect and early literary culture. But with the consolidation of the Spanish empire in the sixteenth century there came a parting of the ways, and linguistic affinity across the border was never to produce political repercussions of any consequence. Internally, despite the later marked economic differences between north and south, Portugal remained a unified homogeneous nation, with increasing agreement on a common standard based on the dialects of the cultural centre, Coimbra, and the political centre, Lisbon.

Similar developments took place in two territories at the northern outskirts of the old empire. The territories of Denmark and Sweden were slowly consolidated within distinctive state structures after the tenth century. The various dialects of the two were relatively close to each other, and for a while it looked as if only one effective state structure would emerge. This possibility was broken by Sweden in 1522, and the Reformation and printing press helped to build two distinctive standards. The oral dialects did not disappear, and in the border areas it was originally a matter of indifference which standard was closer. This explains the Swedish success in integrating Scania and the other territories wrested from Denmark. It also helped that the conquest (1658) occurred before the introduction of compulsory mass education.[5] There was no sudden imposition of a new standard: when people learned to read, they were made familiar with the Swedish standard.

The Dutch case was very different. The Low Countries had once been part of the Roman and Frankish empires, and formally remained imperial territories until 1648. They were typical city-belt territories: instead of consolidation during the Middle Ages, there was a system of interacting principalities and cities under some form of imperial feudal obligation. They were also culturally divided: the line between Germanic and Romance speakers, which today divides Belgium, has remained stable since the fifth century. After a brief consolidation under Burgundy after 1377, the Reformation and the protracted fight against the Habsburg Empire again divided the Low Countries. But this new and essentially religious line traversed the territories further north than the old linguistic divide. These developments left the Germanic regions in three distinctive parts: the southern, Catholic, provinces of

Flanders and Brabant, a Calvinist centre dominated by Holland, and a Frisian north. Economic development and dynamism gave Holland a dominant position in this new structure. Flanders, once the core of early northern capitalism, was left in Habsburg hands and stagnated until the twentieth century. Friesland remained largely a primary-producing periphery that became subordinated to Holland, the centre of the new Dutch state. The medieval literary standard that had flourished in Flanders and Brabant was gradually 'northernized', a process that continued into the nineteenth century.[6] Widespread agreement on a common standard, the 'Algemeen Beschaafd Nederlands', was reached after 1900, and this even broke through in Belgian Flanders in the 1950s. The process of linguistic homogeneity took much longer and was more painful than in Denmark or Sweden, but in the end the result was not too different. Flanders and Holland shared the same standard, which had also swamped Frisian.

English and French were languages of core territories consolidated against the Empire. In both cases there were great variations in linguistic expressions in the Middle Ages, followed by rapid standardization in the wake of the invention of printing. But both languages were still limited to the core territories, facing a number of peripheral languages and patois. There was, however, a marked difference between the two countries in their policies towards these outlying areas. The English, having unified their core territory more thoroughly, were much more tolerant towards their peripheries: they allowed the Scots to retain a wide range of distinctive institutions within the Union of 1707, and for long pursued a policy of benign neglect towards the Welsh and Irish. The peripheries tended to be ignored rather than actively integrated. In France the frustrations of a fragmented administrative structure produced a violent wave of centralization during the Revolution. In practice, this brought with it a further press of gallicization, of forced imposition of the Île de France standard across all territories.[7] The process of integration, however, was slow. It began in earnest only with the Industrial Revolution and the proliferation of new networks during the Third Republic (Weber, 1976; also Serant, 1965). The Jacobin ideology of the unitary nation-state combined with the pressures of the capitalist economy to penetrate and weaken the peripheral cultures. There was definitely a phase of cultural colonialism in France, assisted by the unification of the labour market, with the more backward peripheries treated not very differently from the overseas colonies acquired during the nineteenth century.

Portugal, England, France, Denmark and Sweden all developed strong centres and distinctive standards at the fringes of the old empires. The Netherlands developed a dominant standard within the old imperial territory, but at a slower speed. Within the European urban dorsal spine territorial consolidation was achieved in two steps: before 1648 consolidation came through consociation, the development of polycephalic federations (the Netherlands, Switzerland); after the French Revolution other fragmented territories were brought together under one leading centre without affecting the basic polycephality of the city structure. The two territories so consolidated had both developed strong literary standards of their own long before they were politically unified. In this respect they differed markedly from the empire-nations at the edge of the old empire.

What distinguished the German and Italian trajectories from those of all the other territories was this contrast in the timing of the two processes of unification: they were culturally unified several centuries before they were politically consolidated. The only other country to trace a similar trajectory, at least until the sixteenth century, was Ireland. There, too, the cultures were unified while the political system was thoroughly fragmented: however, the Irish standard did not survive the Reformation and the English ascendancy. In Italy the Church had been successful in maintaining Latin as a standard of written communication after the fall of the western Empire, but this was an elite language remote from the several regional oral dialects. With the rise of commercial capitalism and an expanding literate stratum in the cities, it proved impossible to maintain Latin as the dominant language of long-distance communication. Three standards competed with each other in the early phase of vernacularization: Sicilian, Tuscan and Venetian. By the fourteenth century, however, the prestige of the Florentine culture throughout the peninsula aided the acceptance of the Tuscan standard as the 'umanesimo volgare'.[8] While this did not reduce the distance between oral dialects, there was no serious counter-challenge, and, after the French Revolution and Risorgimento, no serious controversy over the national standard (Serrani, 1972; Bechelloni, 1970).

By contrast, developments in Germany did not start out from a single elite standard. A unified written language was very much a product of the joint colonization of the eastern marchlands and the consequent intermingling of different dialects. The subsequent consolidation of the Hochdeutsch standard was decisively helped by the printing press and the powerful impact of Martin Luther's translation of the Bible. Despite centuries of political fragmentation, Hochdeutsch formed the education standard for both Protestant and Catholic states in the west. With the decline of the Hanseatic League, it gradually superseded Niederdeutsch in northern Germany. To the south, with the spread of trade across the Alps, German had become an important cross-local language of commerce. While the Alemannic Swiss established their independence in the fourteenth century, they did not break with the linguistic culture of Germany: Hochdeutsch was quickly accepted as the language of elite communication. Similar processes occurred in Austria and Prussia, areas that had not developed a cultural standard before the new printing technology changed the conditions for long-distance communication: both accepted Hochdeutsch as the standard of written communication.

The multilingual structures

In six of the cases in Category I, linguistic centralization was a direct consequence of political centre-building, while in Germany and Italy there was a process of linguistic homogenization within a decentralized network of elite interaction within the old imperial structures. We shall now look at the fewer cases of more deliberate linguistic accommodation within multilingual structures. Again, we must distinguish between two sets of original conditions: within the city belt, and on its periphery. The former produced two multilingual systems, Switzerland and Belgium. On the periphery one crusading empire, Spain, had to resort in part to a federal alliance strategy in the conquest of its territories.

Multilingual structures were more likely to develop in territories with strong federalizing traditions, in boundary zones between major language groups, or in military alliances among territorial systems of near-equal strength. However, the cases differ too much from each other and are too few to permit pushing such a simple summary too far. While all are officially multilingual, they differ markedly in the strength of the constituent languages. There was never any question of linguistic equality: in all three cases one language has been historically predominant. The Swiss structure was for long the most balanced, but there was never any doubt about the economic and demographic preponderance of the Alemannic German community. For at least a century after its foundation, the Belgian state had a strongly skewed structure: French was unquestionably the elite language, and it is only since the 1950s that some degree of equilibrium with Flemish has been established. There has been no such trend towards equilibrium in Spain. While the three major regional languages — Catalan, Basque and Galician — have received some minimal level of official recognition, this is counteracted by a marked demographic imbalance. Spain differs also on other counts. Belgium and Switzerland were buffer territories and did not develop indigenous standards, while Spain had at least four endoglossic standards. This contrast corresponds to that between interface and external peripheries: dependence on two or more centres in the one case, dependence on one centre in the other.

For Switzerland exoglossic standardization was perhaps the simplest strategy in the building up of a strong federation. It would have been vastly more costly to enforce one endoglossic Alemannic standard in Germanic Switzerland; this would have given one dialect a distinct privilege. It was much easier to accept an external standard equally remote from all the local dialects, and one least likely to disturb the federation. With geographical expansion the Swiss persisted with federation at all levels except the economic, giving formally equal power to all cantons, establishing religious parity and equalizing the position of dialects by accepting exoglossic standards. The one exception confirms the utility of the linguistic strategy. The Rhaeto-Romansch communities in the Grisons (Graubünden) could not look to any external standard, and perhaps because of this could not agree upon a standard of their own. To the extent that the linguistic groups in Switzerland have accepted a high degree of separateness, the resulting centripetality has paradoxically provided not only accommodation, but also integration (Schermerhorn, 1970: 77-85).

While Switzerland had the good fortune to be caught in a vice between three high-prestige languages, the Belgian state was trapped in a state of disequilibrium. One exoglossic standard was that of a great European power; the other, of a politically much weaker unit. French was the language of the nation-building elites, while Flemish, for all the glories of its medieval flowering, was primarily a set of rural dialects. Attempts to rectify this disequilibrium began in earnest only in the 1950s and have still to run their course. But it seems clear that to solve the problem of multilingualism Belgium has to adopt a Swiss policy of federalization. The difficulty is that the two populations are too intermingled in the Brussels area to allow a straightforward territorial solution.

The situation has been even more skewed in Spain, where whatever is done to devolve decision-making processes to the historic peripheries will probably not result in a federation of equal units of government.[9] Yet Spain began life with strong federalizing characteristics. The Iberian alliance against the Muslims has some parallels with the Swiss fight against the German emperors. However, the Iberian allies were dynastic, not peasant republics or corporations of burghers, while the Reconquista opened up vast territories in the south for colonization. While in the early phase of the Reconquista there was some doubt about the outcome of the struggle for political hegemony, by the end of the fifteenth century the issue was settled. Castille was the dominant partner, acquiring control over large expanses of territory. But Aragon and Catalonia never accepted their fate, rebelling again and again, and refusing to succumb to castillianization. What was even more important was that Catalonia, part of the medieval trade belt, developed great economic strength to compensate for the loss of political power, and, being an independent centre economically aided efforts to maintain a distinctive language. Catalan did not lose its hold on the native population through continuous outmigration: on the contrary, the greatest linguistic danger was the constant immigration of Castillian speakers into the industrial growth centres around Barcelona (Rossingol, 1974; Perez-Alondon, 1979). Such double jeopardy is a common feature of peripheral territories.

Catalonia is more obviously an intermediate case, having much in common with the cases in Category IV. However, it can be grouped with the other two cases, because minimally they do have in common a history of federalization and a tolerant practice of regionally distinctive languages. We might have added Britain to this category, but that would entail some uncomfortable concept-stretching. Whatever the policies towards the Celtic fringe, there was little doubt about the unitary structure of government. And while there was a federal element in the Anglo-Scottish Union, Scotland differs from Catalonia in that the former employed the central language as a standard of written communication both before and after union.

The victorious peripheries

There is no hard-and-fast rule of success for dependent peripheries. Here we shall simply reckon as victorious those that were able to establish and maintain their own linguistic standards, to which the bulk of the territorial population remained loyal. Discounting Catalonia, because its earlier history of centre-building makes it more natural to treat it as a key component of a multilingual system, this criterion gives us nine victorious peripheries: Norway, Finland, the Faeroes, Iceland, Friesland, Flanders, Luxembourg, the Bernese Jura and, more dubiously, Wales. The Nordic victories were the most complete: these peripheries not only established dominant standards within their territories, but also achieved political independence. The Frisian victory was much more severely limited and came very late. Flanders and the Jura are parts of multilingual structures and achieved equality of status within federal frameworks. Luxembourg was caught between two external standards, but succeeded in promoting its local dialect as an alternative standard of official communication. Wales is a much more marginal case. While it had far greater success than the other Celtic territories in preserving a distinctive language, that success was increasingly limited to rural, more sparsely populated, areas. In general we might say that territories that had not achieved independence before the French Revolution could still maintain distinctive standards if there was widespread literacy and some level of mass education before the introduction of universal suffrage, and if the decisive waves of mobilization for the peripheral language came before the opportunities for migration across regions. Clearly, however, such a generalization should be treated with circumspection in discussing several of these cases.

The Nordic cases fit into very different cells in the conceptual maps presented in Chapter 1. Their situation is summarized in Figure 3.4, which brings out the differences in timing in the histories of liberation in the four cases. Two factors proved important: inter-intelligibility of the peripheral and metropolitan languages, and direct demographic contacts between the native populations and settlers from the dominant culture. The distance between the peripheral and the colonial elite language was much

FIGURE 3.4
A conceptual map of the Nordic territories

Peripheral status ↔ Continuous independence ↔ Peripheral status

Strong city network ↔ Weak city network

FAEROES	ICELAND	NORWAY	DENMARK	SWEDEN	FINLAND
Under Denmark, currently in process of reaching independence	Under Denmark until 1944	Under Denmark until 1814, domestic sovereignty under Sweden until 1905			Under Sweden until 1809, a grand duchy under Russia, 1809-1917

greater in Finland than elsewhere. The structure and vocabulary of Finnish were very different, and took a great deal of effort for a Swedish speaker to learn. By contrast, the distance between the Danish metropolitan language and the local languages and dialects in Norway was much less pronounced. In fact, the printing standard established in Copenhagen was for centuries accepted in Norway as an expression of the oral languages, at least as pronounced by the educated elites. The distances to Icelandic and Faeroese were greater, but there, perhaps partly because of their remote locations, much of the older literature was disseminated through locally and manually reproduced versions.

What was different in Finland was the proximity and nature of the Swedish settlement: rural communities in Ostrobothnia and the south-western archipelago, and a set of resource-controlling elites along the southern coast. These two sets of Swedish speakers did not interact closely until the nineteenth century, when they sought mutual protection from the initial waves of Finnish nationalism. While the position of the Swedish minority as a whole was strengthened through this alliance, the Swedish elite had a direct interest in the development of a broadly-based Finnish movement as an essential element in a strategy to protect the inherited structure of government against the Russian centre (Alapuro, 1982). Nationalism served as a civil religion safeguarding the Finnish state, and for this reason it proved possible to reach agreement on measures of accommodation between the two linguistic communities. The Finnish language was placed on an equal footing with Swedish in 1883, and by the time of the 1919 Constitution the process of equalization had gone so far as to make it relatively easy to establish the detailed rules of the 1922 Language Act for the determination of the rights of each community. While the Swedish minority has steadily declined to some 6 per cent of the population, there have been few infringements of their territorial rights. Swedish persists as an important language in Finland, for example in business and commerce, and it is part of an impressive infrastructure of institutions and stigmata that serve the minority. On the other hand, Swedes in local minority situations have increasingly solved the predicament by becoming bilingual (Ågren, 1974).

The situation in Norway was different. Upon independence in 1814 the written and printed standard was Danish, but the language was pronounced differently throughout the country. The history of the liberation of Norwegian from the Danish inheritance is largely the history of the reduction of this distance between the written and the oral language. This process occurred during a period of expanding education, accelerating modernization and widespread political mobilization: the result was protracted conflicts, first over the urban standard due to replace Danish as the written norm, and then between this standard and an indigenous counter-standard developed out of rural dialects. By 1907 the urban standard ('riksmål', later called 'bokmål') was clearly distinctive from Danish, despite some conflict over orthography and vocabulary content. The conflict was reinforced by the powerful upsurge of the intellectual construction of the 'landsmål' (later called 'nynorsk') counter-standard.[10] Nynorsk caught on not only within the rural areas of the south and west; it became an expression of identity for the rising peasant intelligentsia after 1870. The broad left alliance (Venstre) took up its cause and forced through legislation to recognise Nynorsk as an official norm, both of administrative communication and in the schools. But this standard also experienced conflicts between dialects, which could often be resolved only by allowing several alternative grammatical forms. The Nynorsk movement reached its peak between the two world wars: continued urbanization after 1945 reduced its numerical strength (Haugen, 1966: 309), but this popular decline was paralleled by its increasing adoption within intellectual circles, a development that helped to enrich both languages.[11]

In both Iceland and the Faeroes the movement for national cultural independence proved successful, but the conditions for their development were different. Iceland had established a strong literary standard during the Middle Ages, the survival of which was assisted by the island's remote location. It was confirmed after the Reformation with the translation of the Bible into classic Icelandic. As a result, even though Danish increasingly became the language of administration, Icelandic remained the language of the church. The indigenous standard was so well-rooted that, by the time of the nationalist upsurge and the reestablishment of the Althing in the nineteenth century, it was recognized by Denmark as the only official language on the island. Danish intrusion went much further in the smaller Faeroese community, which lacked an effective counter-standard: Danish was used in the church, the schools and in administrative practice. Even so, the 1845 attempt to introduce Danish as the sole language of educational instruction, a move towards total integration, triggered a strong nationalist reaction and efforts to produce a written Faeroese standard. The first victory came in 1912, when Faeroese was accepted in education alongside Danish. In 1938 the latter became only optional in schools, and a decade later was dropped as the official language of internal administration. Again, geographical isolation and a limited and specialized metropolitan settlement may have helped the language to survive.

By contrast to the Nordic cases, the Flemish movement in Belgium and the Francophone movement in the Bernese Jura are cases of successful vindication of linguistic rights within multilingual systems. In both the problem concerned the legitimation of an exoglossic standard in a peripheral territory. Flemish was for long merely a set of dialects of the dominant language to the north: the Flemings were culturally as well as politically and economically peripheral. By contrast, while the French speakers in the Jura had been thoroughly peripheralized both economically and politically, their language was that of a great power, and one that was accepted as a standard elsewhere in Switzerland. There was another difference: the Jura was divided in its religion between a Catholic north and a Protestant south, whereas Flanders was much more homogeneously Catholic. Finally, the Flemish territory was much larger geographically and demographically within Belgium than the Jura within Berne. But whatever the differences in the conditions, the Flemish movement and the Jurassiens, albeit only recently, both succeeded in reasserting the distinctiveness of their territories and language.

The victory was more complete in Flanders. After independence the Belgian elites were uniformly francophone. There was no recognized Flemish standard, and the province was heavily rural. The great change came with World War II. Flanders was transformed into a booming industrial region, and the northern Dutch standard was accepted in the 1950s. Economic change and government expansion generated a growing market for skilled workers, professionals and bureaucrats in Flemish (Heisler, 1974: 200) and a corresponding upsurge of recruitment of Flemish speakers into higher education: it was this new generation that increasingly rejected the dominance of the francophone elites. More generally, despite the elitist position of French, Flemish had survived as the popular language within the province. Partly because of this strength, the Flemings were able, with economic development and political mobilization, not only to win equal rights for their language, but also to secure its exclusive dominance within their own territory. The focus of the Belgian political problem was increasingly the greater Brussels area, historically Flemish but experiencing more and more francophone settlement. Brussels highlighted a question that is crucial not only to Belgium: can you combine a system of territorial federal accommodation with a system of personal rights and communalism? There may well be possibilities of reconciling the two, but any one solution for safeguarding linguistic rights will be costly.

In Switzerland there was never any doubt about the primacy of the territorial principle, at the communal as well as the cantonal level. In the Bernese Jura the francophones could send their children to schools in their own language whenever they were in a majority locally, but only rarely could they gain influence within the large German-dominated canton of Berne. Religion and economics, however, served to divide the French-speaking Jura. The Protestants in the south had always been closer to the German speakers in Berne than the northern Catholics. Moreover, the south had been industrialized over a much longer span of time and was closer to the advanced centres of the Swiss economy. As a result, the southern labour force was more open to recruitment into the German-dominated forms and therefore less likely to insist upon monolinguality. The northern Jura experienced considerable economic progress after World War II, but no more so than the south. However, the general increase in the absolute level of prosperity permitted a large number of Jurassiens to stay within their local communities and reject the lures of the outside labour market. The demand for control over a distinctive linguistic standard was linked to the belief that people could afford to stay in the French-speaking environment, that they did not have to submit to the discipline of bilinguality within a cross-local labour market. In the south the great majority were already in this cross-local labour market. The north-south contrast was heightened because of the primacy in Switzerland of the territorial principle. The demand for an equal status for French could most easily be resolved by the establishment of a separate French-speaking canton, and constitutionally this could be reached only through a series of referenda at all levels, including the communal. It was the referenda at the communal level within the Jura that settled the territorial and linguistic issue. The monolingual canton of Jura established in the 1970s was much smaller than the historic territory, and excluded most of the Protestant south.[12]

Wales was not a victorious periphery in the same sense as the previous cases. It can perhaps be included here as the most successful of the Celtic language communities in maintaining itself against the metropolitan standard. Within the United Kingdom Irish practically disappeared during the nineteenth century and could not be restored to full vigour with the founding of the Republic: at best, it remained a ceremonial language resorted to for historical and sentimental reasons. The situation in Scotland and Cornwall deteriorated even earlier to become still more parlous. While it is dubious whether Welsh is stronger than Breton, its status has been markedly different. Through a series of ad hoc decisions, culminating in the 1967 Language Act, it has become accepted in the courts, in religion and in the schools, as well as being given some space in the electronic media (Krejci, 1978: 147-57). Indeed, the time allocated to broadcasting in Welsh, while very limited, is nevertheless greater than that granted any other linguistic minority in Western Europe (and is the first minority language to have the exclusive use of its own television channel). It is in this sense that Wales can be regarded as a victorious periphery, though 'victory' came too late to halt the inexorable slide of Welsh to become a minority language within Wales. The problem therefore has been that the territory of the language did not coincide with the administratively defined region. The survival of Welsh alone in Britain rests upon several factors. Its early literary strength was buttressed by the Reformation: the translation of the Bible authorized in 1562 legitimized the language as a medium of religious communication. Later, the rise of Protestant Nonconformism and the great educational movements of the eighteenth century (Williams and Hughes, 1978) gave it a grass-roots strength that seemingly could not easily be broken. But broken it was in the wake of industrialization, and the language steadily retreated to the backward rural areas.[13] While there was stability in the absolute numbers of Welsh speakers until World War II, the proportional strength declined steadily from some 80 per cent in 1801 (Rhys and Brynmor-Jones, 1906: 549) to 54 per cent in 1891, and further to less than 25 per cent in the 1970s. The division between the rural heartland of the language and a non-Welsh-speaking majority in the industrial south has been a constant source of conflict between the 'culturalists', who wish to concentrate efforts on the preservation of the language, and the 'separatists', who want to assert the distinctiveness of the entire historical territory. As in Norway, the decline in recent decades has been accompanied by a definite surge in cultural activities, though how far this can be taken as expressing a stable commitment to the language cause is hard to assert. Nevertheless, the new media have helped to build core groups of intellectuals and cultural activists whose life careers are closely tied to the fate of the language, and who increasingly cannot afford transition to another language.

The last two languages in this section are still more marginal than Welsh, but the marginality expresses itself in different settings. Frisian is essentially a boundary language given some status in the Netherlands. A strong medieval language with a considerable literature, it lost out during the Reformation and with the economic rise of Holland. West (Dutch) Frisian was resuscitated in the nineteenth century and a stable standard was developed for written communication: this was eventually legitimized for use in basic education in 1955 and as an optional language in the courts in 1956. Elsewhere, East Frisian, in north-west Germany, has largely died out, though North Frisian, with some 10,000 speakers, lingers on in the islands off the German-Danish coast, but without a common standard. Possibly because of the isolated location of this island language, the German authorities allowed its usage in primary education as early as 1925.

Letzeburgisch, the primary language of Luxembourg, is essentially a Germanic dialect. Its fate was changed by the recognition in 1815 of Luxembourg as a sovereign state. This tiny buffer territory had to develop a policy of flexible adaptation to its giant neighbours: its professionals were trained in either France or Germany, and used both exoglossic standards in administration, law and legislation. The local dialect developed a written standard very late, but in 1912 was introduced as an obligatory language of instruction in the schools. The decisive change, however, came in World War II. As part of the aversion to everything German, Letzeburgisch increasingly replaced Hochdeutsch, and today has equal status with French in internal administration, though the latter dominates in external communications. Letzeburgisch is only one of several dialects in the buffer zone between German and French, but in this one case the dialect was promoted to an official territorial language. The original reflex was to accept two exoglossic standards, but when one of these proved to be unacceptable, the solution was to promote the local dialect as an alternate endoglossic standard, possible because of the independent political status. This decision contrasts clearly with the policies pursued in two other territories, Alsace and Alemannic Switzerland, between the two great language communities. The general tendency in these border areas was to opt for exoglossic standards of written communication: in Alsace the local dialect prevailed, but without official status, while in Alemannic Switzerland the various dialects retained their strength in oral communication, with Hochdeutsch remaining the basic standard of written communication.

Peripheries with weak standards and some level of autonomy

The case of Luxembourg exemplifies one possible path of linguistic upgrading: political independence, then legitimation of a distinctive standard for the territory. Similar developments occurred in Norway. There are also other cases of contrasts in the timing of processes of political liberation and processes of cultural self-assertion. Ireland is the only instance of full sovereignty without successful assertion of linguistic distinctiveness: by contrast, Scotland represents successful maintenance of distinctive identity-maintaining institutions without full sovereignty and without a separate language. There are also some linguistic communities with limited status within federalizing systems: Rhaeto-Romansch in Switzerland, Sardinian in Italy, and Basque and Galician in Spain. In all these cases we deal with languages at low levels of legitimacy, either because of their internal fragmentation or because of their marginal status in education or administration.

What makes Ireland interesting is the failure of the nationalist movement to make the old language an efficient medium of everyday communication. Irish had been the first western European language to replace Latin and Greek as a medium of learning, with a strong literature from the sixth century onwards. Decline set in with the Reformation and increasing English dominance. The great surge of Catholic mobilization in the nineteenth century only served to weaken further the position of the old language: the Catholic Church retained its hold on the peasantry, but did nothing to strengthen the language. Its support for full citizenship for Catholics was not a demand for separate linguistic status: the concern was with control of education and access to the vast English labour market. These interacted in the mid-nineteenth century (Akenson, 1970) to reinforce an already established trend: the Industrial Revolution, by opening up a market for the services

TABLE 3.1
Literacy and language usage in Ireland in the nineteenth century

	*Literacy**		*Language 1851*		
Province	*1841* %	*1851* %	*Irish only* %	*Irish and English* %	*Total Irish speakers* %
Leinster	44	39	0.01	3.5	3.5
Munster	61	55	7.9	36.0	43.9
Ulster	40	35	1.8	5.0	6.8
Connaught	72	66	13.6	37.2	50.8
Ireland	83	77	4.9	45.9	50.8

* Percentage of population aged 5 years or more unable to read or write.

Source: Akenson (1970: 376, 378).

of the Irish peasantry, had already broken down their isolation from the English language. The distribution of language use by province in 1851 (Table 3.1) points to a correlation between the spread of modernity and the switch to English as the main medium of communication. Irish was strongest where literacy was least advanced, in the south and west: it was on its way to extinction in the areas most dependent upon the British economy — Leinster (the Dublin region) and Ulster. Developments in the school system (the teaching of Irish as an optional subject was introduced only in 1900) and the labour market made these trends irreversible. As a result, when the Gaelic League launched its campaign for the Irish language in the 1890s, it was already too late to stem the tide. A desperate effort at revival after independence also proved to be in vain: Irish might have been established as the official language of the new state and been made obligatory in education and as a requirement for some civil service jobs, but this did not make it a living, dynamic language. Moreover, standardization, to the extent that it was achieved, did not come about until the publication of an official grammar in 1953 (O Cuiv, 1969: 22-34).

However, the decline in the active use of Irish did not affect the strength of ethnic identity: there are many other ways of signalling belonging to a 'we' group. In Ireland the distinctive and pervasive presence of Catholicism helped to preserve a sense of separateness, as did the burning grievances over landownership. These were reinforced by the nature of the central British presence, uncaring as much as repressive. And after 1922 the symbolism could be concentrated on the issue of the partition of the island: the border between the Republic and Northern Ireland, one of the least impervious in Europe, has retained a high degree of symbolic rigidity. Similarly, in the protracted sequences of violence in Northern Ireland, some acts of terrorism at least could be construed as alternative expressions of an effort of identity-building on the wrong side of the border, since language is not there as a permanent reminder to people of their identity. Violence polarizes, and the ceremonial reaffirmation of memories of past hostilities and unfinished business is a powerful strategy of identity-building.

The loss of a distinctive language does not of necessity lead to increased violence. This emerges clearly in the parallel, yet contrasting, case of Scotland, where there was no strong political reaction against the Union until the 1960s and none of the violence so characteristic of the transition to independence in Ireland and of the later confrontations between Catholic and Protestant in Northern Ireland. Yet Scotland too accepted the exoglossic standard of the dominant centre, never in fact even trying to replace English, and even the most ardent nationalists have never pushed hard for a distinctive Scots written standard. This goes a fortiori for Gaelic, and there is no possibility that this remote language would acquire even ceremonial status within an independent Scotland. What makes Scotland unique in Europe is the combination of a strong historical consciousness of separate identity with a complete disinterest in the development of a distinctive language. The divorce between a persisting institutional structure and the language parallels that between 'civil society' and the state stressed by Nairn (1977: 139). We might even say that the Scottish elites traded off their right to a distinctive language against the profitable advantages of integration with the English economy. After the thirteenth century a variety of English steadily spread over the whole of the Scottish Lowlands, but it was a variety clearly distinctive from that spoken to the south. At the same time, the

Scottish state was politically flawed, and the centre proved unable to impose any regular administration or an effective standard of communication over all its hinterlands. While Scotland built up an effective range of institutions that served to maintain identity and to act as agencies of indigenous elite recruitment, linguistically it looked to the standard south of the border (Urwin, 1978). Mass education may have come early (at the end of the seventeenth century), but under the control of the Scottish Church the dominant language of instruction was English, even in the Highlands.

The Scottish case clearly illustrates the importance of the timing of standardization and self-assertion. There was no separate Scottish standard before Union and the Industrial Revolution; and once that revolution had produced all its benefits to the Lowland centres of the Scottish economy, there was little incentive to reject English as the dominant standard of communication. In any case, the alternative standard of Gaelic was rejected even more decisively by groups in the Scottish centre. Compared with Ireland, the intermingling with English took place at a very different level. In the Scottish case there was interaction, if not integration, predominantly at the elite and middle-class level, while in the Irish the interaction was more frequently at the working-class level. This contrast in the class level of the process of interaction goes far to explain differences in the character of later political conflicts between the periphery and the metropolitan centre: the concentration on economic issues in Scotland, the cumulation of ethnic, religious and class cleavages in Ireland.

Irish and Scottish developments occurred within a system of clear-cut hegemony: there was never any doubt about the supremacy of the Westminster Parliament. By contrast, the remaining peripheral situations in this group are found in systems with longer histories of, and stronger sympathies towards, federal practice. The Jura represents a case of successful mobilization of linguistic identity within the Swiss Confederation. Developments in the Grisons (Graubünden) were very different. In the Jura there was never any doubt about the vitality of the linguistic standard: it was exoglossic, but made for a unified linguistic community. In the Grisons there was no such unity. At least six different dialects could be found, each with a separate standard. While all were members of the Rhaeto-Romansch language group, the fragmented geography of the region simply did not make it possible for them to accept a common standard. The first organization to defend the dialects, the Lia Rumantscha, appeared only in 1919, yet this was still before the appearance of anything approximating an open labour market. Accommodation was reached in 1938 with a subsidy given to the Lia and the recognition of Rhaeto-Romansch as the fourth language of the confederation. Yet this meant little in practice. Because of the dialectical diversity, the language could be used only in the local schools, and the canton continued to be administered in German. Moreover, despite provisions for language teaching and broadcasting, the number of speakers in the canton has slowly but steadily declined (Steinberg, 1978: 114-16). The developments in the Grisons illustrate the importance of early unification of a linguistic community: the failure to create a viable internal standard led to the penetration of exoglossic standards into dialect areas that were too small to offer adequate opportunities for mobility.

The fate of the Rhaetians can best be explained by their isolated location. By contrast, that of the Sardinian language reflected the geographical openness of an island to a succession of invasions from outside. Of necessity this openness influenced the character of the local language. Sardinian was never unified: there were three major dialects, with important differences in their trajectories. However, there was very little literature in these dialects beyond administrative documents and religious texts. Haarmann (1975) goes so far as to characterize Sardinian as a 'schriftloss Volkssprache', a popular language without writing. All attempts at asserting the distinctiveness of the language were drowned in the great surge for Italian unification after 1848: in fact, it was a handicap for the islanders that this wave of nationalism was spearheaded by an entity called the Kingdom of Sardinia, in practice a network of elites centred on Turin in Piedmont. While the oral dialects survived, complaints against the centre were more of a political and economic nature (Pintore, 1974). Similarly, the decisive incentives to grant some autonomy to the island in the 1970s did not reflect recognition of a distinctive language. Even so, Sardinian has taken some steps back from oblivion: it has now been used by some local councils, and in 1976 the first mass was celebrated in the language.

We find another set of combinations in Spain: strong peripheral identities, but long and bitter conflicts over political autonomy. Spain has had a medieval legacy of federalism, but surges of

Castillian centralization in the sixteenth and nineteenth centuries triggered increasingly embittered responses in the peripheries. Three territories led the struggle against Castillian dominance: the alternative centre in Aragon-Catalonia, the border periphery of the Basque provinces, and the external periphery of Galicia. The three differed markedly in geopolitical and geoeconomic position. Catalonia had been an alternative centre which had never meekly accepted integration into the new Spanish empire. The Basques were never part of an imperial centre. Rather, to protect their border the Spanish kings had given the Basques south of the Pyrenees a number of privileges ('fueros'), setting them apart from the rest of the state's population. This grant of what amounted to collective nobility (Greenwood, 1977) no doubt heightened the pride and separateness of the Basques: they were already clearly set apart from the Spaniards by language. Linguistic tension was accentuated after the Liberal victory in 1833, with the Basques committed to defending the fueros against the centralizing forces in Madrid. Further embitterment over the same theme arose out of the nineteenth-century Carlist Wars and the Civil War of the 1930s, though the Carlist outcome underscored the difficulties of establishing an alliance between the Church and the defenders of the peripheral culture.[14] By the 1970s the Basque culture was severely fragmented along several dimensions — political, religious and economic. One important factor was the twentieth-century immigration into the provinces of more and more Castillian speakers. Immigration was equally important in Catalonia, but there the distance between the two languages was not an insurmountable hurdle. With Basque it was much more a question of either/or. The linguistic distance and the anger of those who feel obliged to speak in what they consider an utterly alien language is often advanced as a primary explanation of the high level of violence, heightened by the decline of Basque on both sides of the Pyrenees. Basque has several other features in common with the other languages reviewed in this section. Linguists normally distinguish seven dialects, three in Spain and four in France, without a unified standard. Moreover, Basque was never given official status until after the demise of the Franco regime. This produced the same kind of tension as in Wales: some protagonists give priority to the fight for the language, others to control of the historic territory.

The Catalan and Basque peripheries differ on many counts, but they have one feature in common: they are economically advanced while politically subjected and culturally opposed to the dominant Castillian standard. In comparing Flanders and the Jura we discussed the importance of affording one's distinctive culture: this was a matter not only of absolute welfare, but also of the fit between the language community and the cross-local labour market. The same regularity can be observed in the Catalan and Basque cases, but there the feeling of pride in local achievements combined with a rejection of the policies of the centre. In addition, the openness of the Spanish labour market created difficulties for the Basques and Catalans in sharp contrast to those of the Flemings and Jurassiens: the flow of immigrants from the political centre to the rich peripheries intensified the difficulties for the endogenous languages.

By contrast to these advanced Spanish peripheries, Galicia is very much a backward territory, a typical external periphery. Its language, too, was always marginal within Iberia. It might be termed a dialect of Portuguese during the Middle Ages, but with the establishment of a Portuguese state there came a parting of the ways. Galician lost out as a norm of written communication in the sixteenth century, and was revived only in the late nineteenth century, with the eventual reconstitution of a joint norm across several dialects, which made it easier to legitimize the language (Díaz López, 1982). But Galician never achieved official status. While it was a subject of instruction in primary schools, it was not an obligatory medium of teaching. For all these reasons, the Galician case is marginal, and its political advances might well be due in part to its location in a state pressed hard by two other much stronger peripheral languages. Despite having over 2 million speakers, Galician shades into the cases covered in the next section.

Marginal peripheries

So far we have concentrated on peripheries above some minimal level of recognition in linguistic, economic or political matters. We shall now proceed to review those territories without any recognized official language of their own, or without any measure of autonomy in their dealings with the centre. There are obvious problems in grading peripheries on these two levels. Marginality is only a shorthand for a complex multidimensional classification, and is not synonymous with externality. We shall not deal here with all the external peripheries as defined in Chapter 2, but only with those with some level of historically inherited distinctiveness. We shall not therefore deal with all the predominantly economic peripheries, those backward areas with only tenuous or dormant historical claims to distinctive cultural identity.[15] The rules of thumb to be formulated for our marginal peripheries might be that an ethnically distinctive subject territory is more likely to lose its separate linguistic identity: (a) the later the establishment of a unified standard of written communication in the territorial language; (b) the greater the differences in resources between periphery and central territory; (c) the earlier the development of a common labour market for both central and peripheral areas and the greater the opportunities for migration into the central language community; and (d) the greater the likelihood of immigration into the periphery in response to opportunities created by the discovery and development of economic resources. For regions with a strong Catholic tradition, we might add a further rule: a periphery is more likely to keep its separate linguistic identity the greater the opposition between the Church and the dominant elites within the centre.

So far we have touched only incidentally upon size as a condition for the survival of cultural distinctiveness. No doubt there is a threshold for the maintenance of distinctive institutions: once a population falls below that threshold, it cannot mount the resources required to resist integration. But size as such is not decisive: what counts is the frequency of internal versus external interactions. This ratio is a function of the density and the isolation of the populations. A nomadic population spreading itself over a large, sparsely populated territory does not risk much exposure to the dominant sedentary communities. The Lapps of northern Scandinavia are a very small minority, but at least the nomads among them have succeeded in maintaining their distinctive language, dress and style of life. Being traditional nomads, they never built up their own agencies for the control of territory: they survived because no other groups laid claim to the inhospitable regions. Where, however, Lapps settled, voluntarily or otherwise, in sedentary communities, they were much more exposed to pressures from the dominant culture and lost much of their cultural distinctiveness. The central authorities began to offer some facilities in education and the media for the maintenance of the distinctive culture only after World War II. But there was evidence of growing tension among the Lapps themselves as they became increasingly dependent upon facilities provided by the dominant cultural agencies. This tension expressed itself in many fields and in a familiar dilemma. A policy of alliance and acceptance increases the risk of inexorable loss of cultural identity: a policy of self-assertion may simply lead towards trivialization and a folklorization of the peripheral population. This dilemma is particularly acute for small ethnic communities surviving within larger and economically more advanced societies, and the Lapps are perhaps the best example in Western Europe.

There are parallel elements of such folklorization in the Scottish Highlands and islands. Much of the outward show and insignia of Scottish identity has its origins in the Highlands and their feudal-military past. The Gaelic language is part and parcel of this ancient heritage, though for long it has been only of limited symbolic significance and of little importance in ordinary life. The long history of tension between Lowlands and Highlands owes something to geography, but a succession of historical developments accentuated the structural and cultural contrasts between the two territories. The Celts, the major survivors of what had been a complex multi-ethnic structure, were gradually pushed northwards and westwards, but the Highlands and islands were never more than nominally subjected to control by the agencies of the Scottish centre (Smout, 1972; Urwin, 1978).[16] The Reformation accentuated the contrast. Calvinism took firm root in the Lowlands, and the Presbyterian Church later came, especially through its control of education, to work actively for the eradication of Gaelic. The final blow came in the eighteenth century. The defeat of the Jacobites and the subsequent Clearances marked the subordination and integration of the Highlands by a larger political entity. There was a lasting decline in population, and the Gaelic language community was doomed to permanent marginality. The economy of the area is weak, and the British authorities have done little to stem the tide. While Gaelic has been an optional subject in the local schools since 1878, there has been no compulsory teaching in the language. In the last resort, Gaelic lost out simply because the local resources were too weak to stem the tide of emigration, while its symbolic heritage was taken over as part of a Scottish identity that accepted English as the basic standard of communication.

We are brought back to the importance of the peripheral labour market for the survival of languages. If there are strong incentives to emigrate, the peripheral language is weakened. Alternatively, the periphery may be rich in a particular resource and attract labour from outside to such an extent as to endanger the position of the language. This is what happened in South Wales, and it was also part of the origin of the rapid decline of the Celtic language in Cornwall. The Cornish Celts were overwhelmed by migrants from outside, coming in because of the county's mineral wealth. By 1800 there were no longer any Cornish speakers. More recently, the discovery of the tourist attractions of Cornwall has brought in an even greater number of outsiders. Attempts have been made to stem the flow and to resuscitate the old language, but the outlook for such movements of intellectualized linguistic activity are not encouraging.[17] The process of integration has simply gone too far.

There are parallels as well as contrasts between the marginal peripheries of France and those of the United Kingdom. The fate of Breton, for example, has some parallels with the trajectories of its sister Celtic languages in Britain. But in the latter there was no sharp divide corresponding to that between the 'langue d'oc' and the 'langue d'oïl', and no interface belt similar to that from Flanders to Roussillon. Above all, there is the difference in the policies of the central elites to the claims of the peripheries. In the United Kingdom the basic attitude to the peripheries was more one of benign neglect, with little conscious official policy of integration. The latter occurred more as a result of the operation of market forces and the pull of the more dynamic economy of the core territory. France, by contrast, was the first country self-consciously to call itself an 'état-nation', a culturally unified, centrally controlled territory. But this was essentially an ideological expression of a strong will to unify: in practice France remained a multi-ethnic empire. Only under Cromwell did England approach this kind of ideology: the Glorious Revolution of 1688, however, reasserted pluralist trimming, a balance between the capital and the provincial elites. In France most of the acquired territories had been able to bargain for distinctive status within the realm, and were only unevenly penetrated by central agencies. The country was criss-crossed by differences in administrative institutions and policies, and the administrators of the 'ancien regime' were constantly frustrated in their attempts to break down these particularisms. The Revolution was in part a response to these frustrations: the Jacobins wanted to equalize conditions and regulations throughout the territory. This policy of ideological equalization served first to centralize decisions further: by preaching equality the Jacobins reduced the people of the peripheries to subjects or at least second-class citizens (de Certeau, Julia and Revel, 1975; also Anderson, 1975).

In Chapter 1 we hesitated in the case of Occitania: is it a failed centre or an interface periphery? At one point in history there was little doubt about the potential viability of an empire centred upon the north-western Mediterranean: whether its centre would be in Aragon, Catalonia or Languedoc was more a matter of guesswork. The reasons for failure were multiple, but perhaps the most important was the competition among several centres of roughly equal strength in the belt of cities from Valencia to Marseilles, none of which had enough empty space around it to succeed. But Occitania was also an interface caught between France and Spain, though not the subject of protracted conflicts. Once they had conquered Occitania after the crusade against the Albigensian heretics in 1229, the French stepped up their measures of control, and gradually moved from political dominance to social and cultural hegemony.

The thirteenth century saw the end not only of southern independence, but also of a flourishing Occitan literature, one of the first in a vernacular in Europe and the first to develop a 'koiné', a cross-territorial standard of high uniformity that was used also in administrative and juridical practice. At its peak this standard embraced the entire south, but could hardly be maintained without unified resources. With the victory of the Île de France the standard disintegrated into a number of dialectical variants, and was gradually replaced by the language of the conquerors. The Ordonnance de Villers-Cotterets of 1539 sealed the fate of Occitan: the northern standard was to be used in all official documents. The southern elites accepted the new standard without much opposition. But while increasingly persuaded to write in the langue d'oîl standard, they continued to speak their local dialects. With the expansion of the educational system, the oral language was also affected, with an increasing gap between the educated middle class and peasants and workers still loyal to their inherited dialects. Most of the successful languages in Europe reached the point of no return during the first century of printing: once a large body of texts was printed in a language, it was much more likely to survive. Occitan shares with Irish, Galician and Norwegian the distinction of having produced an extensive medieval literature only to lose out in the upheavals of the sixteenth century. The gap remained until the eighteenth century when, with the vogue of Romanticism, a number of intellectuals in Provence and Languedoc began to study the medieval Occitanian literature and to urge its revival, provoking a broad linguistic movement, the Félibrige, in the nineteenth century. However, this revival was and still is divided by geography and variations within the old speech.[18] While the cultural importance of this revival is not in doubt, the political impact has been more questionable. In the long run there may be some impact of the Loi Deixonne of 1951, which allowed the use of Occitan as an optional medium of instruction in the schools (though other decrees and bureaucratic practice severely reduced its import), and which perhaps might lead towards an effective joint standard. However, since its 'rediscovery' the southern language has also been constantly undermined by the extension of the national labour market. The French Midi was traditionally more urbanized than the north. Provence and Languedoc were not the earliest provinces to develop mass literacy (Furet and Ozouf, 1977), but they built up effective school systems long before the western periphery. From the Third Republic onwards the Midi produced a considerable surplus of graduates who found an expanding market for their talents in private firms and the public sector agencies of the north. This educated exodus from the south was perhaps as strong a factor as any in reconfirming the dominant position of French over Occitan.

The situation in Brittany was very different (Serant, 1971; Dulong, 1975). The language was distant in grammar and vocabulary from French, the level of urbanization and education was much lower, and the position of the Church was much stronger. Brittany parallels Ireland in its economic backwardness and cultural dominance by the Catholic Church. But the Breton Church differed from the Irish in its persistent opposition to the forces of the territorial centre: it became a staunch opponent of gallicization and was to remain until the twentieth century an effective agency for the maintenance of a distinctive Breton culture. The Breton language had been pushed westwards by the Normans in the ninth century, and Brittany was divided into two parts, the western Basse Bretagne and the eastern Pays Gallo, a line of division that survived incorporation into France in 1491. The division was not without consequences for the Church, which was stronger in the east than in the west (Furet and Ozouf, 1977: 338-40). But perhaps for that very reason the Church represented the most important cross-territorial cultural agency and the main bridge-builder across the line of linguistic division. It built up Breton identity across the dialects and came to the forefront of the struggle for a distinctive culture in the wake of the French Revolution. In this confrontation the Church found its greatest ally in the Breton nobility.[19] The Church and the nobility stood together in the confrontation with the Jacobins: Brittany was with the Vendée a stronghold of royalism, the country of the Chouans. This alliance was at the origin of the great revival of Breton philology and literacy in the first half of the nineteenth century, which helped develop a unified standard for the language, and the years since have seen a considerable flowering of Breton literature.

The alliance of nobility and clergy did help to keep the language alive even though very little was done to support it through the system of education. In all the external peripheries of France the introduction of primary schools was tantamount to gallicization: teaching was conducted exclusively in French, and there were all kinds of sanctions against the use of any form of patois (Furet and Ozouf, 1977; Weber, 1976). What saved Brittany was its geographical isolation and the absence of any extensive system of education before the final decision to introduce compulsory schooling in 1881.[20] The local language was simply reproduced from generation to generation in the absence of a strong alternative imposed from outside. The situation changed with the Third Republic, which not only introduced compulsory schooling, but also developed a national network of communication and created conditions for intensive migration from the peripheries to the expanding labour markets in the capital and the industrial centres of the north (Weber, 1976). But this large exodus did not decisively threaten the language with extinction. Three factors counted heavily in its survival: the high fertility of the Breton peasantry, the backwardness of the economy, and the strong cohesion of the emigrant groups. In this Brittany compares favourably with Wales. In both cases the language was sustained in the economically backward heartland, and given additional strength through the opposition between the local religious bodies and the central authorities. But, at least in terms of absolute speakers, Breton seems to have fared better than Welsh (Haarmann, 1975: 356; Gourvil, 1976: 106-9). This is remarkable in the light of the consistent discouragement of the language by the French authorities: there was no official recognition before the Loi Deixonne allowed optional teaching of Breton during the last three years of primary school (extended in 1970). The family and parish still offer the decisive environments for the reproduction of the language: the schools have essentially served to strengthen the language of the centre.

The situation is again very different in Corsica. The island has been vulnerable to foreign invasion in much the same way as Sardinia (Gregori, 1970). Rebellion against Genoa finally succeeded in 1729, with the establishment of a republic and constitution in 1735. This, however, Genoa did not accept: the island was simply sold to France in 1768. Despite further attempts at rebellion, Corsica was gradually but firmly integrated into France. The coastal urban middle class was thoroughly gallicized, and there was a steady stream of migration to the mainland: the island became a prime reservoir of labour for the army and administration.

Corsica may be integrated into France at the political level, but it is still very much an alien periphery in cultural terms. Yet this cultural distinctiveness finds less and less expression in linguistic communication; given its history of exposure, this is not entirely surprising. Corsicans, particularly those in the interior, may continue to speak their dialect, but there is little written communication except in French. Indeed, Haarmann (1975) treats Corsican as a dialect halfway between Italian and French and not as an independent language, reflecting the fact that the island is not only an external periphery to the French mainland, but also an insular interface between France and Italy. The claims of the language were scarcely heard until the 1970s, and the Loi Deixonne did not cover Corsican. Optional teaching in the language was made possible in 1974, but one year later only some 6 per cent of primary school children had elected to be taught in Corsican (Petrella, 1978a: 222).

Considering its geography and history, Italy is remarkably uniform in its culture. But history has left a few pockets of alien languages. Sardinian was discussed elsewhere, because of the autonomous status granted to the island. Two minor alien pockets are the Friulians and Ladins, both speaking dialects of Rhaeto-Romansch. The Ladins (some 13,500) live in the Dolomite valleys close to the German speakers south of the Brenner (Magnago,

1974). The Friulians, considerably larger — between 400,000 and 800,000, depending on the criteria of 'linguality' employed — are concentrated on the Italian-Slovenian border. Neither can boast a significant literature; they are primarily oral dialects. What is remarkable is that they have survived so many centuries of occupation by stronger powers. This north-eastern corner of Italy was overrun by a succession of outsiders during its long history. An independent duchy of Friuli did appear in the eleventh century, but in the fifteenth it was partitioned between Venice and the Habsburgs. Both parts were integrated into the Kingdom of Italy in 1866, by which time both Friuli and the Ladin territory had been thoroughly italianized. This process continued after 1866, with no evidence that it will be reversed. There had been no teaching in either dialect, and it was only in 1963 that the Italian government acknowledged the special problems of the region. However, the statute of autonomy to the region of Friuli-Venezia Guilia was not a response to pressures by the Friulians to protect their culture, but rather a natural step in the long process of border negotiations with Yugoslavia. The Friulian dialect remained marginal, with no official teaching in the language. By contrast, the Ladins, perhaps because of the much smaller and more isolated population, were allowed to use their language in their schools. This concession, however, was primarily part and parcel of another sequence of diplomatic moves on the border: that which led to the Austrian-Italian agreement on the Alto Adige. While both Friulian and Ladin are dialects of border zones, this does not make their territories interface peripheries in our terminology: in the typical interface, the population speaks a dialect of an external language recognized in the territory as a standard of written communication.

Solutions at the interfaces

The long process of restructuration of the territories of western Europe after the fall of Rome produced several units of varying size along the borders of states. The fates of these intermediary areas, with long histories of cultural and political conflicts and divided loyalties, reflected the oscillations of the larger units on either side. Most fall along the much disputed borders between France and Germany and France and Italy: they are all part of the Lotharingian buffer zone first defined in the Treaty of Verdun in 843.

Let us begin with Alsace, a territory with widespread acceptance of two exoglossic standards, French and Hochdeutsch, and a local Germanic dialect. The position of the two exoglossic standards has varied considerably with the vicissitudes of history. Alsace was brought within the orbit of the French kings in 1648. The language of administration and education, however, remained German until the French Revolution. And even after the Jacobins France continued to accept Alsatian distinctiveness and allowed the teaching of German in the religious schools. The first step towards gallicization in 1853 provoked a great wave of reactions. Indeed, the Alsatian conflict was at the heart of the memorable debate between German and French scholars on the meaning of 'nation'. German historians such as Mommsen and Treitschke wanted to identify 'Nation' and 'Sprache', while French scholars such as Michelet, Taine and Renan defended a broader cultural conception. To Renan (1970: 61-83) national identity was not a matter of language: rather, it expressed itself in a daily plebiscite, a constantly reaffirmed commitment to one's people and their institutions. The German conception won in the first round. Alsace was brought into the German Reich in 1870. Despite a liberal German policy, the population remained divided in identity — closer to the Germans in language, but strongly imbued by the spirit of the French political system. This neurotic ambivalence was intensified over the following decades as the province was exchanged back and forth between France and Germany (cf. Maugue, 1970; Gras, 1982). France introduced a tougher policy of integration after 1925, forcing German out of the schools and making French the official language of administration. These measures increased bilingualism, but did not kill the German dialects: there was simply a more marked differentiation between external and internal communication. The commercial-administrative bourgeoisie depended much more on external communication and was more thoroughly gallicized than the peasantry and working class. World War II pushed the process much further. Nazi policies alienated the majority and increased the distance to Hochdeutsch, which had never been popular in oral communication. This revulsion helped the French cause after 1945, even though partially counteracted by the tacit accusation in France of Alsatian collaboration with Nazi Germany. In any case, France tightened its grip by controlling the language used in the media (cf.

Gras, 1982; Petrella, 1978a: 237) and by limiting optional teaching in German in the schools. While parents may have continued to use dialect in the workplace, French was encouraged at home as they believed that fluency in the language would increase their children's life opportunities. While a more liberal attitude towards language teaching in the schools was introduced in 1971 and again in 1981, the dialect has not been greatly resuscitated, despite an intellectual and folklorish revival: the major compensation has been a more positive central attitude towards the teaching of German. The developments in Alsace resemble those in Luxembourg: the same strengthening of the French standard, continued dominance of the oral dialects in private communication. But Luxembourg was independent and had built up its own distinctive institutions. Alsace was simply two 'départements' administered from Paris, which was keen to weaken, if not eliminate, the endogenous institutional infrastructure. The proliferation of literature in the dialects could not substitute for official action to recognize an endoglossic standard, and the fundamental ambivalence of the Alsatian elite spilled over into politics.

The situation in Lorraine and Franche-Comté was less dramatic. Both provinces were thoroughly gallicized even though brought under French authority some time after the initial conquests in Alsace. In Lorraine it was the rapid development of coal and steel in the nineteenth century that brought in large masses of French-speaking workers, leaving only a few pockets of Germanic speakers. The periods under German occupation (1870-1918 and 1940-45) did little to change this: Lorraine remained thoroughly French in its culture. Further south the western part of Burgundy (the Duchy) was incorporated into France in 1477. The eastern Franche-Comté remained in the empire until 1678. This, however, was not a Germanic-speaking territory: the inherited language was Franco-Provençal, a tongue intermediary between Occitan and Langue d'Oîl, but this standard lost out in administrative practice by the end of the fifteenth century: French was established at the elite level in the Franche-Comté long before the final political conquest, and the territory was soon fully integrated into the French system.

Franco-Provençal was also the language of territories further to the east and south: the linguistic boundary running southwards from a point west of Basle towards the Alps was a line of division between some form of Alemannic German and Franco-Provençal.

The oral dialects of *Suisse Romande*, in fact, have remained close to the latter, though the written standard had become French in the late Middle Ages. More importantly, the Swiss were, from the beginning of their state-building efforts, more ready to tolerate the penetration of exoglossic standards of written communication.

The situation was rather similar in Savoy. This territory immediately north of the western Alps was to offer the basis for a strong effort of state-building during the Middle Ages. As protection against the expansionist designs of France, the Savoyards aligned themselves with the Habsburgs and moved their capital to Turin on the other side of the Alps. This was the beginning of the peripheralization of the old province of Savoy, which went much further when the rulers in Turin moved towards the unification of Italy. Eventually, Savoy, along with Nice, was ceded to France in 1860, to become an economic periphery deprived of its former links with Italy and Switzerland.[21] The cultural base vis-à-vis French was always precarious, and without economic strength offered little opposition to full integration (Lovie, 1977).

Between Savoy and Turin is the interface of the Val d'Aosta, a Franco-Provençal region that was not ceded to France in 1860. The unification of Italy heightened the peripheralization of the area. The construction of a rail link to Italy in 1866 aided emigration to the industrial centres of Piedmont and Lombardy, and subordinated the valley's economic interests to those of Piedmont. On the other hand, the culture and language were well-established, and proved able to survive a campaign of forced italianization by the Fascist regime. The defeat of the latter led to victory for the Valdotains: the new Italian government conceded autonomy to the region (Janin, 1968). But the decision to grant autonomy was not simply a response to pressures built up within the local population: it also reflected change in the geopolitical situation. Italy had lost the war; France was one of the victors and could have claimed the valley.

The situation was very different in another Alpine interface, the South Tyrol, an area claimed by two losers in World War II, where settlement was a slow process punctuated by outbursts of violence (Alcock, 1970). When Austria ceded Venice and its hinterlands to the new Italian state in 1866, it retained a triangle of land south of the Alps, not only for strategic reasons, but also because of the large concentration of German speakers. But there was also a strong Italian population, and the area was seen as 'irredenta', unredeemed Italian territory. The South Tyrol, in fact, was the reward promised to Italy by the Allies for entering World War I on their side. The transfer consequent upon Austrian defeat led later under Mussolini to a policy of deliberate italianization, especially through immigration into the area. But the other language was too well-rooted to be destroyed. In 1946 a statute of autonomy was granted, but to a much wider territory, called Trentino-Alto Adige, in which the German speakers were clearly a minority. German-speaking opposition to incorporation, supported by Austria, continued to express itself in acts of sabotage and terrorism. This violent opposition to italianization reached a peak in 1964. The two governments concerned were forced to set up a commission of inquiry into the situation in Alto Adige, which eventually proposed an accommodation between the two language communities through the proportionalization of public goods and services: this Proporzpaket was finally ratified in 1972, since when linguistic tension has declined significantly.

Along the Mediterranean coast the county of Nice was also ceded to France in 1860. Nice had a vigorous dialect and was open equally to the French and Italian standards (Gonnet, 1977). On this score it came closer to the Alsace-Luxembourg model: a strong local dialect and two exoglossic standards. In 1857 a local census indicated that some 75 per cent of the inhabitants used the dialect regularly. What distinguished Nice was its early cosmopolitianism: the sun and the 'plage' attracted tourists, and the local elites made clever use of the opportunities offered by this influx of foreigners.[22] But there was hardly any separatist or linguistic reaction to these foreign elements: the elites simply exploited the opportunities offered by the interface position. The dominant style of politics since incorporation has been ethnic machine politics: a mixture of Italian clientelism with the ethnic-local appeals so well-known from American cities. Politics was highly personalized. This seems to have been ranked as more important than strict cultural survival. While the significance of the dialect has declined, the years of integration with France have not appreciably changed this style of politics, but when decisive political issues have to be settled, ethnic loyalties count more than other identities. Ethnic mobilization is not necessarily a step towards greater participation in public affairs by ordinary citizens: ethnicity need often be no more than a resource used by established elites in a game of power.

Further west is the interface of Roussillon, Catalan country, originally an autonomous unit under Aragon and, later, Castille. It was annexed by France in 1659 after the Catalan revolt of 1640. But the area was not fully integrated: the two counties of Roussillon and Cerdagne constituted a 'province étrangere' (Marcet, 1977). While the French kings had promised to respect the 'usatges' (equivalent to the Basque 'fueros'), the ancien régime advanced the process of gallicization, a process accelerated and consolidated after the French Revolution. Even so, the language of oral communication remained Catalan, with today some 200,000 active speakers (Haarmann, 1975: 321). The Loi Deixonne allowed optional teaching in this 'regional' language, but its situation in other spheres is weak and under further pressure from French, which dominates completely.

Most of these interface peripheries are the product of wars or diplomatic settlement. Only in Savoy was there a plebiscite before the territory was turned over to France. After 1918, however, the plebiscite became a major instrument of diplomacy: where there was a conflict over a boundary line, the decision was to be based on the wishes of the population concerned, expressed in a plebiscite. The Treaty of Versailles stipulated a number of such plebiscites, and ordered the new League of Nations to administer them. Most bore on issues at the interfaces with eastern Europe, but three affected the western frontiers of Germany: the Eupen-Malmédy area on the Belgian border, the Schleswig problem on the Danish border, and the Saar issue. The Saar plebiscite did not occur until 1935, and overwhelmingly endorsed re-absorption by Germany of this interface, which had little or no marked division of cultural loyalties within its population. The fate of the Germans in Eupen-Malmédy was settled in 1920, and today this tiny German minority is accepted as a further language community within the Belgian structure. By contrast, the Danish-German border issue had been a source of contention ever since the first stirrings of Prussian expansionism. Political control over Schleswig and Holstein had varied through the centuries, reflecting the fluid nature of the old empire, and both areas, especially the former, were ethnically mixed. When Prussia began its drive for German unification, these territories were prime targets and the subject of two wars between Denmark and Prussia. Victory went to the Germans, and both Schleswig and Holstein were brought into the German Confederation. With German defeat in World War I, the Danes successfully called for a plebiscite. The result in 1920 confirmed the actual demographic boundary in Schleswig between a Danish north and a German south that had existed for centuries. However, small minorities were left on either side of the new border. Both minorities have been guaranteed some form of official protection, and have been granted funds to run schools in their own languages. Both have strong organizations and local newspapers that help to retain distinctive identities, but there is also evidence of a decline in ethnic mobilization and the salience of ethnic identity. In North Schleswig the clear-cut segregation at the institutional level is counteracted by the absence of segregation between the two groups at the face-to-face level (Elklit, Noack and Tonsgaard, 1978).

The infrastructural roots of identity

There is an enormous number of distinguishable languages in the world, but only a few of these rate a realistic chance to be transformed into standards of written communication. Such a standard cannot be developed without a centre or network, or a network of centres: writing was originally a prerogative of elites, and could be subjected to some sort of normative prescription only through constant interaction among groups with some competence in the given medium of communication. Once a standard had been established for some time and had found expression in writings of high prestige, it proved hard to replace: the costs of establishing an alternative were very high. Perhaps the greatest source of such stabilization was the technology of mass reproduction of printing. Primarily, stable standards were most likely to develop in consolidated territorial structures built up around unambiguous centres before the advent of printing. There was, however, a second chance. Languages that failed to develop a definite standard with the arrival of printing could still become regular media of written communication if (a) the language was seen by important elites as a symbol of territorial identity; (b) there was a definite drive to reach agreement on a joint grammar and vocabulary for written expansion; (c) there were deliberate efforts to spread this joint version through use in religious or other symbolic ceremonies and through the media of mass education; (d) schools in the peripheral language were established early on. The success of efforts to develop distinctive standards depends very much on the stability of the population: the greater the rate of emigration, the greater the incentive to learn the language of the larger community, and the weaker the support for the distinctive standard. Similarly, the greater the rate of immigration into the territory, the greater the likelihood that the peripheral language will be pushed out by the central one. In practice, this means that if a peripheral standard is to maintain its hold on the territorial population, it must be fully established in the media and in mass education well before the opening up of a wider cross-territorial labour market.

These propositions obviously need further specification. We have tried to apply them concretely in our linguistic presentations, but have been unable to systematize the evidence as much as we would have desired. One source of difficulty in any attempt at systematization is the configuration of ethnic-linguistic affinities. Some languages are close to each other and can be mutually understood by those speaking them: depending upon the political and economic environment, this situation could assist either absorption by one standard or the survival of linguistic heterogeneity. Other languages are so different from each other that speakers of one can master the other only at great cost of time and energy. The difficulty is that there seems to be no easy rule for deciding when the gap between two languages is large enough to generate two different standards, or when it is small enough to be compatible with a single standard. In Spain, for example, it is easy to see Basque, so remote from Spanish, as a potentially distinctive standard. Yet similar claims have been made for Catalan, which is not very far removed from Castillian.

We have also seen that there are great variations in the willingness to accept discrepancies between one dialect and common standards of written documentation. There are at least two distinctive standards in Norway even though the oral dialects are usually mutually intelligible to the speakers. There is a greater tolerance of discrepancies between oral and written forms of communication in Germany, France, Switzerland and Italy. It is difficult to see how these variations in the toleration of discrepancies could be systematically explained within the basic model: one simply has to take the historical evidence for granted without further attempts at explanation. An additional source of difficulty in any comparative analysis is the ambiguity of the term 'language'. We clearly use this term in two very different meanings: simply as a label for a set of mutually intelligible dialects, and as the dialect of the standardizing elites. This distinction is important. There is no difficulty about 'dialect': this is simply the oral medium of communication within a group recognizing itself as distinctive from all outsiders. A language, however, can be one of two things: a set of similar dialects, whether expressed in writing or not, or a standard of written communication accepted by at least some of the speakers of the dialects within the set. In the first sense we deal with a set corresponding to the biological concept of species: dialects close enough to each other to be mutually comprehensible constitute a language. In the second sense we have a convention agreed upon by a group of elites, a set of rules to be observed in writing or printed communications.

This review of the survival of identity across the territories of Western Europe has focused upon their languages, whether oral or written. But while peripheries can maintain their identity without a language of their own, the likelihood of continued erosion of other sources of identity is increased once the language is lost. The less the peripheral language can be used as a diacritical mark in the struggle against the centre, the greater the likelihood of several efforts to rally the periphery around other banners, through stressing the continuity of distinctive institutions or by trying to instil into the population an awareness of separateness through violent action. In this sense Scotland is the clichéd exception that proves the rule. The survival of Scottish identity was aided by the relative disinterest of the English centre in its northernmost periphery and later by the economic buoyancy of industrialization: parallel to these political and economic developments was the emphasis in the nineteenth century upon an ersatz tartan past that became inextricably intertwined with the 'real' historic lore of the land. More generally, however, European history is littered with peripheral linguistic casualties: it is only with the concatenation of specific developments, rarely repeatable, that the loss of this major symbolic ingredient of identity can be compensated by the presence of other symbolic artefacts, for once a system is opened up to a flow of messages from outside, the proportion of people questioning the justification of established customs or institutions would seem likely to increase. This has happened to many religious bodies: why not to territorially based identities? Alternatively, the ability of established customs to survive in an 'alien' linguistic environment and to resist determined efforts by the centre at standardization may be thoroughly undermined: this proposition underlies our comparison of the strategies of the British and French centres and the fate of their several respective peripheries.

The more fundamental question would be: even if a periphery is integrated into a wider linguistic community, even if the population all acquire that wider language, will the periphery in fact be so open to messages from outside? When a periphery has lost its language, people may of course expose themselves to messages from outside, but will they do so? A language is not only a medium of communication; it is also a criterion of membership and identity, a shibboleth. It is quite possible to understand and to use the language of others, and still employ a variety of 'diacritical marks' — accents, grammatical peculiarities, deviant glossaries — to indicate who you are and what group you belong to. And these indications of identity are so much more convincing because they are not subject to wilful change. When you have grown up in a local language (dialect) community, it will be more difficult to acquire another accent and learn another form of intonation, at least sufficiently to be accepted as an indigenous member of the other community. It is often said that language is fate: if you have grown up in a particular community, your chances of acceptance within another are significantly reduced. This is much more likely in isolated communities with low levels of mobility. In highly mobile urban communities there may be much greater toleration of diversity, at least within some spheres of life. The more diversified a community, the more the diacritical marks may prove important in defending separate identities without interfering with specific exchanges in daily life.

During the early phases of urbanization and centralization there was perhaps a tendency to suppress such diacritical marks, a tendency that would have been consistent with the predilections of most central elites. However, with the increase in upward mobility and the multiplication of encounters between groups, the tolerance of diversity has increased. In fact, we have experienced a double movement: increased interaction among people of different linguistic origins, and increased willingness to signal identity by diacritical marks. The great wave of reaction against the anonymity of modern urban society that began in the 1960s found many alternative forms of expression: in the call for a return to the local community, in the cult of smallness, in the ecological nostalgia for simpler forms of life, and also in the accentuation of origins, dialects, distinctiveness. In many countries the contents of radio and television have since the 1960s displayed an increasing diversity of accents, of displays of identity; there was, in short, a decline in conformity to the standard literary language. Another way of describing this tendency would be to say that the spread of the dominant standards of linguistic communication has opened up channels for the fast and efficient diffusion of messages, but at the same time has increased the need to make use of the diacritical marks of the oral language to express one's identity.

Without some such mechanism it is impossible to explain how the Irish, Scots, Occitans or Corsicans have kept so much of their ethnic identity without a standard language of their own. An accent, a system of intonation can replace a dialect as a vehicle for the expression of identity, though as the dilemma of Northern Ireland indicates, two rival identities can still possess the same broad intonational pattern. At the same time, it is worth repeating that the 'new' toleration of diversity came too late to prevent the extinction or revival of previously distinctive languages that were mortally wounded in the aftermath of the printing revolution, the Reformation, the French Revolution and industrialization. Paradoxically, the new electronic age has posed an acute challenge to peripheral languages, one as serious as those of the invention of printing and the establishment of a cross-territorial labour market. While television stations have a more limited range than radio stations, they have become vastly more important because they are both oral and visual. While this may have aided the use of diacritical marks within one language, it has rarely benefited peripheral languages. Television is a costly medium, and outside federalizing accommodation situations such as Belgium and Switzerland it is, from central perspectives, financially indefensible to allow peripheral languages their own television channel. In this respect interface peripheries are at an advantage; they can often receive television programmes beamed from the neighbouring state with its accepted or understood standard. For the rest, television and even radio time are exceptionally limited (see for example Tudesq, 1977): from data collected by Petrella (1978a), Wales is the linguistic periphery best served by the state to which it belongs, and even that is dismissed as far too meagre by the defenders of the Welsh language.[23] For many cultural minorities, the possession of television facilities has become a shibboleth, in much the same way as possession of a steel industry has for long been accepted as the essential hallmark of a country's having arrived industrially.

Dialect and language, then, must be treated together. We could, in fact, establish a gradation from the local we-group to the cross-territorial network of exchange. At the lowest level there is full conformity to the same accent, the same way of speaking the particular dialect as defined by its phonology, morphology and syntax. At the next level there is communication among we-groups using different dialects, but still with enough conformity of structure to allow easy intelligibility across the groups. At yet another level the languages differ sufficiently in phonology, morphology and syntax as to make them difficult, if not impossible, to understand without thorough instruction. As we move from level to level, the diffuse identity-building function of language decreases, and the purely instrumental message-transmitting function predominates: indeed, at the highest level a central language can have an identity-destroying function as it whittles away at the overall infrastructural roots of a peripheral identity. The process of territory-building in Europe found one of its expressions in the drive to develop standard languages. This in turn could smooth the task of sustaining ceremonies that transmitted the lore of the land and/or reaffirmed the territorial identity of the state: while these tasks could be effectively carried out by an efficient institutional network, the symbolism they were intended to convey would be much stronger if language and state were coterminous. The word 'nation' had a meaning before the French Revolution very different to what it had afterwards. The original sense was the collectivity of those with the same 'pays de naissance', those born within the same historic space.[24] The French Revolution pushed the term one notch upwards: it was to refer to all who lived within the entire territory of the French state and who understood the dialect of the Île de France. Nation-building accentuated the inter-intelligibility of dialects within the larger territory: the strategy was to create greater identity with the centre by increasing communication across localities with different dialects of what was defined as the same language. A linguistic map of France in the nineteenth century (Figure 3.5) would show how difficult a strategy this was: the great majority of communes outside the central region between the Seine and Loire spoke what officialdom called 'patois' — sometimes simple oral dialects remote from the langue d'oîl, in other cases completely foreign languages with separate standards. What the French drive to nationhood showed with such great clarity (and something that also

FIGURE 3.5
The extent of the French language in France, 1835

Note: The stippled line encloses those départements either wholly or mainly French-speaking.
Source: Weber (1876: 68).

emerged from other state experiences, such as the British) was that it was quite possible to build up a standard that could be intelligible at the elite level across the entire territory and still leave the lower strata of the population communicating over shorter distances only in their inherited oral dialects. These class differences in the reach of communication could be overcome to some extent through education, migration and occupational mobility, but this still left a difference in both intensity and style between exchanges at the we-group level and those at the cross-territorial level of the nation-state community.

It is tempting to compare this development towards political-administrative unification with the earlier process of religious unification within the great cross-territorial churches. When Buddhism, Christianity or Islam spread messages of ultimate salvation across communities of very different ethnic origins and cultures, the local we-groups were not dissolved: as well as maintaining their identities, they were made aware through the institutional organization of the church of their links with a wide range of different groups sharing the same faith, rituals and holy places. Something very similar happened in the building of national communities. There is much to be said for Hobsbawm's (1972; also 1977) interpretation of nationalism as a civil religion, a body of conceptions, rituals and rules of behaviour linking local communities together in a wider system.

The point to underscore is that several such religions can share the same linguistic standard, as in the German and French language areas, if there is sufficient distinctiveness in the other elements of identity. It is also important to point out that, where two groups share a common language and many other cultural characteristics, religion itself can take over this civic role of identity-building and boundary maintenance: Northern Ireland is a possible case in point. This is where Ernest Renan was right. The standard language of writing was not as important as the varied repertoire of signals and stigma of identity available to every individual in the immediate community, such as participation in rituals and ceremonies, observance of inherited customs and awareness of a shared past. But Renan was only vaguely aware of the *layering* of such expressions of identity: some accentuated membership in the local we-group, while others were shared across a range of communities and signalled loyalty to the wider territorial system. Individuals can possess more than one identity, and several layers of identity can exist within a single territorial system: whether these multiple identities are benign or antagonistic depends in each instance upon the particular political concatenation of events, policies and trends. The building of a national territorial community in fact forced the great majority of subjects into some level of bilinguality: one language for close interaction within the immediate community, and at least one other for communication over longer distances. The first is the language of the home and local friendship circle, the other of markets, networks of external contacts and agencies of control and administration. This distinction applies whether the standard of long-distance communication is unique to the system or is shared with another.

Whatever the structure of the territorial system, there will be at least two layers of language and identity: what counts is the distance between them and the costs of moving from one to another. In the classic nation-state the distance is taken to be small or even minimal: the medium of local communication is simply one of the set of inter-intelligible dialects spoken across the entire territory and therefore very close to the standard developed from one or some subset of these. In practice there are much greater variations in the distance between the two layers. We can distinguish at least four gradations of distance between the home standard and the territorial standard:

1. The two are mutually intelligible: both are members of the same linguistic species. This is the classic case of easy transition from dialect to standard. The country closest to this type of minimal bilinguality is perhaps Sweden.

2. The two are not mutually intelligible, but the home dialect is a member of a linguistic species expressed in a distinctive and recognized alternative standard within the territory. This situation corresponds to those prevalent in what we called successful peripheries and multilingual systems.

3. The two are not mutually intelligible, and the home dialect and its standard are not recognized by the central authorities. This situation is prevalent in what we called marginal peripheries.

4. The two are not mutually intelligible, and the home dialect is a member of a linguistic species expressed in an external standard centrally established in a neighbouring territory and officially recognized within the territory of the speaker. Alternatively, the exoglossic standard may not be recognized within the territory of the speaker. These situations are those in our interface peripheries.

These gradations in distance have sharp implications for the equality of citizenship. We can distinguish two very different kinds of citizen rights in a system of democratic pluralism: the right to respect for community of origin, whatever its language or ethnic composition, and the right to opportunities for full use of individual abilities within the wider territorial network. We can call the one the right to roots, the other the right to options. Roots are important because they help you know who you are and whom you can trust: they are the lifeblood of cultural identity. But options are equally important. You may not want to be locked in for ever within the same community; you may wish to find a wider arena for the use of your talents. The problem is to find some acceptable fulcrum between these two orientations. Domination by roots may end up in social, cultural and even economic serfdom. The multiplication of options may result in anomia: a decrease in predictability, increased irresponsibility and a heightened depersonalized anonymity. Conservatives since Burke and de Maistre have given priority to roots; liberals, priority to options. Socialists have tended to oscillate between an anarchistic emphasis on the virtues of the small community and the protection of roots, and a centralist emphasis on the liberation of individual energies within large systems. Such ideological contrasts are also reflected in the positions taken in the controversies over peripheral languages. Conservatives and anarchists have tended to agree on the need to cultivate roots and the home dialect; liberals and centralizers have tended to agree on the means, on the need for a territory-wide standard, but not on the goals, the maximization of individual options versus the opening up of opportunities for collective action in the building of strong organizations.

We can establish a set of gradations for the 'fullness' of citizenship parallel to gradations of bilinguality (Figure 3.6). This is obviously a crude typology, but it does help to focus attention upon one aspect of the peripheral predicament, the potential tug between roots and options, which can heighten a distinctive identity and generate peripheral political discontent and mobilization. Only in the first situation is this possibility more or less unlikely. At the

FIGURE 3.6
Language and citizenship gradations

	HOME DIALECT	STANDARD	CITIZENSHIP
(1.1)	Close to Standard A	A: centrally established within territory	Full citizenship: both roots and options
(1.2)	Remote from A, but within same linguistic species	A: centrally established	Limited citizenship: fewer options
(2)	Not of species A: dialect of species B not inter-intelligible with A	B: officially recognized as peripheral standard	Full peripheral citizenship: roots protected, options at least within periphery
(3)	Not of species A: dialect of species C not inter-intelligible with A	C: peripheral standard not given official recognition within territory	Minimal citizenship: no protection of roots or options
(4)	Not of species A: dialect of species D represented by standard external to territory	D: exoglossic standard recognized within territory	Full peripheral citizenship: roots protected, options at least within periphery
(5)	Not of species A: dialect of species E represented by external standard	E exoglossic standard not recognized within territory	Minimal citizenship: neither roots nor options within the territory

other extreme we have two cases of minimal citizenship: situations (3) and (5) represent infringements on basic human rights. If you have been brought up in a home dialect of a linguistic species different from that of the dominant authorities of the territory, you have the right to expect full recognition of the standard of written communication corresponding to your oral dialect. This would be a recognition not only of your need for roots, but also of your need for options. The recognition of a peripheral standard not only helps to strengthen identification with the community of origin; it also opens up a wider range of opportunities of choice within a larger territory. It is in this sense that language is at the heart of cultural identity, or rather, perhaps, at the heart of its potentially explosive political consequences. Other stigmata may be important, but without language their capacity to resist incorporation may be greatly hindered. The ability, for example, of Scotland to sustain a distinctive infrastructure of identity-maintaining institutions without a language of its own may in the last resort be due not to any inherent strength of its own identity base, but to its good fortune to be incorporated by a centre that for long was content to ignore or benevolently tolerate such cultural deviations. Finally, the contrast between roots and options may enable us to focus more clearly upon the interplay between cultural identity and the costs of economic opportunities and expectations within the cross-cultural labour market. Where options inside the periphery are under pressure, either through economic decline or in-migration of cultural outsiders, or where they are seen to be clearly inferior to those available elsewhere in the political territory, the resulting sense of economic deprivation and perceived inequalities may act as another kind of catalyst upon the roots of identity and transform cultural distinctiveness into political protest. It is to the more specific theme of the politicization of peripheral predicaments that we now turn.

4

The Politicization of Peripheral Predicaments

In the 1960s and 1970s there flowered in Western industrial societies a conspicuous peripheral protest against regimes and political centres. This 'pronounced and sudden increase' (Glazer and Moynihan, 1975: 3) was, in the hyperbolical language of Isaacs (1975: 3), a 'convulsive ingathering of people in their numberless groupings of kind', where a quest for the roots of identity superseded a concern with the options of equality. The renaissance took several forms: a re-emphasis upon the peripheral language, and even phoenix-like attempts to revive some long defunct as modes of living speech; demands for the right to use the minority language in specific situations, in education, the mass media, and in dealings with government agencies; and, at the extreme, renewed or original claims for the right of self-determination. It shook to the core the concept, held for much of the twentieth century, of the nation-state as the norm for territorial organization, with Western Europe as its home, and challenged the validity of prevailing theories of social mobilization, economic development, political integration and the successful impact of distributive welfare policies.

While not many had heeded the warning by Geertz (1963: 154) that there is nothing automatic about the integrative process (it 'does not do away with ethnocentrism: it merely modernizes it'), this is not the place to elaborate upon the traditional approaches and the dissenting and revisionist additions that have subsequently enriched them. Let it suffice to say that there has been a sea-change, correcting the bias prevalent in much political science writing of a scant sympathy for groups that were regarded as having definitively lost in the historical game. Conventional wisdom now accepts that most, if not all, states in Western Europe have several layers of identity with real or potential political significance. The previous chapters demonstrated the historical origins of these layers: the fact that they are historically derived does not necessarily make them anachronistic, without relevance in the modern industrialized world: 'the argument can no longer be made that inexorable historical forces such as urbanization, industrialization, secularization — in short, mass society — will automatically pulverize communal identities below those attaching to the national state' (Young, 1976: 10). However, to accept the existence of multiple identities, mutually compatible or not, within a territorial state says nothing about the metamorphosis from social distinctiveness to political expression.

The context of mobilization

Much of the recent literature implies a mere revival of the kind of ethnic or linguistic concerns that were manifest in 'pre-modern' periods, and so a less than perfect, or even temporary, incorporation of such interests in Western European political or state-wide party systems. Certainly, the potential of such concerns goes back to the French Revolution and the injection into politics of the notion of popular sovereignty, where the right to rule was vested in a populace that was ethnically defined: as a consequence, political legitimacy would always be less than perfect in any territorial unit that did not conform to the pure nation-state. While peripheralization is an ongoing process, our analysis so far has indicated that the kinds of peripheries that can be identified in Western Europe have retained the same characteristics — economic as well as cultural — over long periods of time. It was, in fact, the city and the alphabet that heavily influenced the fate of the territories of Western

Europe. The geography of trade routes made for differences in the resources of state-building, while the invention of printing aided the emergence of vernacular standards of communication which in turn prepared the ground for the relative success or failure of later stages of nation-building at the mass level. In effect, there has been a progressive freezing process in the territorial and group structure of Western Europe; peripheral political protest, both current and previous, must be considered not only as a reaction to contemporaneous economic problems, political trends and cultural dilemmas, but also against the backdrop of the geoethnic, geopolitical and geoeconomic heritage of the continent.

The French Revolution represented a crucial notch in this freezing process. One of its consequences was that, with democratization, political mobilization in western Europe came more and more to mean party mobilization. The assumption of a general revival of earlier ethnic or linguistic concerns cannot by itself account for the failure for most of this century of separatist or ethno-national movements. Until recently, indeed, it was more conventional to stress the integrative functions of political parties since the early phases of mass politics, which in a sense was but a further step in the temporal freezing process (Lipset and Rokkan, 1967; Rose and Urwin, 1969, 1970, 1975; Urwin and Rose, 1970).

Within this political universe, many of the current regionally based parties (and other politically active organizations) can nevertheless trace a pedigree back to the opening phases of mass mobilization, and perhaps beyond. Alternatively, regions and groups that today provide a home for such movements have in the past almost invariably displayed some political manifestation of discontent. Let us, for example, compare two countries that today represent, as it were, the extremes of the strength and consequences of regionalist mobilization. In France, the first — and primary — country self-consciously to seek the status of an état-nation, peripheral politicization along ethnolinguistic lines has always been totally marginal in its effect upon the mainstream of French political life. Even the determined agitation of Alsatian nationalism in the 1920s and 1930s failed to wring any concessions from the monolithic Jacobin state (Gras, 1982). Yet it has always been there, not moribund or dormant, but a continuous and integral thread of politics, a perpetual irritant for the état-nation. Its seeming recent 'prominence' may be no more than a return to normality after the nadir of the first postwar decade when, because of unhappy wartime experiences, opposition to the état-nation fell to its lowest ebb. By contrast, Belgium has been regarded as the most likely victim of disintegration arising from the political pressures of culturally distinctive groups. Again, however, this is not new. The cultural structure of the Belgian population has been politically salient (if not obviously so in party politics) ever since the establishment of the state in 1830. Indeed, the inauguration of mass politics in the late nineteenth century, far from providing a basis for an integrative revolution, generated a heightened crisis between Fleming and Walloon which was defused only when involvement in World War I helped to smother it through a stress on an overarching national loyalty. A somewhat similar rise and fall occurred in the 1930s and 1940s. As in France, the immediate postwar decade is more an aberration from the normal state of affairs than a culmination of a process of national integration that suddenly collapsed.[1]

The image of a revival is further complicated by the fact that in several instances there have been and are a number of mutually opposed movements competing against each other to be the true voice of the region or group. Moreover, a heightened mobilization of peripheral regions or groups over the past two decades was by no means general. There are even areas historically distinctive in some aspects of identity, for example Schleswig, Alsace or Bavaria, which have displayed a steady decline in both the strength and vitality of region-specific political mobilization and the scope of the territorial/group demands laid at the door of the political centre. In short, there has been a political revival or a growth in strength of only some cultural expressions of identity.

In this context it is appropriate to accept that 'ethnicity is highly malleable and responsive to the circumstances in which groups find themselves' (Greenwood, 1977: 101). Malleability, in the widest possible perspective, refers simply to the contextual framework. While it is undoubtedly important to incorporate a regionalist perspective into an analysis, the centre cannot be ignored. Simply because it is the centre, it occupies a crucial political position in determining not only the generation of peripheral aspirations, but also their content and likely future. The symbiosis of centre and periphery has been a major theme of the two historical chapters. Here we shall focus on the contemporary phenomenon more through regional eyes, reserving the centrist perspective to the next chapter.

It is merely banal to state that peripheral movements are only one kind of political expression within a state. There can be many kinds of regional, peripheral or ethnic demands that may be translated into political movements. In some instances, their salience may even be muted at the mass level, no matter how much the issue agitates the political system. In Belgium, for instance, Zolberg (1977: 104) suggests that the mass interest in linguistic issues has remained relatively low, a factor that the politicians could take into account in their deliberations and manoeuvrings. In the world of mass politics, the regionalist party is only one form of expression in what amounts to a complex mosaic; and in itself it may be a relatively minor one. Ethnic consciousness, or a concern with cultural identity and roots, may be universal: nationalist movements are not. If we take the exhaustive lists that have been compiled of linguistic minorities in Western Europe, then in only a few instances has the associated sentiment upset the prevailing forms of political activity by becoming a significant issue or organizing force to be taken into consideration at the state level of politics. Moreover, assuming we know what is ethnic, whether it be self-identification, lineage, possession of distinctive cultural stigmata or artefacts, or even membership in organizations and institutions, we cannot immediately proceed to accept that the ethno-national assumption that state legitimacy and ethnicity are linked is incompatible with loyalty to an existing state.

Again, the case of France is illustrative. A recent article (Beer, 1977) listed by name no less than 101 ethnic activist associations in six French regions, mentioned the existence of a further 86, and stressed the exclusion of regional organizations without any specific ethnic content in such 'pure' French regions as Picardy and Normandy. This can easily conjure up an image of frenetic activity which, however, does not readily fit with the more imperturbable reality of the French state. Their fragmentation and the lack of devolutionary success point to the paucity of regionalist resources as well as to the nature of the Jacobin state. The regional units established in France in the 1970s came out of a nexus of national party politics, bureaucratic rivalries and economic initiatives upon which ethnic activism had very little influence (see Wright, 1979; Gourevitch, 1978, 1981). We may identify ethno-national groups and accept that they are equal theoretically: to assume that they are all equal empirically is misleading. While regionalist demands for some form of adjustment to the territorial structure of the state, or

small quantity

for special treatment for a specific group, may be traumatic for a state, under certain circumstances their political impact can be negligible.

To paint the scene in this manner is important, for it illustrates the labyrinthine nature of the landscape and re-emphasizes the necessity of relating current peripheral politicization to the broader geopolitical vistas of state-building and nation-building. And it is with the state as a territorial concept that we should begin a review of politicization in order, within the perspectives of territorial strains and centralizing strategies, to seek to disentangle the relationship between territorial regions and regionally concentrated groups with distinctive sociocultural characteristics. This implies that we should consider the politicization and activation of cultural differences along the two interrelated dimensions of 'membership space', that is, membership of a group that possesses, and is probably aware of possessing, some common sociocultural stigmata, and 'geographical space', that is, identification with and occupation of a specific piece of territory.[2] While the kinds of political movements that concern us here tend to identify themselves with both a territory and a group, the two dimensions are not necessarily coincident. Not all people in a territory may identify with or support a regionalist movement and its political demands. Yet the latter may demand control of, or significant structural adjustments in the control of, a specific territory, and hence over all those who live there, irrespective of their political opinions or sociocultural stigmata. This holds true whatever the size of the group or territory, whether it is an all-embracing demand for independence, or even whether the territorial claims (which often are based on past settlement distributions or patterns of political control) extend far beyond the current extent of territorial occupation.[3]

For peripheral mobilization the most appropriate starting point might well be territory. A neutral concept, territory becomes politically significant because of the interpretation and value placed upon it by people: it becomes 'a concept generated by people organizing space for their own aims' (Gottman, 1975: 29). While there is no one-to-one fit between territory and population, the fact that in almost all of our peripheries not all the population bear the associated cultural stigmata or wear the tribal badges means not only that the peripheral minorities are socially constituted, but also that categorization of groups related to history and territory can often be more important in defining cultural groups than the stigmata themselves (Allardt, 1979: 26-30). This is the framework within which we can consider the basic questions surrounding the politicization of peripheral predicaments: what are the conditions of group identity, and what are the conditions that lead politicized groups into active conflict and struggle? The first question in particular relates to resources available to groups in relation both to the centre, which claims legitimacy over the territory, and to the external links to other centres outside the political state.

Resources are necessary, but not sufficient, conditions for mobilization. The latter occurs when catalysts operate upon the resources to transform cultural distinctiveness into political action. The writings of conventional literature on political sociology and mobility can be extended beyond classes to embrace other types of groups, a point we have already touched upon in our discussion of roots and options. Groups tend to be territorially and economically distributed unevenly in any one political unit. Accommodation between them might be expected when the whole society is totally interdependent, where no group can survive in isolation, or when there is a clear, stable and accepted hierarchy of functions. Conflict emerges more readily with change, that is, with increasing and disturbing cross-group contacts and marked shifts, for better for for worse, in the situation of one group.[4]

Resources and catalysts

Let us first look at the resources available to a group: these are territorial, cultural or economic in nature. Before we do so, however, we should seek to fix the discussion to the cases of peripheral mobilization that form the basis of this chapter. The Western European peripheries vary greatly in their 'natural' resources, and so their dilemma and importance to the core will also be different for each dyadic pair of centre-periphery relationships. In Figure 2.12 we presented a chart for the location of peripheries within the overall structure of Western Europe. We have chosen here to utilize this chart and for each of the peripheries to indicate the major political organization or the style of mobilization (Figure 4.1).

FIGURE 4.1

A chart for the location of peripheral movements within the overall structure of Western Europe

	Seaward peripheries		Coastal plains		Central plains/Alps			Germanic marchland		Landward peripheries	
	1	2	S	3	C	F	4	L	5	6	7
	No or only incipient medieval state formation	Distinctive medieval state, but dis-continuity	Continuous state formation since the Middle Ages	Western interface territories	Continuous state formation since 14th-16th centuries	Early state formation, later absorbed within larger systems	Internal interface territories	Continuous state formation since 13th-17th centuries	Eastern interface territories	Distinctive medieval state, but dis-continuity	No or only incipient medieval state formation
Arctic peripheries	GREEN-LAND: separate party system FAEROES: separate party system	ICELAND: separate party system									LAPPLAND: limited cultural organization
Protestant territories		SCOTLAND: Scottish National Party WALES: Plaid Cymru	CORNWALL: Mebyon Kernow	SCHLESWIG: Slesvig Parti (in Denmark); Südschleswig-scher Wahler-verband (in W. Germany)			FRIESLAND: Frysk Nasjonale Partÿ (in Netherlands); limited cultural organizations (in W. Germany)		FINLAND: Svenska Folkparti		

FIGURE 4.1 continued

	Seaward peripheries		Coastal plains		Central plains/Alps			Germanic marchland		Landward peripheries	
	1	2	S	3	C	F	4	L	5	6	7
Mixed/ national Catholic territories	N. IRELAND: several political organizations	BRITTANY: Union Démocratique Bretonne (+ several other parties/ organizations)		ALSACE: Mouvement Régionaliste d'Alsace-Lorraine JURA: Rassemblement Jurassien OCCITANIA: Partit Nacionalista Occitan; Lutte Occitane (+ several other organizations) ROUSSILLON: Several political organizations VAL D'AOSTA: Union Valdôtaine (+ several other organizations) CORSICA: Union di u Populu Corsu (+ several other organizations)		PIEDMONT: cultural organizations SARDINIA: Partito de Azione de Sardegna	BAVARIA: Bayernpartei (+ several other organizations) GRISONS: cultural organizations				

FIGURE 4.1 continued

	Seaward peripheries		Coastal plains		Central plains/Alps			Germanic marchland		Landward peripheries	
	1	2	S	3	C	F	4	L	5	6	7
Counter-Reformation territories		GALICIA: several political organizations NAVARRE: Union of Navarrese People BASQUE LANDS: Partido Nacionalista Vasco; Euskadiko Eskerra (+ several other organizations); Enbata (in France)		BELGIUM: Volksunie (in Flanders); Rassemblement Wallon (in Wallonia); Front Démocratique des Francophones (in Brussels); Partei der deutschsprachigen Belger (in Eupen/Malmédy) CATALONIA: Pacta Democratico de Catalunya (+ several other organizations)			TYROL: Südtiroler Volkspartei (+ several other organizations) VENETIA/FRIULIA: Movimento de Friuli; Movimento per Trieste		CARINTHIA: cultural organizations BURGENLAND: cultural organizations		
Mediterranean territories			ANDALUSIA: Partido Socialista de Andalucia								

Territorial responses

We can begin with territory, which is a sine qua non of geographical politics. Possession, says the proverb, is nine points of the law. Any group that is not regionally concentrated and in physical occupation (whether wholly or partly is for the moment irrelevant) of a territory — even if they may claim some identification with a territory elsewhere — will be a much more difficult mobilization target for any movement with political regional pretensions and aspirations: without territorial occupation, challenges may be dissipated by institutional arrangements. The peripheries in our universe are all populated at least partly by a distinctive cultural group with historical ties to and roots in the area. One important group, however, cannot lay claim to possession of a distinctive piece of territory within the state where it resides. In this sense the Swedish Finns, far from being a model of integration, constitute an exception. The Swedish Finns are not exclusive occupants of any one clearly defined piece of territory, apart from the tiny Åland Islands, and some 23 per cent, including those middle-class elements putatively most qualified to provide a territorial political leadership, reside and work in Helsinki. In other words, quite apart from the constitutional safeguards granted to the Swedish Finns after 1918, it may be suggested that their 'passivity' and the central position of their party, the Svenska Folkparti (SPP), is due precisely to their lack of territorial occupation, to the physical presence of a large proportion of the group in the Finnish centre.[5]

In a pluralist democracy, electoral competition and performance are the most obvious and impressive indicators of the ability to mobilize mass support. The electoral record tends to confirm the importance of territorial occupation as a resource. In the United Kingdom, with its plurality electoral system, only Irish nationalists have ever looked beyond their own bailiwick for electoral support, but primarily contesting only a handful of Liverpool constituencies. Neither Plaid Cymru nor the Scottish National Party (SNP) has attempted to tap the Welsh and Scottish populations residing in England. But similar constraints seem to apply in more liberal proportional systems. Few parties look beyond their 'own' region, and those that do are perhaps relatively less successful in mobilizing support there than in the indigenous territory.

Historically, geopolitical location has been a major factor

enhancing the political value of territory, with the decisive emphasis being upon military-strategic importance. Today, however, economic weight and geoeconomic location are probably more significant considerations than strategic location.[6] Nevertheless, the previous possession of value can be used as a resource to press claims in the same way as previous independence. Both may create a mythology that becomes incorporated into the identity, lore of the land and infrastructures of the group and territory concerned. Historically, for example, the unique privileges granted collectively to the Basques by the Spanish crown were due in large measure to the strategic geopolitical position of the provinces. As military considerations declined in significance, the Basques found it increasingly difficult to resist a centre that stressed more and more the values of centralization and standardization. Geopolitical location may be a particular key resource for interface peripheries. For them the political border itself can be a positive or negative resource in a way that is not possible for external peripheries, which do not have a landward border or cultural link with a neighbouring state. Interface peripheries have, by the mere existence of an alternative cultural centre, assets beyond those of external peripheries, and this different situation may well offer a number of different and extra political options which themselves might be converted into political pressures that can be brought to bear upon the centre (Figure 4.2). Although internally divided as to where its ultimate allegiance lay, during the past century the political

FIGURE 4.2
The political resources of peripheries

Degree of dependence on centre of own state		AVAILABLE TO EXTERNAL PERIPHERIES	ADDITIONAL TO INTERFACE PERIPHERIES
	High	Monocephalous state; dominant capital; nil/few resources	Regional economic centre dependent on trade across border
	Low	Polycephalic urban structure with economically strong peripheral cities	Strong extra-national urban centre, which also serves as a cultural focal point

football of Alsace illustrates perfectly the dilemma and the advantages of an interface situation. Some help was always available from the neighbouring state, which could also serve as a refuge for those actively hostile to, or discriminated against by, the political centre (Silverman, 1972; Gras, 1982). Similarly, Austria was positively engaged in the Alto Adige conflict on the side of the German-speaking population (Alcock, 1970).

It might be expected that the larger the size of the territory or the cultural group, the greater the resource. But size is a double-edged weapon. Very small areas may still generate significant political mobilization and, as the experiences of Northern Ireland and the Alto Adige indicate, can have a strong potential for trouble. Size, moreover, does not necessarily constitute a viability barrier against independence or a demand for independence, as the experiences of Iceland and, more recently, the Faeroes illustrate. Size must be linked to geopolitical location and distance, and with the political costs of control. Very small groups may have a weaker human resource with which to press their claims; yet because their smallness per se may pose less of a territorial threat, the centre may accept that the price of compromise will be considerably less onerous than the costs of resistance. This is true both along the interfaces and, even more so, in the more remote external peripheries. Distance and difficulty of communication are key factors in understanding the Icelandic and Faeroese situations.

Cultural responses

Religion has been a powerful driving force in European history, frequently providing territorially peripheral groups with a cultural standard and a major, if not sole, means of indigenous elite recruitment, as well as being a potent structural force in the formation of party systems. Particularly during this century, however, religious issues have largely disappeared from the Western European political agenda, either by their complete removal from the public sector (for example, through the separation of church and state) or by the formalization of equity within the public sector, as in Belgium. The displacement of religion as a partisan structuring force has not, however, followed on at the same rate: religiously based parties still exist. And as part of this general survival, religious unity or distinctiveness, as both a belief system and a territorially based organization, can be a potential source of territorial mobilization. However, its significance for territorial issues seems today to be more than tenuous primarily in Northern Ireland, where it is worn almost as a tribal badge.[7]

Language is the key resource for many who stress ethnonationalism. A distinctive means of communication can clearly be a powerful resource, and formal or informal bilingualism, as we have seen, almost inevitably places pressure upon the minority language. The case of Belgium is illustrative. The blossoming of linguistic politics in the 1960s was not essentially over whether there should be two linguistic regions: that was by and large accepted. Nor was it really an issue of public discrimination. Rather, it arose from a perceived lack of regulation, from linguistic freedom, whereby Flemish parents seemed increasingly willing to educate their children in French, and whereby French spread outwards into the Flemish countryside with the expansion of the Brussels conurbation. For those with a vested career interest in Flemish and others concerned with the fate of the language, the latter was an obvious rallying point for mobilization as well as the central issue. Language, however, can be a two-edged sword in those areas, like Brittany and Wales, where there is incongruence between identity and language, where too strong an insistence upon language may alienate those who do not speak it, even though they may still identify with the territory and the group. In such circumstances language can become, as it were, a negative resource that constitutes a ceiling on the potential of political mobilization. Nevertheless, language is a potential resource in the way that religion cannot be, first because in practice it does tend to be linked intimately with identification with and occupation of territory, and second because it cannot be removed so easily from the public agenda. While religion can be a private affair, language is an exchange medium and collective good that must be shared by all, including, at the extreme, those at the centre: this at least is the ultimate implication of linguistic parity and bilingualism. As Zolberg (1977: 140) has shrewdly observed, a state can pretend to be blind, but it cannot pretend to be deaf-mute.

Past historical developments may have produced in a territory a surviving pattern of identity-maintaining institutions, as with law, education and religion in Scotland or the Basque 'fueros', or a set of (greater or lesser) devolved powers of administrative decision-making. These may provide at the least a degree of cultural autonomy and local indirect political control as well as ensuring the recruitment of indigenous elites. Decentralization may also offer a more limited objective that could be captured by mobilization; but it can also serve to defuse regional tensions by permitting the resolution of problems and complaints at the regional level, and so avoiding the involvement of the whole state. Even without the presence of obvious cultural stigmata such as language, this distinctiveness would nevertheless imply some degree of consciousness of separateness, where the impact of history upon identity is that of ensuring the retention of 'collective memories' (Strauss, 1969: 167-8). Indeed, such an infrastructure might be a more appropriate resource for mobilization than language, since it implies the existence of a coherent organizational framework. We may divide the authority of the political centre into two categories: the core of rule-makers, and the agencies of rule implementation. The result is an institutional network for implementing those aspects of national identity deemed particularly important by the lawmakers (Figure 4.3). We may also distinguish within the peripheral population those who have roles in the institutional network of cultural exchanges, and identify two types of middlemen: government agents and mobilized community leaders or spokesmen. Typical government agents would be local schoolteachers, local mayors (under a Napoleonic regime), or local ministers of a state-established and state-controlled church. Where there appears cultural tension between centre and periphery, or where the centre increases pressure upon this local institutional network, these agents may be confronted with a dilemma. They can act primarily as the extended arm of the central authority, or they may choose to view themselves as spokesmen for and defenders of the peripheral population, utilizing their institutional links with the central authority to gain access to the political core of the state.[8] Mobilized community leaders, by contrast, owe their position not to the institutional network of government, but to the indigenous social institutional network supported by the peripheral community. These are people who in Chapter 1 we described as having invested time and effort into acquiring command of the artefacts of the periphery's cultural heritage and who hence wish to maximize distinctiveness and to profit from it. Here there is no division of loyalty; these people have no access to the centre. It will therefore be easier for them to oppose pressures of standardization rather than to seek mediation. Figure 4.3 is a crude attempt to illustrate

FIGURE 4.3

The institutional context of central cultural standardization and peripheral counter-cultural defence and mobilization

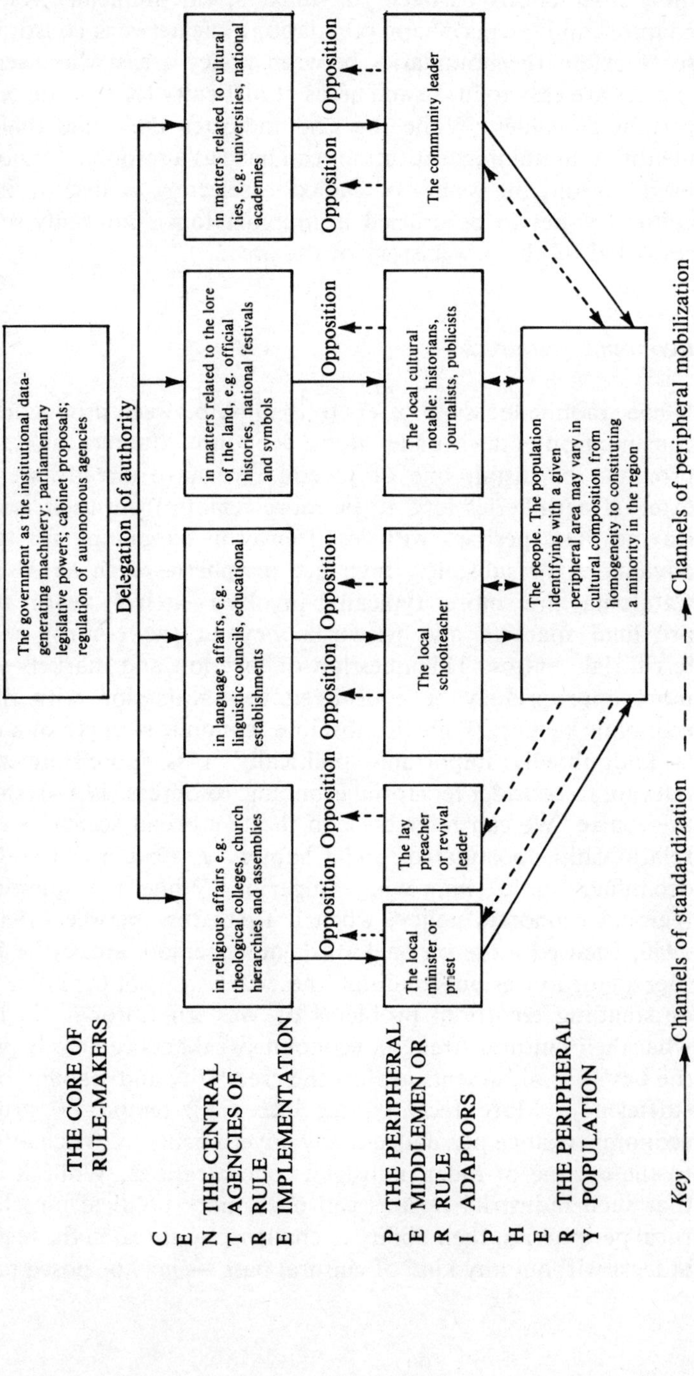

these interactions between rule-makers, rule-implementers, rule-adaptors and the peripheral population. The network constitutes to some extent the boundaries between policy areas where regional choices are easy to make and areas of difficulty for a protagonist of peripheral values. While the grid indicates the value that such identity-maintaining institutions can have as a resource for political mobilization, the reality of choice in selecting or discovering the cultural issues to be utilized in mobilization is normally severely restricted by the past history of the area.

Economic resources

'Geoeconomic location' refers to the link between production and consumption in the broader global economy. Markets can be either proximal or distal, one or several. We have already seen that external peripheries tend to be more remote from their markets, leaving them perhaps with less leeway in bargaining for trading advantages or subsidies. Interface peripheries such as Alsace or Catalonia are more typically involved actively with several proximal markets and networks beyond the control of their territorial centres. This question of location and markets should more appropriately be considered in conjunction with that of economic weight. While the absolute economic strength of a region is undoubtedly important, politically it is more immediately relevant to consider territorial economic resources vis-à-vis those of the centre. We can refer back to the five broad scenarios of this relationship postulated in Chapter 2: backward/stagnant, declining, static, improving, superior. While the question of regional economic policy, when it first arose between 1930 and 1950, focused more on backward, more remote areas (the Italian Mezzogiorno was outstanding), these areas are not the home of the outstanding territorial problems of Western Europe. No matter what their cultural strength, economic weakness can easily provide the basis for arguments against the credibility and viability of self-sufficiency. More recently, an increasing tempo of structural economic change persuaded many governments to switch attention to the decline of older industrial concentrations. While it is true that such industrial regions can pack more political muscle than rural peripheries, their ability to challenge or threaten the regime — at least without any kind of cultural base — may be posed more in political-economic than in territorial terms (for example, by attempting to extract more from the centre through redistribution of financial aid). The major territorial challenge may well come from economically superior or improving regions: these have an economic weight that more demonstratively can support independence and/or counterbalance the political resources of the centre. Flanders, Catalonia, the Basque provinces and perhaps Scotland all fall into these two categories.

Catalysts

Looking at territorial structures in terms of resources goes a long way towards understanding the relationship between territory and politics, plotting kinds of peripheral predicaments and mobilization responses. It would be a mistake, however, to allot equal weight to each resource, or to assume that by themselves they constitute anything more than a potential. The peripheral predicament arises out of the syndrome of cultural identity and territorial identity, a syndrome that over the centuries has been constantly under pressure from central policies of standardization and regulation. While political mobilization and the desire for political autonomy may incorporate some degree of concern with economic problems of distribution, the latter is not a necessary component. That is the historical heritage of territorial and group identity, which can be invoked as a source of both rights and a dream of a golden future. The combination of cultural identity and economics, where it does appear, may be concerned more with deprivation and may pose similar problems only in its acute form, a kind of economic division of labour based upon an ethnic hierarchy: 'internal colonialism' is the term most frequently employed to describe this situation.

Figure 4.4 indicates the position of the most important peripheries in terms of the strength of their cultural identity and their relative economic weight: the placements are derived from the analyses of the two previous chapters. However, it must be reiterated that these resources constitute only a potential. Zolberg (1977), for example, suggests, by his description of the Belgian political elite as both the firebugs and the firemen in linguistic-territorial affairs, that there has been a large degree of passivity at the mass level, while Linz (1973) has argued that the Basques on the

FIGURE 4.4
The cultural and economic strength of peripheries

CULTURAL STRENGTH	RELATIVE ECONOMIC STRENGTH: High ←		→ Low
High	Catalonia Basque country Flanders	Scotland Wales Jura Wallonia	Sardinia Val d'Aosta Alto Adige N. Ireland
↓ Low		Alsace	Galicia Schleswig Friesland Brittany Occitania Corsica Friulia

whole are not very concerned about the fate of their language. Political mobilization occurs with the injection of catalysts, capable of metamorphosing this potential into movement, organization and demands. At a minimum these catalysts can be subordinated into two basic waves of change that have affected the continent in the past century.

The diffusion of democratic principles and structures emerged within an era of heightened interstate tension and conflict. These two phenomena combined to generate a greater belief in the desirability of, and urgency of establishing, an integrated nation-state and a more effective penetration by the centre throughout its territory. Most of the territorial-peripheral problems of Western Europe, the untidy fragments of earlier efforts at state-building, originated in the decades before 1914. Some contemporary peripheral political movements are direct creatures of the national revolution in nineteenth-century western Europe or — as with the Slesvig Parti or the Südtiroler Volkspartei (SVP) — are a consequence of the collapse in 1918 of the central European efforts at empire-building. Others are built upon the ruins and traditions of earlier movements, which themselves can trace a lineage back to the previous century. Of the significant organizations of today, only the French-based Rassemblement Wallon and Front Démocratique des Francophones (FDF) in Belgium seem to be exceptions, without any such pedigree. The Russian Revolution introduced a new twist to integration. Socio-ideological unity began to compete with national-linguistic unity, to be reinforced after 1945 by the new pattern of global superpower politics and an emphasis upon the state as a security community. It might be hypothesized that in the 1960s and 1970s the views of those who had remained loyal to the peripheral group/territorial identity gained greater prominence and their cause greater respectability with the growing toleration of the risks of thermonuclear war, which reduced the perception of the state as a guarantor of security.[9]

Paralleling these political developments was a process of socio-economic change through the modification of capitalism towards the welfare state. The Industrial Revolution produced distinctive geographic patterns in each state, which, on the whole, remained undisturbed until the emergence of a 'second industrial revolution' after 1945. The effects of this varied. In some instances it exaggerated existing centre-periphery gaps and tensions: elsewhere it led to the industrialization of peripheries that had succeeded in retaining cultural distinctiveness precisely because of their isolation from the industrial mainstream of the state. In yet others it produced economic decline and perhaps 'de-industrialization'. At least in the first two situations, language abilities (or disabilities) received enhanced importance, especially in skilled and managerial work, and greater costs were imposed on the cultural minorities. At the same time, the latter, through the new mass media, could be made more immediately aware of their disadvantaged situation, of their predicament. Finally, the establishment of the welfare state in a sense consolidated the political and economic expansion of the centre through increasing the extent of the public domain and through the scope and need for greater regulation, standardization, distribution and redistribution by the central regime (Peacock and Wiseman, 1967: 119). Concomitantly, the combination of economic growth and welfare services weakened the decisive structuring role that class and religion had played in the generation and organization of political activity.

While these phenomena affected every western European state, their effect upon centre-periphery structures and tensions was not necessarily the same or of the same degree everywhere. In each instance their consequences were modified by the nature of the existing identity structures and style of central control. But at any rate, they provided the catalysts of mobilization. At an absolute minimum, there have been two waves of mobilization. The first arose from the nineteenth-century democratic and industrial revolutions. The introduction of democratic principles and a greatly extended suffrage permitted the organization in the electoral arena of parties for the protection of minority interests or conversely, where the latter were very small, of swamping them entirely. By contrast, democracy also implied greater standardization and centralization, while industrialization allowed more rapid communication and greater territorial interaction and exposure. The most obvious field in which identities clashed was that of language, with education perhaps as the most bitter arena. In the late nineteenth century the surviving peripheral standards came under even greater pressure: to a considerable extent, the long retreat of minority languages within states was hastened by the introduction of universal education.

The second wave, more modern, arose more specifically from a combination of economic discrepancies and the more rapid tempo of economic change after 1945, and the heightened egalitarian thrust of the modern democratic state which increasingly produced centralization of functions (Ashford, 1979; Peacock and Wiseman, 1967). Demographic changes may also be a catalyst, but as Katzenstein (1977) points out in his study of the South Tyrol, these may be both cause and consequence of conflict, and therefore inappropriate as explanations of the waxing and waning of the latter. It may well be that the cumulation of cultural and economic inferiority provides fertile soil for peripheral mobilization: more significant, however, is the question of inconsistency between economic strength/potential and cultural status. As many social psychologists have argued, a well-structured set of identities is a precondition of an individual's ability to function in balance (Isaacs, 1975: 26-37).

In a broader sense, the waves of mobilization have in common a confrontation with change: processes of state-building such as linguistic and educational standardization; economic expansion or decline; a heightened awareness of the outside world through more obvious government activity within the local horizon, improved communication, higher levels of education, geographic mobility and a more penetrative mass media. In the case of Scotland, for example, discontent with London hardened when the two societies, Scottish and English, ceased having parallel but separate economic and cultural existences; but as long as there was a British partisan alternative, first Liberal and then Labour, that seemed to defend peripheral interests, discontent could be contained within the national framework of politics — in the early 1920s Red Clydeside was not only anti-Conservative and anti-capitalist, but also anti-English. The dramatic upsets after the mid-1960s might be traced to a combination of factors: a stronger awareness of Labour, when in power, as a national British and centre-oriented party; government propaganda on the virtues of regional economic policy; a belief that the latter had failed in Scotland; and, later, optimism in the economic opportunities offered by North Sea oil (Urwin, 1978). To contrast Scotland with the northern shires of England, where many of the same considerations apply, is to emphasize that economic change in the broadest sense may be necessary but not sufficient. There must be something upon which territorial mobilization can be built, and that something is a form of cultural identity that possesses, both subjectively and objectively, distinctive and potent stigmata and artefacts. Together, cultural base and economic catalyst provide a base for mobilization.[10]

If we now turn to the universe of peripheral movements listed in Figure 4.1, we may first identify those that less ambiguously are part of the first wave. There are a few parties that to a greater or lesser extent succeeded in establishing themselves as durable, even electoral, forces. The Svenska Folkparti (SPP) is perhaps the best example, with a sense of solidarity that was forged by the attempts at finnicization. Although there was a Swedish elite in Finland, most Swedish speakers were to be found in manual and agricultural occupations, and the mere fact of speaking a common language had not been sufficient to cement an overriding common identity. Other small parties, for example the Slesvig Parti and the Südschleswigscher Wahlerverband (SSWV), also fall into this category. A second group consists of movements coming from regions and populations that hitherto had not only been relatively isolated, but also had enjoyed sociopolitical privileges and/or a distinctive institutional infrastructure. The Basque provinces and Scotland are examples. But the contrast between the two is instructive, for one experienced early and significant peripheral political mobilization, the other did not. Any comparison would have to build upon cultural distinctiveness to incorporate patterns of central control — the more assertive centralizing efforts of Madrid versus the more indirect collaborative style preferred by London — and upon economic factors such as in- and out-migration. Along with the parties in Schleswig, the Südtiroler Volkspartei (SVP) more clearly introduces the international element common to interface peripheries in this first phase. Through to the later 1950s, the policies and aid offered by Austrian governments were equally as potent for continued protest and mobilization as, for instance, Mussolini's policy of italianization (Alcock, 1970; Katzenstein, 1977).

Economics occupies a more central role in the mobilization of the other contemporary movements. The Volksunie is unique in coming from a region that holds a majority of the state's population. The advance of Flemish nationalism was accelerated when the psychological perception of (rather than actual) cultural inferiority could be coupled with demonstrated economic improvement. The continued economic strength of the Basque provinces and Catalonia, and actual and potential central discrimination (especially under the Franco regime) have helped to sustain the possibility of regional mobilization there. Positive economic change and a potential prosperity from North Sea oil were contributory factors in the delayed upsurge of Scottish political nationalism: they increased the political and economic value of Scotland in the eyes of both the SNP and Westminster, an increase reflected in the subsequent actions of both. By contrast, the Rassemblement Wallon is an example of a party stimulated by economic decline and a challenge from other, more prosperous regions. In the Jura, too, the separatist movement corresponded to negative sociostructural and economic change. But whatever the economic movement involved, all are also grounded in some form of cultural identity and territorial loyalty.

Aims and strategies

That identity, with both population and territory, provides peripheral mobilization with a common set of aims, while the strategy adopted to pursue these aims is heavily conditioned by the structure of the state, by the style of central control and response. The aims of mobilization can be summarized in a deceptively simple way: to live in one's own country, to speak one's own language ('le droit à la parole'), and to be autonomous.

However, to study the aims of mobilization, it is necessary to distinguish between two important aspects: (1) aims as the final outcome of the processes of peripheral identity-building and the territorial differentiation of political authority, and (2) strategic aims. What do mobilized nationalist groups claim to be their final

FIGURE 4.5
The pyramid of peripheral aims:
desired outcomes ranked by degree of independence

Types of peripheral ideology, defined in terms of desired final territorial solution	*Stages of escalation, from full integration in a state to full independence from a state*	*Examples of political movements likely to be relevant to each stage*
FULL INDEPENDENCE ↑		
Separatism/ irredentism	Full independence / Transfer to neighbouring state	Wars, acts of terrorism, state-level negotiations
Confederalism	Regional autonomy with a central authority only for the regulation of inter-regional problems	Loosely constituted party system of statewide alliances between regionally based parties
Federalism	Shared autonomous powers between a central government and all provinces	Several regional parties contesting national elections
Regional autonomy	Autonomous status for only one peripheral region, to be treated differently from the rest of the state	Peripheral party with strong electoral support contesting national elections
Regionalism	Preservation of the cultural characteristics of a peripheral population	Stable peripheral party tending to compete only in local and regional elections
Peripheral protest	Putting peripheral demands on the agenda of the central political system	Statewide party with high degree of electoral support in the periphery
Peripheral identity-building	Arguing for the unique character of a given territory and its population and urging the preservation of its distinctive artefacts and stigmata	Cultural defence associations
	Province of a state with no separate cultural identity	
FULL INTEGRATION ↓		

aim at any one time? A common way of specifying aims is to point to the relationship between the periphery in question and the core of the state after the conflict has been resolved, as perceived by the movement. These alternatives are summarized in Figure 4.5, where the central column shows the content of each final aim. The pyramidal shape has been chosen because it reflects the tendency that, the more profound the desired changes, the smaller the popular base is likely to be. The right-hand column lists examples of different kinds of political associations likely to be active at each level of aim. The left-hand column uses what may be described as peripheral ideologies, which express the structural solution equivalent to the level of demand. The range extends downwards from full independence or secession to a concern for peripheral identity-building, even though the latter may often be regarded as a first stage in a chain reaction up the pyramid: certainly, opponents of such minimal demands may fear them as the thin end of the wedge.

In Figure 4.6 we have used this typology of goals to classify some of the peripheral cases. To avoid the possibility of single entry cells, we have collapsed some of the categories in Figure 4.5. To root the classification more firmly in the historical developments and processes of sociopolitical change discussed earlier, we have incorporated, first, an economic dimension, distinguishing between current highly developed, declining industrial, and semi-industrial or underdeveloped peripheries, and second, a dimension of past traditions of political organization, tapping whether or not a periphery has previously experienced autonomy or independence. The stated aims of the various movements (or at least of what seems to be the majority opinion within them) lie overwhelmingly at the modest end of the pyramid. Figure 4.1 indicated that in several peripheries there has appeared a proliferation of political groups and movements, among which there may often be those dedicated to achieving the ultimate aim of independence directly through violence and even guerilla warfare. Although only the Basque ETA groups and the Irish IRA have achieved prominence through a sustained level of activity, all these movements could be placed at the summit of the pyramid, since all tend to have a restricted membership.

Aims as the selection of political strategies are also of two types: pursuing a given final goal directly, and gradual change accompanied by pragmatism in a continuous chain — definition of

FIGURE 4.6

A chart for locating peripheries by economic vitality, historical tradition and peripheral demands

Aims	PAST INDEPENDENCE			AUTONOMIST TRADITION			NO PREVIOUS AUTONOMY, INDEPENDENCE		
	Economically developed	Early industrialization reconversion problems	Semi-industrial, under-developed	Economically developed	Early industrialization reconversion problems	Semi-industrial, under-developed	Economically developed	Early industrialization reconversion problems	Semi-industrial, under-developed
INDEPENDENCE, IRREDENTISM	Catalonia	Wales Scotland		Basque Provinces (Spain)		N. Ireland Faeroes			Alto Adige
CONFEDERALISM, FEDERALISM			Bavaria	Flanders	Wallonia	Jura			
REGIONAL AUTONOMY, PERIPHERAL IDENTITY-BUILDING			Brittany Savoy Schleswig		Alsace	Val d'Aosta Friuli Friesland Occitania Roussillon Basques (France) Grisons			Corsica Galicia Sardinia Andalusia Lappland

immediate and limited aim, success, definition of new aim and so on.[11] In the latter instance, the continuous production of new aims as old goals are attained places the endorsing movements and the peripheries concerned higher up the pyramid of independence. Even if the regionalist parties in, for example, Belgium are regarded as having regional autonomy as their primary 'independence-oriented' ideology, it would be a fallacy to assume that this aim will necessarily restrict the movements in the future (Buch, 1979). A successful partial devolution might limit further demands, or even remove them entirely from the agenda: equally, it might encourage further intensification. The historical precedents are on both sides. The Proporzpaket of 1969 and 1972 seems to have successfully defused the escalating conflict in the South Tyrol, but this can be counterbalanced by the Norwegian struggle for release from the personal union with Sweden, where the years between the 1860s and 1905 saw a chain of escalating goals during which time the satisfaction of one demand simply stimulated the generation of another that was even more far-reaching.

A successful peripheral strategy can be defined as one in which choices are made that maximize the realization of the desired outcome, if possible with minimum costs. Such a definition makes success independent of desired outcomes, being tied exclusively to the attainment of the planned political outcome. Hence the IRA and ETA have been less successful in reaching their aims, which both organizations have operationalized in terms of direct, final goals. A movement with more modest demands has a higher likelihood of success. In Friesland, for example, the chief concern seems to be preservation of the language. Here political mobilization has progressed only one step beyond cultural defence associations. The Frysk Nasjonale Partÿ contests only local elections: in general elections it is content to endorse statewide parties that declare themselves willing to support the Frisian language cause. In short, the main objective is merely to place the latter on the central political agenda. It might be argued that behind the rhetoric foliage this is also the aim of many small movements, such as those in France. Similarly, one of the most successful contemporary peripheral movements, the Rassemblement Jurassien, did not organize itself as a fully fledged political party, remaining a non-partisan umbrella organization that could pressure all parties as well as the Swiss and Bernese authorities.

However, general trends and patterns are strongly modified in each case by the particular concatenation of circumstances appertaining there. The demands expressed by and within the various peripheral populations can vary greatly. Plaid Cymru might place Welsh independence at the top of its agenda, but it simultaneously can campaign for more realistic, limited and ad hoc measures aiding the extension of facilities where the Welsh language can be used. In Flanders, even within the Volksunie, a number of bizarre final goals can be found existing alongside the conventional one of Flemish independence.[12]

Ultimately, the nature of the goals depends upon what has already been achieved in the past and the historical status achieved by or granted to the stigmata of cultural identity. In Finland, for example, Swedish is already constitutionally accepted as a national language, with several clearly defined rights in administration and education. Here, the emphasis in the maintenance of mobilization has been less on pressing for new, unachieved goals than on ensuring that governmental authorities conform with the constitutional provisions (Miljan, 1976). Similarly, to press for a new canton of Jura was more realistic in Switzerland than a similar claim anywhere else, as it would not and did not per se impose any additional burdens upon the Swiss confederation as a whole, while the language of the Jura already enjoyed high status as an official language of the Swiss state.

FIGURE 4.7
The political aims of peripheries

DEGREE OF CONSEQUENT CHANGE IN THE TERRITORIAL STRUCTURE OF THE STATE		OPTIONS AVAILABLE TO EXTERNAL PERIPHERIES	ADDITIONAL OPTIONS AVAILABLE TO INTERFACE PERIPHERIES
	High ↑	Separation	Irredentism
		Increased devolution	Increased interregional, supranational cooperation
	Low ↓	Demands for larger share of state resources	Comparisons across borders to evaluate and participate in economy and distributive efficiency of neighbouring state

We should not forget the question of the geopolitical location of peripheries. This too can be decisive in influencing demands. Figure 4.7 illustrates how on each rung of the scale of desired change interface peripheries have options (and hence possible goals) in addition to those available to external peripheries. Let us compare Brittany and Alsace, the former with a distant memory of independence, the latter with some tradition of autonomy, both contained within a French state historically opposed utterly to any kind of decentralization. The options available to Brittany have been very limited, and in a sense Breton nationalism has been forced to align itself with the cleavage patterns of the French polity: Paris versus the provinces, Right against Left (Braud, 1978; also Reece, 1977). With the failure of the autonomist agitation of the interwar years and the gradual fading of passions aroused by the wartime situation, Alsace more recently could utilize its interface position to seek some flexibility in language and economic affairs, not least because of the EEC membership of both France and West Germany. To Paris, German became more acceptable as a language (and this was accepted by Alsace in preference to insisting upon a higher status for its own particularistic dialect), while France could be absolved to some extent of responsibility for the structural problems of the Alsatian economy through the possibility of commuting across the border to and employment in the more buoyant West German economy.

To achieve the desired aims, mobilized groups and aspiring peripheral leaders can choose among a host of strategies with which to attack the centre and achieve a united and distinctive organization. The means adopted, by both centre and periphery, constitute some of the more dramatic expressions of identity conflicts: their newsworthiness, unfortunately, has often allowed the form of the acts themselves to dominate the information about territorially based political struggles and so to oversimplify the issues involved. It is nevertheless fairly easy to operationalize such differences in political methods. The most visible expression is that of violence and terror, shading into large-scale civil disobedience. The most institutionalized is electoral competition, the formation of a specific political party to defend and advance the perceived interests of the territory and identity group. Then follows, in order of descending magnitude, the penetration and colonization of statewide parties, the establishment of an umbrella organization to press for a non-partisan approach, the supportive approach of providing basically non-political services to the community, petitions directed to institutional authorities, and general propaganda aimed at both the centre and the peripheral group. Clearly, these alternatives are not mutually exclusive. The simultaneous employment of multiple strategies is as common as the existence of different, but related, organizations — for example, Plaid Cymru and the Welsh Language Society, the Slesvig Parti and the Bund deutscher Nordschleswiger — pursuing different strategies. Indeed, the simultaneous deployment of different strategies can be related to organization differentiation, as with Sinn Fein and the IRA in Northern Ireland. The selection depends upon the combination of the perception of their relative value, the resources available to the potential organization and the context — which includes an interpretation both of the past and of the anticipated reaction of the centre.

The success or failure of any mobilization effort depends upon its dissemination of information and viewpoint. Hence, propaganda, the spread of value-laden information, is the basic activity for anyone wishing some change in the structure and style of territorial government. Propaganda serves the dual function of mass recruitment and central elite persuasion. By itself, though common to all the movements listed or implied in Figure 4.1, it is rarely sufficient: especially where the first objective is attained while the second fails, other strategies become necessary. Petitioning institutional authorities is a more sophisticated propaganda version in that the messages are specifically directed towards preselected targets. Though concentrating on individuals in positions of political and economic influence, the objective is ultimately the same: to attempt to convey the impression to decision-makers that there exists a broad climate of opinion in favour of the desired changes.

A supportive strategy, through the provision of essentially nonpolitical services to the peripheral community, might be called less high-powered. The immediate objectives are the strengthening of the communal network, the stiffening or erection of barriers against penetration from outside, and the stimulation of the consciousness and salience of identity. Where some political objectives are involved, they may entail also the fostering of the belief that something can be done to alleviate the peripheral predicament and the hope of a spillover effect into political nationalism. This would seem to imply, however, the survival of an institutional infrastructure that will assist in maintaining the stigmata and artefacts of the distinctive society. Survey data from the northern linguistic peripheries of Spain in 1977 illustrate this point. In Galicia, with weak barriers and low levels of consciousness and salience, 51 percent considered the region too weak economically to be independent: in the Basque provinces and Catalonia the figures were 31 and 14 percent respectively. Similarly, only 28 percent in Galicia believed that regional progress would be a positive benefit of having a regional government, while the Basque and Catalan figures were 52 and 56 percent (Del Campo, Navarro and Tezanos, 1977). Overall, this approach by itself is not directly political, and the expected political returns will almost certainly not meet the costs involved, since it by no means denotes a *positive* action, that is, bringing pressure to bear upon the centre: it merely represents a defence against the centre.

Alternatively, mobilization may be sought within the political system. The most broad-ranging option is to seek to work upon and within the statewide parties, with the same objective of portraying a wide non-partisan consensus. Whether true or not, the territorial/identity problems are presented as not being a divisive issue for established political organizations and their aims. The most common feature is the endorsement of individual candidates across party lines, though infiltration is not uncommon. The problem here is to generate some momentum and maintain the salience of the issue without allowing it to become merely another issue between parties. The Rassemblement Jurassien has perhaps been the most successful exponent of this strategy: the Rassemblement did not contest any public office itself, but it sponsored, endorsed or opposed individual candidates of whatever party according to their attitude towards the demand for a separate canton of Jura. However, this is an exception rather than the rule. Very few umbrella organizations have emerged, and their fate is typified more by the formation in 1969 of the federative Défense et Promotion des langues de France (DPLF) through a merger of eight regional movements. The DPLF was consciously non-partisan, but failed entirely to rock the French political system. In essence, it rapidly was forced back to a supportive strategy, to concentrating upon limited practical aspects of linguistic defence.

Rather than adopt an all-party strategy, a group may seek to insert itself within, or ally itself with, a single statewide party. This might imply that, for the politically active in the periphery, one party seems a more natural home, and the design is to turn the peripheral issue into one of partisan politics. In Flanders in the 1930s, for example, while three Flemish parties had succeeded in winning parliamentary representation, all still actively pursued the hope of being incorporated within the large Catholic party, a party that enjoyed an almost hegemonic position in Flanders and which was the largest Belgian party. Such a partnership, however, is rarely one of equals. Almost invariably the periphery will be more dependent upon the party than vice versa. While the addition may strengthen the host party, this always has other and more important bases of support. While the nationalists may be highly dependent upon the host's success, the dilemma is that the greater this becomes, the less the party will need peripheral support — to which must be added the problem of the possible alienation of the other major parties.

This dilemma is equally acute where an alliance is sought with a national party, an option that is more usual for miniscule political organizations or groups in decline. In Denmark the German population has steadily declined since 1920 to around only 5 percent of the population of South Jutland. Its party lost its Folketing representation in 1964. With no hope of arresting the decline, the Slesvig Parti in 1973 concluded an alliance with the new Centre Democrats, after which the party's leading candidate, placed first on the joint constituency list, was elected to the Folketing.[13] By contrast, this strategy seems to have been a satisfactory arrangement in the northern Italian peripheries. In both the Val d'Aosta and the Alto Adige the major local parties have worked in close harness with the Christian Democrats, in the former perhaps partly because of the tiny size of the province and the limited nature of the demands raised. In the Alto Adige the SVP until 1959 consistently rejected all overtures from other regional groups, preferring to be an election partner of the Christian Democrats, despite the latter's dwindling sympathy for regional devolution. However, specific Italian circumstances also played a role. At that time the Christian Democrats were seemingly entrenched for ever in government, and therefore the only party that could satisfy peripheral demands, while the anti-clerical nature of the major opposition parties would certainly not be attractive in a strong Catholic area.

One further interesting possibility that should be noted is negative mobilization, a political equivalent of the supportive approach — defensive rather than positive. Especially where the target population is so small that its representation would be swamped in a national legislature, a peripheral movement might be tempted towards the path of passive non-cooperation. In the 1965 French presidential election, the Centre d'Études Régionales Corse urged abstention: 44 percent of the island's electorate did not vote (up to 85 percent in some communes), compared with a French figure of 15 percent. The Centre pursued a similar strategy in 1972 on Pompidou's referendum on regional reform: the turnout in Corsica was 41 percent.

The most extreme strategy is violence. Bombing and assassination may be good propaganda which can serve to quell possible objections from the peripheral population and to impress upon the centre the high costs involved in any attempt to eradicate the violence. It is doubtful, however, whether violence as a strategy can be structurally predicted. The existence of a clandestine military tradition dating back to violent historical events seems to be more important than contemporary characteristics of the communities: ETA and the IRA have more in common with each other than with the Basque and Northern Irish communities. Overall, violence is more likely where there seems to be little or no support for the policy, or where other avenues for pursuing demands are closed: it is very much a costly policy of last resort. The stance of the centre seems to be less important than the structure of the periphery. While it might be argued that intransigence by London and Madrid contributes to the high level of violence in the Basque provinces and Northern Ireland, the one major common problem relates to the divided identity nature of the provinces.[14] Austria provides a similar example. While Austrian governments have been sympathetic and positively oriented towards the Carinthian Slovenes, their policies have been sabotaged not only by the violent reaction of a tiny Slovene activist segment (a classic example of identity being invested in past rather than present occupation of territory), but also by the German-speaking majority in Carinthia (Haas and Stuhlpfarrer, 1977).

In the last resort these alternatives all are perhaps an admission of weakness or uncertainty. They are linked to barriers that can hinder peripheral mobilization. One important obstacle is the combination of institutional structures and previous mobilization. The rules of the game in different countries will obviously influence the nature and availability of access to the political arena, as well as determining what issues are accepted and how readily they are accepted. One crucial factor is the gatekeeping function of the electoral system. A plurality system, as in the United Kingdom, increases the costs to a peripheral party of breaking into the system, and these are high in relation to the expected successes. Proportional representation, perhaps, affords an earlier recognition of the utility of the electoral alternative. Even so, life may not necessarily be easier. In most Western European countries the switch to proportionality was one of the last stages in the democratization process, usually occurring some time after the extension of suffrage and the consequent pressure on political leaders and activists to establish mass organizations. A statewide party system, with what that entailed for mobilization, existed, at least in embryo form, before proportional representation reduced the costs of establishing a viable peripheral party. For the latter, it would be less a question of mobilizing than of switching the direction and content of mobilization. Within the statewide party system, the regionally skewed support of statewide parties may be more meaningful for peripheral demands. The social base of Plaid Cymru indicates that it tends to be in the same electoral market as Labour, rather than Liberal or Conservative. And the power of Labour in Wales may be at least as meaningful for Welsh demands as for British integration, and more so than Plaid Cymru. In Spain politicians from the small-town and rural province of Galicia have always been prominent in Madrid, a tradition that was continued after Franco with the electoral success, nationally and within Galicia, of the Union Democrático de Centre (UCD). Most Scottish members of Parliament are strongly Scottish-oriented, working hard for distinctive policies and benefits (Keating, 1978). Even the successful SPP cannot claim to be the exclusive spokesman of the Swedish Finns: it has held only some two-thirds of the Swedish speaking deputies.

A second barrier is internal group or territorial variation, which may then turn potential into negative resources. Language can be a two-edged sword where there is incongruence between it and identity. Plaid Cymru's identification with Welsh, despite its bilingual protestations, is a stumbling block, and the party's performance has not matched the 18 percent who in 1968 agreed with independence for Wales, let alone the 55 percent who desired some kind of political devolution. The Jura has consistently been divided over its future since the Congress of Vienna, with French Catholic juxtaposed against German and French Protestant areas.

In Northern Ireland the River Bann effectively divides the province into a largely Protestant east (especially if we exclude Belfast) and a largely Catholic west.

Differences in attitudes towards territorial change are frequently related to internal social structural characteristics. No ethnic or linguistic group is monolithic. While regional activists seek to stress what the group has in common, other factors may divide it politically. It is, in fact, rare for the periphery to be populated only by a single ethno-linguistic group. Unity, where it appears, is more common in remoter external peripheries which are economically less developed and less attractive to outsiders other than those posted there to serve in central agencies. Here, out-migration tends to have been a dominant social feature since the Industrial Revolution. Economically advanced regions have tended, through in-migration, to become more like interface peripheries, with a more mixed population. Wales experienced a large English and Irish migration into the southern coalfields. German speakers began to move into the Jura in the early twentieth century in the heyday of its industrialization. Perhaps the most marked in-migration patterns are to be observed in Spain, where both the Basque country and Catalonia received floods of immigrants from less prosperous parts of Spain. The problem of different identities in these provinces was heightened in the Basque case by the high opportunity costs imposed by the great gulf of the cultural distance between the two groups. The extreme distinctiveness of Basque from Spanish may make the Basque language a stronger resource as a cultural stigma. But by the same token, in the minds of Spanish speakers its distinctiveness constitutes a formidable hurdle in learning costs and facilitates alienation from any political movement that stresses priority for the language. These facts are reflected in Table 4.1. The numbers in the Basque and Catalan regions favouring territorial change are higher than elsewhere (except the extreme case of the remote Canaries), but not perhaps dramatically so. And the figures do not correspond to language as such, since only a minority of the Basque population can speak the language. Nor is it wholly congruent with identity. Of the Catalan sample, only 56 percent identified themselves as Catalan, and 38 percent as Spanish. The number of Basque identifiers (32 percent) was lower than Spanish identifiers (41 percent), even lower than Galician identifiers (44 percent), and only marginally higher than those registering an Andalusian identity. When looking only at those born in the region, the Basque figures did not greatly increase, while the Catalan figure (71 percent) was much higher (Del Campo, Navarro and Tezanos, 1977). These data indicate the lesser costs involved in assimilation within Catalonia.

TABLE 4.1
Attitudes towards regional autonomy in Spain, by province

	Desired form of government structure for province			
	Status quo %	*Regional autonomy* %	*Federal status* %	*Independence* %
Catalonia	35	32	12	5
Basque country	21	32	24	6
Galicia	49	16	13	1
Andalusia	52	18	8	1
Valencia	50	23	6	1
Canaries	34	50	10	0
Castille	49	21	9	2
Total	44	24	10	2

Source: Del Campo, Navarro and Tezanos (1977).

The data in Table 4.1 shows a sparse pro-independence position, though rather more (13 percent) did believe in the right of regions to secede: not surprisingly, the Basque and Catalan figures, 32 and 20 percent respectively, were rather higher (41 and 27 percent among native Basques and Catalans). This limited appeal of independence is a general phenomenon, and most peripheral movements, certainly the larger ones and those that strive for respectability, concentrate, at least in the first instance, on some form of decentralization.[15] Despite the widespread presence of favourable attitudes towards some form of change — regularly around 80 percent in Scotland throughout the 1970s, and even between 67 and 85 percent in French polls in 1975 — this option of the middle range is the most diffuse and the most susceptible to attack, not only from the centre, but also from more extreme versions of territorial change. Outright independence or a radical territorial restructuring (federalism) are in a sense easier to concretize and hence to mobilize. What this means is that political mobilization itself can be dissipated among several movements espousing all the various options from cultural defence up to and including violence. There are at least five alternative Basque views on the relationship between the provinces and the rest of Spain, and the Partido Nacionalista Vasco (PNV), with its Christian Democratic line, has to face not only the pro-Spain element, but also more radical groups within the Basque camp. Similarly, the Pacta Democrático de Catalunya (PDC) has had to face other regionalist movements, such as the remnants of the prewar Lliga and Esquerra. Even what seems to be a reasonably solidly based party like the Volksunie has been opposed by more extreme groups hostile to what they see as concessions made to the centre. A proliferation of groups seems to be the fate of French peripheral mobilization, and this is also characteristic of political life in the tiny Val d'Aosta. Parties such as the SPP, SVP and SNP, which enjoy a hegemonic position within the pro-periphery political camp, can therefore deem themselves fortunate, and are the exception rather than the rule.

The electoral record

While nearly all the current peripheral parties possess a lengthy pedigree, all tend to operate in the shadowy area between party and other forms of political agitation: almost inevitably, because of the nature of their claims, they tend to be broadly aggregative in intention and bifurcated in behaviour between party and pressure group. Many, again, such as the Movimento de Friuli, Union Démocratique Bretonne (UDB) or Frysk Nasjonale Partÿ, do not contest national elections, or do so as very junior partners of a statewide party.

None of these parties has achieved its potential (as opposed to a reasonable) electoral strength. Few, if any, of the peripheral parties upon which academic and media attention has focused in recent years have achieved even the levels of a long-established party such as the SPP or the post-1945 SVP. The latter has consistently secured around 60 percent of the vote in the Bolzano area in both national and local elections, while some 75 percent of the Swedish Finn population are to be found in the ranks of the SPP. By contrast, the Catalan nationalist vote in 1977 (shared among an alliance of parties) was only 27.9 percent, far below the hegemony of pre-

Franco days. The Volksunie has improved upon the interwar Flemish nationalist vote, but not overwhelmingly so. In other instances, previous peripheral political distinctiveness has not been repeated. Alsace, for example, displayed a very distinctive political style during its sojourn in the German Reich, and in 1928 autonomist groups garnered 40 percent of the Alsatian vote. For the rest, the most impressive performances have been those of the SNP (30.4 percent of the Scottish vote in October 1974) and the peculiar case of the FDF (almost 40 percent of the Brussels vote in the 1970s).[16] But these are totals that most peripheral parties can only dream about. The French case is representative of the other sorry extreme.[17] But weak regional/local performances are not restricted to France. They have been repeated by, for example, the rejuvenated Bayernpartei (BP), the Movimento de Friuli, and the Partito de Azione de Sardegna.

Of those areas with 'major' peripheral parties that contest national elections, only in Scotland, Wales and the Belgian provinces is there a more or less complete congruence between territory and identity. In the first two, at least, there is no great clash between holding both peripheral and British identity: the relationship in practice is largely benign. The problem in Belgium is not so much one of antagonistic identities as of the very low level of identity with Belgium as a territorial and political entity. Elsewhere, the territory for which the party claims to speak is more clearly populated by groups with different identities, an incompatibility that may well reinforce a party's commitment simultaneous with making its task and objective more difficult. In all but three cases (SNP, nationalists in Northern Ireland, and BP — to which we might add a further German case, the Deutsche Partei (DP) of Hanover), the identity claimed by the party is fortified by the linguistic distinctiveness of its presumed social support. The SPP is a deviant case: language may be the basis of political mobilization, but identity is a domestic concern. The Swedish speakers are Finnish, not Swedish.

Survey data on these parties are rather unsatisfactory, especially with regard to the interchangeability of identity and language: in several instances one is used as an indicator of the other. Similar problems emerge with aggregate data, which is rendered almost useless by the paucity of these parties' electoral performance. Hence, it is almost impossible to indulge in a systematic comparative analysis similar to that attempted in Chapter 2.

The core parties are those competing in territories where language and identity are mutually reinforcing, that is, areas that possess a language distinctive from that of the state. Of those that have regularly contested statewide elections, these are the Slesvig Parti, SPP, SVP, SSWV, Union Valdôtaine, and the parties of the northern Spanish peripheries. The SSWV attempted to mobilize and protect the interests of the Danish-speaking population of South Schleswig, though with a declining social base its activities have gradually become more those of a cultural defence association. North of the border its counterpart, the Slesvig Parti, endeavoured, with some success, to do the same among the German-speaking population: 85 percent of German identifiers support the party, while 91 percent of its support is derived from those with an unambiguous German identification (Elklit, Noack and Tonsgaard, 1978: 176). Some three-quarters of the Swedish speakers in Finland have supported the SPP (Miljan, 1976), while in Italy the SVP and Union Valdôtaine are respectively restricted almost exclusively to German and French speakers. In the Basque provinces and Catalonia a large proportion of the population is not indigenous to the region or language. In 1977 language/identity did serve to differentiate the parties in Catalonia. The parties within the Pacta are strongly integrated with Catalan cultural organizations, while the high Socialist (PSOE) vote seems to have come more from the large immigrant community in Barcelona. The Basque case is more clear-cut. Some 66 percent of the territorial population profess no knowledge of Basque, yet 93 percent of PNV supporters and 96 percent of the more radical Euskadiko Eskerra (EE) claim some comprehension of the language, compared with only 10 percent for all other parties in the province (Linz, 1978). In 1978 an overwhelming sense of Jura identity was recorded among Rassemblement activists. This is especially noteworthy because 75 percent also stressed a religious commitment and 60 percent a class commitment: yet these latter were ranked only third and fifth respectively when the respondents were asked to rank the importance of their membership in five different social groups (Campbell, 1982).

The circumstances of the other parties are more disparate. More than most, the Belgian situation is perhaps sui generis. Two (or three) identities exist underneath the concept of being Belgian, itself very weak.[18] The sheer bulk of Flanders has meant that French, at least in the past few decades, might be regarded as a regional as much as a central language. At any rate, each of the three major regionalist parties is confined to its own region, recruits from its own linguistic group, and must compete not only against statewide parties in its own region, but also against the other regionalist parties.[19]

Two German parties — BP and DP — and the SNP have operated in regions with a distinctive identity, but where the language is that of the centre. In the case of Scotland, all but a handful of immigrants have a Scottish identity, which both limits and permits the use of the latter as a basis for mobilization or partisan differentiation. The problem here, one that the moribund German parties failed to resolve, is not just to focus on identity, but also to turn the multiple identity with state and region from a benign to an incompatible, even antagonistic, relationship.[20] By contrast, in Northern Ireland there are antagonistic identities, but a common language. The context of Plaid Cymru has been different again: while the sense of Welsh identity might be pervasive, language reinforces identity for only a minority of the population. Recent surveys show that only some 17 percent of Welsh speakers (23 percent of fluent speakers) support Plaid Cymru, compared with 4 percent of non-Welsh speakers. Regionally, the party has the allegiance of 25 percent of Welsh speakers in the cultural heartland of the north and west, 16 percent in north-east and mid-Wales, but only 9 percent in the populous south. Paradoxically, while Plaid Cymru has identified, and is identified, with the Welsh language, the distribution imbalance of the Welsh population means that just over one-third of the party's support is non-Welsh-speaking (Balsom, 1979). An analysis of aggregate data (Table 4.2) confirms this anomaly. While the party's electoral successes have been in constituencies within the heartland counties of Gwynedd and Dyfed, these sparsely populated areas gave it only 37.8 perçent of its total Welsh vote in 1970, the year of its best electoral performance: one-half of its votes came from the populous south.

Other cultural variables do not seem to play a prominent role in electoral mobilization. Few regions that have spawned regionalist parties possess a distinctive religion or are divided between two religions. As a mobilizing force the latter appears most conspicuously in Northern Ireland where, at least in popular terminology, the dividing line separates Protestant from Catholic: Irish nationalist groups are mobilized almost exclusively from the Catholic population. Elsewhere, religion seems to have played a muted role in the Jura, Scotland and the Basque country. Bassand (1975) found an ecological link in the Jura between religion and issue alignment. However, the detailed survey analysis by Campbell (1982) suggests that the religious factor was linked to, and part of, the wider question of territory of origin and territorial identity: it

TABLE 4.2
Distribution of population, language and Plaid Cymru support in Wales, by county

Region	*County*	*% of Welsh population, 1971*	*% of Welsh language speakers, 1971*	*% of votes cast for Plaid Cymru, 1970*	*% of total Plaid Cymru vote, 1970*
North and West	Dyfed	11.6	40.6	17.8	20.4
	Gwynedd	8.1	61.3	22.0	17.4
Mid- and North-East	Clwyd	13.2	20.6	6.8	8.3
	Powys	3.6	24.2	7.9	3.4
South	Mid Glamorgan	19.5	9.4	18.7	21.9
	South Glamorgan	14.2	5.0	6.5	8.0
	West Glamorgan	13.7	19.5	9.6	12.8
	Gwent	16.2	1.7	4.4	7.9

Source: based on data in McAllister, Parry and Rose (1979); Craig (1972).

was non-Jurassian immigrants who formed the Protestant opposition to territorial change. In Scotland the SNP failed to make any great headway among the large Catholic minority (mainly of Irish descent) in the industrial heartland of Glasgow: even at its peak of optimism, considerably less than 10 percent of Scottish Catholics indicated a preference for the SNP.[21] Religion seems to be significant in the Basque country as the factor that most effectively distinguishes between the support of the various pro-Basque parties.

The traditional view of the socioeconomic basis of peripheral parties was that they were likely to be agrarian-based or to reflect the whole spectrum of socioeconomic characteristics. In fact, none can be described as agrarian-based, and few have a significant agrarian support. Since 1945 the largest figures have been recorded for the German regionalist parties. Elsewhere, available data point to strong farming support for the Slesvig Parti: 31 percent of its support comes from farmers (Elklit, Noack and Tonsgaard, 1978: 179). While these parties may not be agrarian, their mobilization is skewed in a rural direction. Similarly, in the Alto Adige the mass base of the SVP is primarily rural (Katzenstein, 1977: 315), as is that of Basque and Catalan nationalism, even though the origins and leadership of the former at least are primarily urban (Heiberg, 1982). The Basque experience is repeated in Scotland. While the origins of modern organized nationalism in Scotland lay in dissidents from left-wing socialism, in the long decades of quiescence and introspection the party activists and support came more from middle-class elements in small-town Scotland, most specifically in the more industrialized central belt. Political take-off in the 1960s repeated that of Basque mobilization a half century earlier: expansion into the more rural areas of the country. In the 1979 collapse, SNP strength suffered much less in the geographical and economic peripheries of Scotland.

The notion that peripheral parties are broadly aggregative across socioeconomic groups is borne out to some extent by ecological evidence. An aggregate analysis of socioeconomic variables in Scotland suggested that, in contrast to both the Labour and Conservative Parties, the SNP vote was unrelated to any distinct social attributes: few correlations were significant, and only the two collinear variables of farmers/agricultural industry were positive (Jaensch, 1976). Similarly, the socioeconomic basis of the Rassemblement Wallon has resembled that of Wallonia as a whole (Hill, 1974: 48-9). In South Jutland supporters of the Slesvig Parti, whose common bond was their German identity, when asked what they would have done if the party of their choice had not contested the 1971 election, gave responses that were distributed among the other (mainly socioeconomically based) parties in a ratio that approximated statewide party strength (Elklit, Noack and Tonsgaard, 1978: 181-2).

More typically, however, survey data tend to suggest a refinement of this proposition. While peripheral parties do succeed to a considerable extent in mobilizing support across socioeconomic boundaries, that support tends to be strongly skewed in the direction of middle-class groups. In both Wales (Balsom, 1979) and

Scotland (Brand, 1978) the middle-socioeconomic status categories have been the strongest pillars of nationalist support. In Belgium both aggregate (Frognier, 1975) and survey (Hill, 1974: 48-9) analyses stress the strong middle-class cohesion of the FDF and a not too dissimilar bias within the Volksunie.[22] Strong minority consciousness in Spain can be found in cities like San Sebastian and Barcelona. We might therefore expect mobilization to be successful in this urbanized environment: given, for example, the considerable socialist (30 percent) and communist (20 percent) triumph in Barcelona in 1977, it seems reasonable to assume that the PDC vote (15 percent) was biased more towards middle-class groups. That working-class members of peripheral minorities are less prone to support their 'own' peripheral party is also supported by evidence from Scandinavia. Only 18 percent of the Slesvig Parti's support comes from workers, compared with 31 percent in the total sample (Elklit, Noack and Tonsgaard, 1978: 179). In Finland only about one-half of Swedish-speaking workers are to be found in the ranks of the SPP.

There is, then, a wide range of variations in support. A simple reference to ethnic identity cannot be sufficient to explain what they have in common. If that were the case, then all perhaps should be branded as failures. A more detailed mapping must incorporate an attitudinal dimension of identity. Within the group-identity context, the natural reservoir for these parties comprises those electors for whom identity is so salient that they desire independence or at least some degree of territorial-institutional change. In most instances this core potential is limited. We have already referred to Spanish data that indicate a very low level of endorsement of independence as an option in the Basque country and Catalonia, though in both provinces the numbers accepting the status quo were the only mainland instances that were lower than the national average. Similarly, throughout the 1970s, while only some 20 percent of Scottish samples were adamantly opposed to change, only a further 20 percent opted for independence, and almost all of these had already found their way into the SNP camp (Urwin, 1978: 127-8). It is the middle ground, consisting of an interest, no matter how vague, in some degree of change, that offers expansionary opportunities to these parties and that, given the right set of conditions, can pose problems for political centres and territorial integrity.

A cohesion based upon identity and attitudes is perhaps tautological. What is more interesting is the middle-class predominance. The middle-class weight is even more pronounced when attention is focused more narrowly upon party leaders and activists, even where the electoral base is more clearly rural. While the SNP candidates in 1970 and 1974 were broadly middle-class in background, those of Plaid Cymru were overwhelmingly from professional groups (Butler and Pinto-Duschinsky, 1971: 301; Butler and Kavanagh, 1974: 211). This phenomenon is repeated in non-partisan, non-electoral organizations like the Rassemblement Jurassien, among whose activist ranks the liberal professions and middle management are strongly represented (Campbell, 1982). In the multitude of peripheral organizations in France sampled by Beer (1977: 151-2), no less than 75 percent of the activists interviewed were professional or white-collar workers: the level was consistent across all the regions examined, and contrasts with a figure of 29 percent for the total French work force.

Middle-class preponderance fits well with conventional interpretations of the rise of 'historic' nationalism in the nineteenth century, and with explanations of the original crystallization of autonomist sympathies in these regions. Heiberg (1975; 1982), for instance, argues that Basque nationalism was essentially a middle-class response to economic change and the expansion of Spanish socialism among the (immigrant) working classes after the 1890s. Within the context of recent volatility, postulated or proven, in European party systems, this middle-class manifestation may well be part of a more widespread phenomenon of insecurity. Where, however, there exists the possibility of identifying with a distinctive region or group, this can provide an alternative base for mobilization and/or political discontent. In this sense there is no incongruity with explanations of earlier nationalist mobilization. What we are confronted with is a sense of marginality arising out of a more direct experience of change and discrimination, and out of the dissonance between perceived status and perceived political efficacy. This is most acute among those who have invested educational and occupational time in the cultural stigmata and artefacts of the distinctive identity. Two features seem to be new. First, in some instances there is a dissonance with economic efficacy in the case of middle management: a feeling that industrial plants essentially constitute a branch economy seems to have emerged in declining industrial regions such as central Scotland, the Jura and Wallonia, with perceived deleterious consequences for these people in terms of promotion prospects and job security. Second, this middle layer between centre and peripheral mass (Figure 4.3) cannot serve as a screen as effectively as a century ago. While greater central activity is more prominent in the peripheries, the fact that this may aid the process of peripheral mobilization where the extent and style of this activity provokes negative peripheral reactions is counterbalanced by a less obvious fact: centres do not need to rely exclusively on middlemen. Through, for example, the electronic mass media and effective distribution and communication networks, centres can directly or implicitly place barriers between the potential peripheral leaders and their target electorate.

Common links in mobilization do not necessarily mean uniformity in subsequent electoral fortunes. Deploying a party's vote as a continuous variable makes available several measures for assessing electoral change in terms of trends and fluctuations (Rose and Urwin, 1970). Trends in party strength may be appropriately measured by regression lines, a statistic that provides a simple indication of both the direction and the magnitude of a trend. Two measures of fluctuation will be used. The 'steadiness', or 'variability', of a party's vote refers to its normal range of fluctuation, controlling for an extreme result: the standard deviation from the mean vote of a party is an appropriate statistic. By contrast, a party that is gaining or losing strength at a steady rate will plot an increasingly variable course because of its persisting pattern of change. The standard error from the trend line provides a straightforward index of the 'persistence' of party strength: a party that consistently deviated from its trend line would have a higher standard error.

These simple measurements of change have been applied to 13 peripheral parties which have contested at least three general elections as separate entities since 1945, and which have gained at least 5 percent of the vote in a region.[23] As a point of reference the results will be contrasted to the average for a universe of 142 elections in Western countries between 1945 and 1969 (Rose and Urwin, 1970). Table 4.3 plots the data for the 13 parties, measured as a percentage of the national vote over all elections since 1945. Change at a rate of 0.25 percent per annum has been taken as the minimum meriting description as meaningful change, even though it represents only a 1 percent change in voting strength over a four-year period. In general, one-third of the parties in the wider

TABLE 4.3
Trends and fluctuations: national level

Party	*Per annum trend*	*Cumulative trend*	*Standard deviation*	*Standard error*
Volksunie	+0.35	+8.40	3.4	2.2
Rassemblement Wallon	+0.07	+0.91	1.8	2.2
Front Démocratique des Francophones	+0.24	+3.12	1.5	1.2
Slesvig Parti	–0.01	–0.17	0.1	0.1
Svenska Folkparti	–0.10	–3.00	1.0	0.1
Südtiroler Volkspartei	0.00	+0.02	0.1	0.1
Union Valdôtaine	+0.01	+0.19	0.1	0.1
Scottish National Party	+0.07	+2.38	1.0	0.6
Plaid Cymru	+0.02	+0.68	0.2	0.1
Irish Nationalist	0.00	+0.07	0.2	0.1
Bayernpartei	–0.17	–3.40	1.6	1.3
Deutsche Partei	–0.09	–0.72	0.4	0.4
Südschleswigscher Wahlerverband	–0.02	–0.24	0.1	0.1

Notes: The cumulative trend is simply the per annum trend multiplied by the total electoral lifespan since 1945 of the party. Irish nationalist consists of a merging of several different nationalist parties.

universe displayed a meaningful rate of change. Moreover, a standard deviation of 2.6 with a distribution skewed in the direction of steadiness, and a median standard error of 2.8, indicated a very limited overall amount of fluctuation. Judged by these standards, the figures in Table 4.3 are remarkable in stressing the most extreme steadiness. Only the Volksunie displays any kind of meaningful trend and a standard deviation above this Western average. These figures, however, are indicative less of steadiness than of the extremely small size of most of these parties in a state-wide perspective. They confirm the view that miniscule parties do not contribute much to an understanding of national party systems in this kind of aggregate analysis. However, since we are concerned with peripheral parties, it makes more sense to explore tendencies towards change only within the peripheries, looking at these parties' share of the peripheral vote (Table 4.4).

TABLE 4.4
Trends and fluctuations: regional level

Party	*Per annum trend*	*Cumulative trend*	*Standard deviation*	*Standard error*
Volksunie	+0.63	+15.12	6.1	3.9
Rassemblement Wallon	+0.21	+2.75	5.4	6.6
Front Démocratique des Francophones	+2.16	+28.11	13.5	10.8
Slesvig Parti	−0.14	−3.36	1.6	1.3
Svenska Folkparti	−0.24	−7.20	2.4	0.3
Südtiroler Volkspartei	+0.16	+4.96	2.5	2.2
Union Valdôtaine	+0.60	+18.60	13.7	13.9
Scottish National Party	+0.76	+25.73	10.0	6.1
Plaid Cymru	+0.32	+10.89	3.9	2.0
Irish Nationalist	+0.01	+0.34	4.8	5.3
Bayernpartei	−0.88	−17.60	8.0	5.7
Deutsche Partei	−0.80	−6.40	2.9	2.2
Südschleswigscher Wahlerverband	−0.28	−3.36	1.3	0.6

Notes: Since the Swedish Finns do not occupy a distinctive periphery, an artificial territory has been created from the only constituencies where the SPP has always and exclusively nominated candidates. Otherwise, see Table 4.3.

The variations across the parties are now considerable. At one extreme are the non-ethnic German parties with a marked downward trend, eventually to disappear from the national scene. At the other is the explosive positive trend of the FDF, a party that represents the total opposite of a peripheral predicament. The Volksunie, SNP and Union Valdôtaine have also experienced positive trends, while the Rassemblement Wallon, Slesvig Parti, SPP, SVP and Irish nationalists evince little change. Similar distinctions can be seen in the standard deviations and standard errors. Those parties with a more limited trend also tend to display a more marked steadiness and persistence. For the Belgian and British parties the high statistics reflect the more sudden increase in support in the 1960s and 1970s. The figures for the Union Valdôtaine are due almost entirely to the extreme deviancy of its first electoral performance in 1948: if this result is excluded, the party shows nil change. More important, perhaps, than the considerable variations across parties is the fact that these statistics tend to be higher than the median Western figures reviewed earlier. In most instances these are due more to electoral movements during the past two decades, and in that sense there has been electoral volatility, with the presence of peripheral parties being a destabilizing factor. But it remains the case that these are limited to a few countries, that the territories tend to be small in a statewide perspective, and that these statistics say little about the significance of peripheral parties. Electorally, contemporary peripheral mobilization has not been very successful. However, peripheral parties constitute only one brick in a far more intricate game, and by themselves cannot provide a full picture of the peripheral predicament and its politicization.

5

The Central Response: Policies of Accommodation

For any state the territorial objectives are twofold: to preserve the integrity of the territory, and to ensure legitimacy within these boundaries through popular support for and acquiescence to its political authority. While several central responses to peripheral demands are available, because of the peculiar territorial and membership qualities of the latter, all except expulsion of a peripheral group from the state entail some impact upon territorial structure. The dilemma for centres is that even the slightest concession might be taken to be, and might become, the thin end of a wedge that might ultimately threaten these regime imperatives, for at the furthest edge peripheral demands challenge the unity of the state. While the progressive freezing of the territorial structure of Western Europe has meant that over the past century the catalogue of peripheral demands has been a chronicle of failure rather than of success, this is of little consolation to any regime confronted with such a situation. The challenge, whenever it arises, emphasizes the dangers of the potential conflict between territorial integrity and complete political legitimacy. Where a periphery rejects compliance with central authority, the consequent course of action can be assessed in terms of the resources available to the periphery and the price that the state is willing to pay. At the extreme, where a periphery repudiates the state utterly, the centre might be forced towards two equally abhorrent and costly alternatives: to introduce coercive measures in order to preserve existing territorial integrity, or, by conceding peripheral independence, to violate that imperative in order to guarantee full legitimacy within a territorially truncated state. This is the major theme of this chapter. First, however, we shall review two other facets of the central response: that of statewide parties confronted with peripheral mobilization, and the centre's efforts to come to grips with regional economic disequilibria and problems.

The party response

Since the late nineteenth century, the context of politics in western Europe has been one of democratic pluralism. In Chapter 4 we indicated how this variety was replicated in the peripheral world: a range of various organizations adopting different strategies. However, while peripheral issues have always been present in modern European politics, they have not figured prominently in party systems. Hence the more conventional approach of stressing the integrative functions of political parties: small parties other than those that deliberately restrict themselves to one region, such as the British Liberals or the Belgian Communists, may have a skewed territorial support, but even in their 'core' areas they rarely approach the weakest levels of support for those major parties that by any definition are nationwide in both intent and performance. However, party systems are not immutable, and existing parties have to come to terms with peripheral phenomena when the latter are injected into the political arena, most obviously when a peripheral party enters the competition for votes. While there are relatively few parties that appeal on territorially distinctive lines, their presence is less important than the existence of clearly distinctive regions. Given that most Western European countries possess peripheries distinctive in some form of identity, it can be asked how this affects the party system, or more specifically what effect political parties have upon unity or division in conditions of territorial diversity.

The first possible option is to intensify pressures and tension by deliberately appealing to territorial sympathies through an explicit and overt promise to push for the realization of peripheral demands. In short, they may side with the periphery in threatening disruption of the regime. This would be an extreme option for parties with pretensions of statewide power: if disruption and severance did come about, the party itself would necessarily be weakened. In the sense that they effectively prevent parties mobilizing across them, national boundaries are still highly significant.[1] This kind of response has manifested itself only in Belgium, especially in the case of Wallonia. The inability of the major Liberal, Christian Social and Socialist parties to resolve the pressures arising from the basic linguistic fact of Belgian life has resulted in all three being effectively fragmented along territorial lines. In effect, there are no statewide parties in Belgium; only regional parties, which unite across the linguistic divide on certain issues, and regional party systems. More generally, to appeal to a periphery may in the long run alienate other groups, and is perhaps a profitable exercise only when the social make-up of the periphery pushes it strongly in the direction of that party. The Jura question, for example, was first tapped politically by the Catholic Conservative Party after 1867. Since this party was largely confined to Catholic areas and bound by their memories of the Sonderbund war, this move entailed little risk of losing support elsewhere or of preventing it making inroads into hitherto untapped, but likely, reservoirs. Catalonia, however, may be more typical in that all parties in the province have come to terms with its identity and sentiment. All now have an 'autonomous' Catalan section, or at least declare themselves to be pro-Catalan. The centre-periphery polarity runs within the parties in Catalonia, each of which has a pro-Catalan wing (which in most cases is dominant).

Alternatively, parties can ignore the territorial question, declaring it not an issue — the traditional stance of British parties before the SNP rise forced them towards some declaration of intent on devolution. In its Welsh stronghold the Labour Party made no distinctive statement about the status of the Welsh language. It fought Plaid Cymru only in the 'normal' socioeconomic arena, and has not been opposed to the use of Welsh. On the other hand, it has never actively campaigned for Welsh, and its commitment to devolution is only halfhearted and was adopted only in the wake of the need to do something about Scotland. In France too there has been a tendency to ignore the issue, but there discontent has served more to nationalize regional politics, rather than the reverse.

In the monolingual states of Europe, with strong centres and relatively weak peripheries, statewide parties have little inclination to mobilize the territorial question, even when, as with the British Labour Party, their ability to gain control of the national centre is highly dependent on the high level of support they receive in the peripheries. In the last resort, it all depends on the strength of the centre and the external relationships of the peripheries. Weaker centres may find it advisable not to ignore the question, especially with interface peripheries. France and Denmark illustrate the two extremes: no compromise and studied disregard in the former, acceptance in the latter. Even so, the major Danish parties did not go out of their way to court the German vote: the first was the Centre Democrat fragment that seceded from the Social Democrats in the 1970s. Moreover, as far as is possible, statewide parties attempt to maintain the concept of unity by excluding peripheral parties from political influence through government participation. It was its minority situation that made the 1974 British Labour government conducive to seeking a form of cooperation with the Scottish and Welsh nationalists. Similarly, despite their growing electoral strength and the seeming salience of the linguistic-territorial issue, the Belgian regional parties were excluded from government, and were not regarded as possible partners, until 1974.

By contrast, parties may consciously aim at cross-regional mobilization: in their drive for votes, party leaders can decide to seek support across localities and across identity boundaries in whatever linguistic medium is appropriate for the people to whom it appeals. Alternatively, they may simply tolerate or accept the differences, though whether this is genuine tolerance or a fear of the consequences of spotlighting the problem is more open to question. Certainly, either strategy is more appropriate in multilingual situations, and in Switzerland, Norway and Ireland language is not normally raised as an issue in party politics. However, either cross-regional mobilization or attempted toleration is a difficult task once identity issues become salient. In Belgium, both the Socialist and Christian Parties had a degree of bilingualism built into their organizational structure: the latter especially maintained a dual structure with parallel and largely autonomous wings coming together in peak organizations. Yet even this rather flexible arrangement did not enable the elites successfully to apply the traditional accommodational practices to the linguistic question: one effect was deep internal dissension within the major parties and a de facto divorce in each between their

Flemish and Walloon wings.

The options available to statewide parties in situations where identity issues have become salient are all fraught with peril. All can have unforeseen consequences and detrimental costs. It is in their interest to seek to remove territorial demands from the political agenda. In this sense party responses, whether in government or opposition, to territorial demands are linked to regime responses. At the extremes governments may accept secession or resist totally. Because of the territorial imperatives of any regime, the former is highly unlikely. The tendency of any regime is to centralize and standardize, which implies that even accommodation of conflicting identity interests is not a normal tendency: 'Governments have a natural tendency to integrate the societies they govern. The protection of minorities is not natural to governments' (LaPonce, 1960: 43). Nevertheless, total resistance has been, or has become, a costly operation, and in many ways is an option of the last resort. More typically, governments will respond by seeking to accommodate the demands within existing boundaries. Peripheral demands are often a mix of cultural and economic discontent. Regimes have the option of pursuing an economic or more specifically political response. The former may be more costly in terms of money, but in the the long run entails less risk to the territorial imperatives of the state. The latter may be endangered more by attempts to accommodate the political demands of the periphery and its inhabitants.

The economic response

In Chapter 2 we discussed the concept of a European core and indicated how it could be measured. Its origins are firmly rooted in the capitalist revolution of the sixteenth century, and were scarcely disturbed by the introduction of a coal-steel economy. Today, whatever might be the exact dividing line, the distinction between core and periphery can be illustrated by a few simple indicators. Areas beyond the core are more likely to have out-migration, to experience higher levels of unemployment and lower standards of socioeconomic life, and to be recipients of aid programmes. This overall picture must be modified because of the intrusion of central policies of administration, economic encouragement, standardization and redistribution. Two points are important for our theme.

First, there was no uniform economic placement of culturally distinctive peripheries across Western Europe: we might expect that peripheral economic demands would also vary over and above the common view that 'something should be done' in the way of central policy. Second, centre-periphery gaps tend to be greater at the fringes of the European core.

There does not seem to be a consensus of opinion on the nature of changes in centre-periphery gaps over the past decades. Some see an amelioration in interregional differences in, for instance, gross regional product per capita and income per capita. However, the significance of such an increase must be qualified. First, it is doubtful if this reduction of gaps in material standards of living has been effective. Second, if there has been a reduction in some instances, this has sometimes been paralleled by an accentuation of others: this is more visible in countries bisected by the boundary of the core. Alternatively, it may have been that the inequalities were originally very weak, as in West Germany.[2] Moreover, an increase in, for example, the income per capita of the poorest regions may be little more than a statistical consequence of a population reduction arising from emigration. More important, an increase in gross regional product in underdeveloped regions can easily distract attention away from the unequal impact of technological development. Despite state policies, the European core has been the major recipient of high-value and technologically intensive industry and of the strengthening of the quaternary sector. In short, the innovatory and command functions have increased both relatively and absolutely in both the core and the central region of each state: centres have become more central.

This has had variable consequences, not only in the economic peripheries. Where central political and economic functions have been territorially divided, as in Spain, any increase in the proficiency of the economic centre has been counterbalanced by the generally greater role of the political centre in territorial control. Only where some form of territorial accommodation already exists, as in West Germany, can this problem be less serious.

Contemporary territorial economic disequilibria have their roots in the historical reorganizations of the European economy. Generally, efforts to come to grips with and rectify these inequalities were generated only when they were seen as a barrier to further development of the state economy as a whole. While this recognition came only after 1945 in Western Europe, regional 'policy' in one format or another has a fairly long history. Yet economics played only a limited role in the first wave of peripheral mobilization. Regional economic problems in the late nineteenth century were viewed more as a social problem by the established central elites: the more dehumanizing aspects of industrialization led to concepts such as Disraeli's two nations or the distinction made in Italy between the legal state and the real country. While an awareness of unequal regional development concentrated on economic peripheries, it took the view that economic backwardness was not due to socioeconomic factors that could be eliminated by government action: rather, it was to be explained by a variety of social Darwinism. It was caused by specific cultural and biological features of the peripheral population. This inaptitude for development could be overcome by central action, but only through an increased tempo of standardization.

This was the background against which the need for economic policy was gradually accepted. The debate was more pronounced in countries that lay at the edge of the European economy, though towards the end of the nineteenth century only in Britain and Italy did it assume the dimension of a 'national' question. Nevertheless, the themes of protectionism for peripheral agriculture, fiscal policy and investment to aid development, and emigration to ease over-population and underemployment, were widespread. The debate raised the question of how the state should intervene: by some kind of global policy for the whole state, or by a series of ad hoc legislation? It was the latter alternative that won.[3] Though there were some extensive debates after 1918, especially in Italy (Mioni, 1976) and Britain (Brown, 1972; McCrone, 1969), the interwar period evidenced little change. After 1945, despite the new belief in growth that was in part fostered by Marshall Aid, the old territorial problems not only remained, but worsened. Growth was concentrated more evidently on the European core, and within states on the more developed regions (with the notable exception of Flanders). This led to a deterioration in underdeveloped regions as well as contributing to the decline of some older industrial concentrations.

Regional economic policy began, then, with false premises. The basic central ideology was that regional inequalities were not a direct and inevitable consequence of the economic system, that they would ultimately be eradicated by an improvement in the overall national economy. The key word was growth, to be achieved by a 'natural' diffusion of technological benefits outwards from the centre which would guarantee maximum benefits to all without imposing undue costs on the community as a whole: maximum economic growth with minimum social costs, however, are conflicting goals (Monod and Castelbajac, 1971). All it would take was time and patience; it depended on the erosion and removal of those sociocultural factors in the peripheries that inhibited development. In short, 'policy' was conceived as merely correcting irrationalities and reducing existing undesirable aspects in the statewide distribution of capital and technology.

Two principal motivations lay at the heart of the original formulation. In stressing the future development of the national economy, such a relative redistribution was also deemed advantageous for the most developed regions through stimulating domestic demand, as well as aiding territorial deconcentration of economic growth. More implicitly, the redistribution of capital resources was considered a necessary instrument for guaranteeing the continued supremacy of the political centre, and hence political stability. The sporadic application of this strategy produced an opposite result. Investment in the poorer regions benefited the developed regions more than the former: almost inevitably, the development of the poorer areas took the form of special welfare programmes and ad hoc compartmentalized action.

A greater institutional effort emerged only in the late 1950s.[4] These were more deliberate attempts to coordinate and structure state intervention more organically, in accord with the declared objective of efficiency. They very easily switched from the problems of backward rural areas to those of older, outdated industrial concentrations, whose current or projected obsolescence through changing technologies and locational requirements was deemed to have even more significant consequences for the national economy (Fleming, 1967). The new key words were priority zones and sectors according to the dominant theory of poles and axes of development (Perroux, 1961; Petrella, 1971; Hansen, 1972).[5] At any rate, the 1960s saw a rash of public and quasi-public regional institutions. But while the forms may have become more institutionalized, the basic logic behind regional policy remained unchanged.

Three basic strategies were employed: direct assistance, the carrot, and the stick. In the past direct assistance had been the hallmark of intervention in agriculture and service infrastructures:

in line with the new emphasis, it was now also adopted in industry. However, despite the expressed intentions and attempts at more coordinated management, it was often transformed to mere aid and subsidies, and in addition the desire to switch direct assistance towards the industrialization of backwards areas often conflicted with the view that sociocultural factors inherent to the region hindered its development.

The carrot was used to lure entrepreneurs to and to encourage capital in the designated development regions. We could construct a long catalogue of attempted measures across Western Europe, but these do not vary much from country to country, indicating that, whatever their other differences, states and economic systems reflect a fundamentally similar logic of development and spatial model. Even so, the effectiveness of the carrot and development zones has been disputed, although any evaluation depends upon whether the criteria used to measure the results are in accord with the declared objectives.[6] The flood of evaluations ranges from those stressing the weak impact on decisions about the localization of investment on the private sector (Wolff, 1974) to those stressing its importance (Moore and Rhodes, 1974), and from those allotting a positive influence on regional development and inequalities to those accepting only a limited short-term impact, but negative long-term consequences (CREGE, 1968). The EEC (1969: 46-7) made the following comments about this seeming difficulty in furnishing an objective appreciation of the measures and their consequences. First, the place that the various enterprise aids occupy within instruments of regional policy were not always in accord with the necessities of structural adaptation; in particular, the infrastructures and environment were less adapted to modern activities. Second, there was a detrimental tendency towards outbidding between states and between regions, which in a sense resulted in the squandering of public funds.

Central regimes were aware of some of these problems. Hence, the recourse to a stick policy, a series of restrictive measures of control over the location of new industrial activities: the objective was to transfer them away from concentrated zones to either underdeveloped or declining industrial regions (Bergan, 1975; Thoss, 1977; Durand, 1974). The difficulty is that, if it is true that there has been a relative deconcentration of industrial activities, it is more likely that this has responded, and responds, to more general trends in the reorganization of productive capacity (de-industrialization, suburbanization).

Over and above state efforts, the question of international co-operation in regional policy has been attempted by the EEC, though its history is perhaps too short for any coherent conclusion to be drawn. The programme, however, has suffered from a lack of funds, which contributed perhaps to the rather restrictive criteria adopted for regional aid. The major defect of the infrastructure that has been developed is the absence of any comprehensive economic planning of regional policy on a Community level. Given the complexity of central activities that can have an effect on regional economic imbalances and development, this is hardly surprising: the OECD (1968: 5; also Shoup, 1967) pointed out during the high period of popularity of regional policy that 'the problem of who, on balance, is subsidizing whom is made even more difficult by the fact that national policies that were not designed specifically as regional policies may nonetheless have important differential regional consequences'. European integration, in the form mainly of a customs union and a common agricultural policy, has pushed for a common market to the detriment of any comprehensive and successful common economic policy. While it may not be possible to establish a causal relationship between the emergence of a common market and the development of the various regions, it would perhaps be reasonable to state that the increase in internal EEC trade between economically unequal regions has not operated unequivocally to the benefit of the poorer. If anything, the reverse is true: EEC policies have tended to benefit the richer regions (Petrella, 1978b; Agostini, 1976). A continued outflow of capital and labour has simply reinforced dependence on the richer regions, whose interests have also been served by public investment in the poorer. In the absence of a common economic policy, the problem of regional imbalances remains an internal matter for the states. We are still a long way from realizing Article 2 of the Treaty of Rome.[7]

At any rate, by the 1960s most Western European states came to erect national and regional planning as a bulwark of socioeconomic policy. The latter had several common features: growth zones of preferential location (Britain, West Germany, Sweden); the establishment of targets for public and private investment and employment in agriculture (France); growth poles to counter excessive population and industrial concentration (Norway; Spain). Overall, the chosen strategy was influenced by the style of government and territorial organization. States with centralized institutions preferred a broader policy with wide objectives, where progress towards allowing the regions a greater fiscal responsibility has at the least been very slow; those with a decentralized administrative structure preferred more limited objectives.

During the 1960s a whole range of further public and quasi-public agencies to promote regional development were added to the existing structures. Yet the original flaw in policy conception remained. In retrospect, the 1960s have been viewed as a golden age. Certainly, there was at the time a prevailing optimistic belief in the inevitability and durability of economic growth, which supported the confidence that a national increase in the quality of life justified the existing territorial inequalities of economic life. The rich would pull the poor along behind them. Centres persisted in placing the regional question in the perspective of the national economy, in seeing the issues of backward areas and industrial decline essentially in terms of an improved management and efficiency of the economy across territory (EEC, 1964: 23-5; Robinson, 1969; Hansen, 1974). Where inequalities were too gross, they were to be redressed by corrective rather than innovative action.

The extent to which regional policy has been effective depends upon how its objectives have been defined. In terms of improving the quality of life everywhere, it has probably been successful. If, however, we look at its ability to stem or reverse the migration flow from the peripheries, it has been less effective. In other words, if we define success in terms of improving the economic welfare of peripheries as territories, regional aid has had some considerable achievements. If its objectives are defined in terms of enabling more of the indigenous peripheral population to live, work and enjoy within the periphery a standard of living comparable to that of more central regions, it has more clearly failed. The former has been the viewpoint of the centre; the latter was increasingly stressed by those wishing some radical form of territorial restructuring. While regional policies did not dramatically reduce the disadvantages of poorer regions, they did introduce some new elements into the picture. To some extent they reshaped and improved economic possibilities in the peripheries, and growth may have increased, where appropriate, awareness of a distinctive identity, and so the possibility of territorial political mobilization. Coupled with the increasing amounts of information relayed by the mass media, economic improvement underlined the value of being able to afford one's own culture, and so may have contributed towards the 'viure al pais' sentiment.

These are hypotheses that we cannot here test systematically across states and peripheries. What is clear is that regional policy has been based on central premises, and that its implications can go far beyond mere economics. One major stumbling block has been the inability to provide autonomous development independent of the central regions: states are economic systems, and it is almost impossible to insulate one area from the rest of the system. It is central agencies that manage the funds made available to peripheral regions and that control the instruments employed. Planning, however, is a two-tier process 'in which national objectives, strategies, and policies, as well as the coordination of regional and local plans with national input and output targets, is determined at the national level; while the extent and manner of the development effort in each region or locality is determined in the area concerned' (Waterston, 1974). This implies that the regions must participate actively in planning for their areas. While the peripheries are directly or indirectly associated with the centrally directed agencies, the range of public bodies that sprang up in the 1960s generally have no real power independent of that of the central regime, and no democratic base. Moreover, the resources made available to them have been limited, and their main function often restricted to consultation, study and recommendation. While the nature of the exercise has inevitably produced the decentralization of at least some functions, this has not been accompanied by a more than minimal transfer of resources. The problem is that centres persist in denying a role for decentralized politics in regional development, while increasingly accepting that this is a decentralized process (Watson, 1978).

We might go so far as to say that there can be no favourable conditions for autonomous economic development until the peripheries obtain the ability to control the appropriate means and instruments. Such a transfer of powers implies that the peripheries should receive the financial autonomy that centres have consistently refused to grant.[8] However, to raise the question of regional control is to go beyond the central concept of planning to the political question of devolution. It is here that the central premises of and desire for economic growth can meet the resistance of the distinctive peripheries. The latter have not contented themselves with demands for more money and employment possibilities. It is but a short step to the basic desires for political autonomy in order to protect cultural identity.

Recent decades have seen a cumulation of contradictions between centre tendencies and peripheral aspirations. Since 1945 there has been a reinforced cross-territorial division of labour and geographical specialization, which has increased the necessity of geographical mobility; a reinforcement of the centralization of economic and financial power; the bureaucratization of the public sector and heightened social regulation, which have forged closer links between technological structures and state intervention in production; and an increasing press towards uniformity in the mode of life. Central economic efforts at regional planning have occurred, and solutions have been sought, within the framework of these tendencies. But these have not been exactly the concerns of the peripheries. Their aspirations have revolved around a broader concept of territorial justice: the desire to work in one's own 'country'; a growth strategy that would conserve the indigenous quality of life and resources; the safeguarding of cultural diversity and linguistic freedom; and the autonomous generation of resources within a reorganized political-institutional framework.

These peripheral concerns have survived over time. It is perhaps only in the immediate postwar years and their problems of reconstruction and the Cold War that they apparently sank from public view. Their re-emergence was to some extent obscured by the optimism of unbounded growth that persisted well into the 1960s. As the European economy began to falter, particularly in the wake of the 1973 energy crisis, the discrepancies between central claims for the virtues of regional policy and its ability to deliver the goods through either sustained growth or the liberal application of money became more obvious: indeed, since 1973 a stronger emphasis upon national growth has meant a lesser emphasis on regional policy. For economic peripheries this heightened the risk of intensified centre-periphery gaps. For cultural peripheries it prised open further the Pandora's Box of autonomy. In a way, centres contributed to their own dilemma, not only because their planning efforts so often failed to live up to expectations and the claims made for them, but also because regional planning brought territory to the fore. The region was elevated from being a purely statistical and geographic entity. It was recognized as an economic entity, for which functions and responsibilities were claimed. By so doing, it brought into the open the more fundamental issue of how space is to be managed. Western European states have become slightly more decentralized, even though centres have refused to recognize fully the implication of political decentralization stated many years ago by Jean Monnet's Union of European Federalists: 'from the smallest village up to the federal government, all matters . . . that can be adequately settled by a lower tier of government must be settled at that level' (Rhodes, 1974). The peripheries may have been more aware of these implications, but their ability to capitalize upon them has been determined by the nature of their resources. Above all, an economic strategy will always be unsatisfactory for culturally distinctive peripheries: their basic demands are political and require a political response.

The political response

The two extreme political responses available to centres are to accept secession or to resist totally. The former violates the basic regime imperatives, while the latter is fraught with risks and high costs. More typically, Western European regimes today, despite past drives towards state-building and increasing centralization, are more likely to show willingness to accommodate the demands and defuse them within existing boundaries. Regional economic policy can be regarded as an example of a limited alternative that avoids the more thorny political questions. Where it is necessary to come to grips with the latter, the number of available options might well shade into infinity. However, these may be subsumed within two broad alternatives: centres can seek either group or territorial accommodation.

To understand these alternatives more fully, we have to return to the discussion in Chapter 3 on geographical and membership space. These simple definitions of space can be linked to our earlier review of the structure of Western Europe. Geographical space implies monocephality; polycephality is more characteristic of membership space. A territorial definition might be related historically to dynastic expansion and conquest, where a single centre has effective control of a large territorial area. Consequent upon the establishment of secure boundaries there is a more deliberate effort of unification through an efficacious system of administrative control and policies of cultural standardization. The objective is to make identification with the state and occupation of territory synonymous. By contrast, a membership definition can be approached through the Weberian concept of 'politische Verbänd', the coming together of local groups, each with a distinctive identity, for specific political or economic purposes. Through agreement these groups establish a covenant of mutual toleration and protection. To preserve the covenant is to preserve polycephality, the retention of territorially varying rights and identities.

These ideal constructs can be used analytically in an examination of central responses by relating them to our discussion of the historical sources of strain and strategies of unification. They can be disaggregated into state-building and nation-building continua. The latter may be divided into four broad categories.

1. *Territorial space dominant.* There is an unambiguous central control in all three dimensions of spatial differentiation, with little in the way of an infrastructure that could shelter and nourish a distinctive identity or counter-mobilization. Without a distinctive identity, political protest would not have any strong territorial perspective: it would tend to be anti-centre, rather than being specifically in favour of some other territorial entity, and so constitute only a minimal challenge to the prevailing territorial structure of the state.

2. *Territorial space dominant; strong membership characteristics.* For most of the territory identification is synonymous with the state. In some areas, however, there is a membership identity distinct from that of the state territory which can serve as the focal point of counter-mobilization.

3. *Membership space dominant; strong territorial characteristics.* While the notion of a covenant prevails, the membership format is diluted by cross-local strains arising from the emergence of one or several competing centres with dominating or standardizing tendencies. These can give rise to regional strains and conflict.

4. *Membership space dominant.* The ideal construct of a covenant prevails. There is little or no conflict between the several units, each with its own centre. Acceptance of differences does not give rise to tension and territorial mobilization directed against the structure of the state.

The characteristics of institutional-structural maintenance in the ideal constructs relate more to strategies of unification. We may again begin with a simple dichotomy: centralizing strategies where all areas are incorporated within one universal system of standardization, and strategies of federalizing accommodation where all areas, while belonging to one territorial unit and subordinated to one centre in some policy matters, nevertheless retain some guarantees of protection for and independence of their separate identity. Between these two poles there is a large grey area of mixed strategies: separate and varying arrangements for peripheries that have persisted in expressing a political will to remain distinctive; standardization of legal rules, but provisions for equal or separate status for some cultural standards. While strategies of unification have varied with conditions in each territory, we can bring some order to the picture by creating a fourfold continuum of state-building similar to that done for nation-building.

1. *The unitary state* is built up around one unambiguous centre enjoying economic dominance and pursuing an undeviating policy of administrative standardization: all areas are treated alike and all institutions are directly under the control of the centre.
2. *The union state* does not enjoy direct political control everywhere. Incorporation of parts of its territory has been achieved through treaty and agreement; consequently integration is less than perfect. While administrative standardization prevails over most the territory, the union structure entails the survival in some areas of variations based upon pre-union rights and infrastructures.
3. *Mechanical federalism* is introduced from above by constitutional means. By contrast to union states, a pattern of territorially diversified structures exists across the whole state. Nevertheless, this pattern is accommodated within a hierarchical system of control with one centre which is 'primus inter pares'.
4. *Organic federalism* is constructed from below, the result of voluntary association by distinctive territorial structures. These retain their separate institutional outlines with wide discretionary powers. Control by one centre is severely limited.

These continua are necessarily crude, and it is not difficult to see that there is a large degree of overlap between the two dimensions. This, however, is little more than a reflection of the complexities of reality. To combine them in a simple typology of Western European state- and nation-building (Figure 5.1) provides not only a useful summary of the continental mosaic, but also a background to the

FIGURE 5.1
A simple typology of state-building and nation-building processes

SPACE/IDENTITY CHARACTERISTICS

Strategies of unification		Territorial space	Territorial (+ membership)	Membership (+ territorial)	Membership space
Centralizing ↑	Unitary state	France, Denmark, Norway, Italy, Iceland, Sweden, Portugal, Ireland	Finland	Belgium	
	Union state		Netherlands, United Kingdom	Spain	
	Mechanical federalism	Austria		West Germany	
↓ Accommodating	Organic federalism				Switzerland

fundamental choice of centres that wish to accommodate territorial demands between territorial and group accommodation. Federalism, as in West Germany or Switzerland, is the ultimate pattern of territorial accommodation. Group accommodation, by contrast, is a form of 'verzuiling', seeking consociational solutions where power, jobs and resources are to be shared or duplicated among the competing groups.

Figure 5.1 shows a reasonable distribution of countries across the matrix, from the cluster of unitary, standardizing states to the federal covenant of Switzerland. The northwest-southeast diagonal represents a good fit between state- and nation-building histories. Placement in cells away from this diagonal indicates the degree to which there is incongruity between the two processes, and so the potential for varying kinds of territorial politics. The figure also provides the basis of discussing possible central solutions that might satisfy contemporary peripheral demands. While the typology is suggestive only, and the location of some countries problematical, we can see that movement along the gradient away from the unitary position would be a move towards both some kind of territorial decentralization of decision-making and the setting up of some kind of covenant that would accommodate distinctive groups. Putting forward options that would move the state structure further below the diagonal is to propose a territorial solution. Conversely, a group solution would move the state further to the left in the matrix.

While Switzerland emerged historically as a consociational structure, it is the territorial principle that has been used to resolve conflicts within the confederation. It was in fact a territorial solution that the francophone movement in the Jura demanded: the establishment of a separate French-speaking canton. Under the constitution this solution could be reached only through a series of positive referenda results at all levels of the confederation: national, cantonal and communal. Positive approval throughout Switzerland would mean very little dislocation, as the establishment of a new canton would not seriously affect the overall structure of the confederation. The consequences were otherwise for Berne, which in this context might be regarded as a unitary state: it would have to give up territory, hence its attempts first to ignore the issue and then to seek accommodation by other than territorial means. While it is clear that the Jura could never have succeeded in seceding from Switzerland, Berne had eventually to resign itself to the inevitable. Referenda decided the issue, and those among the Jura communes settled the boundaries of the new canton. The north voted overwhelmingly in favour, the south equally emphatically against. It was the north that was given cantonal status within the confederation, leaving the aspirations of the nationalist jurassiens only partially fulfilled. This solution left perhaps a more bitter taste in the Jura than in Berne or Switzerland, for what was created in structures and practices conformed to Swiss institutional norms (Ruffieux and Prongué, 1978). In some respects the demands and implemented solution in the Jura resembled that in Ireland: there, too, much of the bitterness was centred on the boundary between seceding and unionist territories, though in the Jura there was only occasional violence.[9]

The modern prototype of group accommodation is not in Switzerland, but in Italy. The award of the South Tyrol to Italy after 1918 and Mussolini's policies of italianization hardened the discontent of the German minority. An agreement on the status of the South Tyrol was reached in 1946, but when Rome eventually introduced legislation for the area, it was a territorial option and an attempt to move to a union from a unitary state. Autonomous status was given to a wider territory, Trentino-Alto Adige, which had an Italian majority. If anything, the conflict worsened, reaching a peak of violence in the early 1960s. A commission of inquiry backed by Italy and Austria presented a detailed review of the areas of friction between the two language communities: education, police, administrative communication, the courts, the naming of buildings and streets, language quotas for recruitment to the civil service. The commission proposed a 'Proporzpaket', a package agreement calling for the proportionalization of public goods and services between the two communities. This was finally ratified in 1972. The Proporzpaket was hailed as a great achievement: certainly, much of the tension has disappeared, and prosperity has increased.

Between 1946 and the Proporzpaket Italian efforts at accommodation involved some degree of quasi-federalism and the territorial option. The 'final' solution in the Alto Adige is clearly a group option, as the consociational element predominates. In this sense the Proporzpaket is different from the Italian solutions applied in the Val d'Aosta, where the grant of autonomy was rapid and undramatic, or in Sardinia. In the latter case the establishment of autonomy did not reflect recognition of a distinctive language:

the decisive incentives were political and economic. By 1980 Italy had introduced a wide degree of decentralization throughout its territory. This new quasi-federal structure and the acceptance of a group solution in the Alto Adige may have come about less because of a positive central commitment to decentralization than because Italy has been a weak unitary state, with insufficient central strength to resist pressures for concessions.

The Belgian situation is more complex. A unitary state, Belgium has, less successfully, pursued a mix of the two approaches: more territorial in Flanders and Wallonia, a kind of 'proporz' in Brussels. The former were clear territorial entities with virtually monolingual populations.[10] If the will was present, territorial accommodation could be attempted without too severe a dislocation. The first step was the broad acceptance of a language border, with monolingual usage on either side. The second was 'dédoublement', the splitting of some government ministries (education, culture) into linguistic agencies. That the territorial movement stumbled was due not only to simple intransigence, but also to the complication of Brussels, a primarily French-speaking city located within Flanders. The Brussels problem was aggravated by the situation in the suburbs, historically Flemish but increasingly invaded by francophones from the expanding capital. To solve this dilemma of territorial versus group rights, the regime proposed in 1976 the Pacte d'Egmont, a consociational device that would allow the suburban francophones to establish fictive addresses in bilingual communes with Brussels. This would enable them to enjoy their linguistic rights without moving out of the suburbs. A cumbersome ploy, the Pacte was at the heart of the Belgian dilemma: how to combine a system of territorial federalism with one of group and personal rights. In a federal structure cultural distinctiveness is given territorial status by majority decision. There may be some provision for the protection of cultural minorities within the designated territories, but there can be no absolute guarantee for minority individual and family rights. In a communalist system with group accommodation the individual or family would register as members of a cultural group and be provided with facilities whatever their residence.[11] By 1981 institutional reform in Belgium had produced four linguistic regions for the application of rules on language usage, three cultural communities with Cultural Councils, and three political-administrative regional councils. The Walloon region, for example, has limited economic powers, while the French Cultural Council (Wallonia and Brussels) possesses cultural/linguistic powers: the Flemish region combines these functions. This is a complex picture, in which the status of Brussels remains unsatisfactory to protagonists on all sides. The final outcome remains unclear, though Belgium now has de facto 'federalization without federalism' (Zolberg, 1977).

Just how impervious a unitary state can be to territorial decentralization is well illustrated by France. Both politically and economically, the country is highly monocephalic, yet historically it has been culturally polycephalic. There could have been the potential for a strong territorial conflict between centre and periphery. Yet the French centre successfully overcame most of its peripheries through policies of cultural standardization that ignored whatever peripheral privileges had existed. The fate of Savoy might be taken as typical. France sabotaged the economic agreement that had been part of the 1860 transfer of the province, rejected the 1922 verdict of the International Court which had upheld the Savoyards' complaint, and in setting up the new regions in the 1970s incorporated Savoy within a broader Rhône-Alpes region dominated by the French cities of Grenoble, Lyons and St Etienne.

Those French peripheries that succeeded in retaining a high degree of distinctiveness have consistently seen their claims for recognition of that distinctiveness rejected by the centre. Breton aspirations have always suffered from the political fragmentation of Breton nationalism. But Alsace, with a high degree of unanimity in the interwar period, discovered how easy it was for a determined French centre to ride out a storm of autonomist agitation. The fate of Brittany and Alsace illustrates that the centre-periphery cleavage in France has been part of the ideological left-right cleavage over the constitutional structure of the state. Rather than disrupting the political mould, peripheral mobilization has been nationalized. When France moved towards decentralization in the 1960s and 1970s, it was because Paris was convinced of the virtues of a functional economic approach (Wright, 1979). Gourevitch (1981) suggests that no French government has felt secure enough to concede power to locally entrenched opponents, though none has felt weak enough (unlike Italy) to have to make such concessions. What this implies is that decentralization would come not through peripheral pressure, but because of central convictions. The statements of the 1981 Socialist government under President Mitterrand seem to confirm this interpretation, and by 1982 plans were well advanced to grant a decree of political autonomy to Corsica, in many ways the most peripheral and least 'dangerous' outpost of France.

By contrast to France, the United Kingdom has been a union state. The English centre has persisted with a differentiated treatment of its territories since the Middle Ages (Urwin, 1982b). The union structure lends itself more to a territorial option, and this has been the chosen course of British governments in the twentieth century, first with the establishment in 1922 of the Stormont regime in Northern Ireland, and then in the 1970s, in the wake of peripheral nationalism, in the abortive attempts to provide devolution for Scotland and Wales. Discrimination by the Protestant majority in Northern Ireland indicate the perils that are attached to a territorial option in a culturally divided situation: yet the power-sharing experiment of the 1970s was an attempt to seek a group solution that failed, primarily because the Protestant majority refused to accept the idea of consociation. The United Kingdom is the prototypic union state, with an accumulation of disparate historical variations. The centre has responded with ad hoc proposals for specific problems as they arose, without any overall strategy, and in this way has sought to maintain a middle ground between a unitary structure and federalism. In the more complex society of the modern world, a major problem is that an attempt to solve one peripheral problem cannot be insulated from the rest of the state: a spillover effect is almost inevitable.

Spain is another union state, but one with more pronounced unitary characteristics than the United Kingdom. The establishment of the Catalan Generalitat in the Second Republic offered a territorial precedent that could be repeated in Catalonia by the post-Franco regime (Camilleri and Galiay, 1980), and one that in a sense 'fitted' with Spanish history. By contrast, given the large non-Basque population, whether group or territorial accommodation would be more appropriate in the Basque context is more debatable. What is clear is that, in order to prevent charges of pandering to Catalan and Basque nationalism being laid at its door, the Spanish centre has opted for a general programme of territorial decentralization, which is pushing the state in the direction of federalism.

What this review of cases indicates is that circumstances have to be in conjunction. Katzenstein (1977), for example, stresses that the

South Tyrolean package had to wait upon three developments: the acceptance by the minority of Italian political practices at the provincial level; the acceptance by Rome of the idea of regional reform across the whole territory; and the diffusion of the appropriate clientelist practices throughout the country. These matured only in the 1960s. It is a pattern that seems to have been repeated in Spain, though not in Britain. In other words, the options available to any regime are circumscribed by the group configuration, the institutional style of centralizing politics, the territorial/membership style of nation-building and the costs involved. Accommodation is easier where nation-building in the past has been a built-in feature of integration. It is easiest where strategies of central control have involved some kind of formal federalization, less so in union states, and most difficult in unitary states. Without an existing decentralized structure, as in Switzerland or West Germany, a territorial solution entails a radical break in the style of government; and without the trauma of some earth-shaking crisis, the lifting of the psychological block might well be possible only in the case of miniscule, remote and placid communities.[12] Even so, most centres have given only a few limited concessions to such communities, usually on language usage and instruction. Very few have gone so far as Finland in the case of the Åland Islands. The uniqueness of Finland is worth repeating. The granting of some territorial autonomy to the Åland Islands in 1922 (and additional legislative powers in 1951) could not be repeated in other parts of the country. There, only a form of group accommodation was possible.[13]

In the last resort, everything boils down to cost. Regimes will pay a high price to maintain their territorial integrity and control, especially where the dissenting regions have a high economic or strategic value. A high value may be an important card for the periphery, but it can equally stiffen the centre's resolve to hold on to what it has. The Tyrolean Proporzpaket was financially as well as politically an expensive solution, involving a tiny percentage of the Italian population. Such costs will rise steeply with the size of the group involved, a point illustrated by the several Belgian efforts. It is estimated that the capital outlay and operating costs of dédoublement alone were at least 30 percent higher than if the reform had not been introduced. Both these attempts at accommodation began in what, in retrospect, came to be viewed as the halcyon 1960s, when affluence could offer opportunities through buying time, if not peace. In the starker economic climate that emerged in the 1970s, with scarcer economic resources, budgeting for resolution through the liberal application of money became more difficult and problematical (Heisler and Peters, 1978; also Wildavsky, 1975: 220-49).

Centre-periphery prospects

We have attempted to present a catholic overview of the territorial structure of Western Europe as the essential backdrop against which any comparative assessment of regional political mobilization must be made. In electoral terms the peripheral unrest of recent decades has in most instances been little more than an irritant. It nevertheless has strong links with the past fate and mythology of territories, and is an expression of identities that to a greater or lesser extent have survived incorporation within a nation-state ideal. At the same time, contemporary mobilization is a reaction to present conditions, and its demands are for adjustment to the current status. Potentially, it could contribute to that intensified identity crisis and 'ontzuiling' process that some observers have argued is a feature of Western Europe today. But if the latter is a general phenomenon, peripheral mobilization can be only a contributory factor — or perhaps even a consequence, for it has not been universal. The concern with identity has been a stable feature of Western European politics over time, albeit one that rarely has been more than marginal. None the less, it does seem that recent changes in society have been accompanied by what we described in Chapter 3 as a concern with roots.

It is easy to overdramatize the strength of peripheral mobilization: no peripheral party is large, and very few are more than medium-size in their own territory. Most, moreover, are not socially radical: their aims are limited, and there is not a total congruity between economic expectations, cultural autonomy and political aspirations. While this may help to explain their relative lack of success, that is not the main point. Because peripheral mobilization introduces questions of territorial structure, its impact can be more poignant. There are no grounds for assuming that failure will lead to death, or that peripheral political mobilization will disappear once its wishes are granted. Though in decline, the SPP has not died, even though it achieved its most important victory as long ago as 1922; nor has the SVP showed any weakening since the Proporzpaket. The task for such parties changes to ensuring that the concessions granted are put into practice and maintained. Similarly, the nationalist jurassiens have charged themselves since the referenda with the task of converting those 'recalcitrant' communes that stayed with Berne. One wonders whether the IRA or ETA would accept voluntary liquidation if independence were ceded. In short, such organizations are likely to be a continuing factor in the politics of these territories.

Survival entails difficulties determined by the context. Outright opposition to the regime might lead to oppression and illegality. To insist on cultural purity may run the risk of alienation from the bulk of the territorial population. Collaboration may have the same consequences. As the SPP has discovered in its long occupation of government office, collaboration means a concern with national and not just regional/group interests. The three Belgian linguistic parties have had to take a position on a wide range of issues that do not fit easily with their identity concerns (Frognier, 1978; Dierickx, 1978). Where there does not seem to be any hard issue, and little regime opposition or regime unconcern, collaboration might lead to assimilation, as it did for much of German political regionalism. Going national is a choice fraught with dangers, and perhaps almost impossible in multi-cultural situations: the only major postwar example is the Norwegian Christian People's Party.[14] Perhaps a more common fate is that of the Deutsche Partei (DP). With a core vote in the old Hanoverian provinces, the DP attempted to become a national conservative party (Meyn, 1965). Not only did this fail: its efforts distanced it somewhat from its origins and contributed to the almost total erosion of its once impressive regional strength.

In short, peripheral mobilization and agitation will not simply disappear. It may retain its confusion value in any situation short of outright independence, with a consequent effect upon the party system and regime. In general, the central response has been slow, but positive. This in turn may confuse peripheral mobilization and/or lead to a war of attrition in which the more likely losers will be the peripheries; and collaboration within the centre may increase the confusion and stress (Lefevre, 1977).

But how important is it that peripheral and culturally distinctive parties are large or small, survive or disappear? What counts in the long run is the resolution of territorial and identity complaints:

even the presence of weak parties may force the state and party system to take cognizance of the fact. It is in this sense that there has arisen a new concern with territory, paralleling that with roots. While the great political debate of the twentieth century has been focused upon the issue of distribution at the individual level, there seems to have emerged in recent decades a heightened concern with the territorial distribution of resources and opportunities. The reasons are several: alarm over industrial decay; governments arguing for regional economic policy but refusing to see its logical political implications; a general unease over central management of socioeconomic change within a welfare state framework. This can be potentially, but not inevitably, dangerous wherever there are regionally concentrated groups with distinctive cultural traits.

In Chapter 3 we referred to how we can identify two different kinds of territorially based citizens' rights in a system of democratic pluralism: the right to roots and the right to options. It would seem merely trite to say that what is required is a balance between the two. But that is precisely the problem. While perhaps the only lasting solution is to accept both orientations and needs, and to use public resources to strengthen both, politically the need to reconcile roots and options, to reconcile identity and the costs of economic opportunities and expectations, runs headlong into the opposition between the peculiar political demands of peripheral mobilization and the nature of the state's imperatives. This is the framework within which we have attempted to chart Western European developments. Our survey has illustrated that the geopolitical, geocultural and geoeconomic map of Western Europe constitutes a veritable mosaic, where explanations that seem to be valid in some situations are not so in others. We have to consider not only the different strategies of state formation and central control, and varying patterns of historical strains, but also their legacy. No group, no territory, is totally monolithic. Other loyalties and cleavages — some traditional, some characteristic of modern societies — are also present. It is not simply a matter of centre versus periphery, of recalcitrant regions. If it had been the whole Jura versus Berne, if there were only Basque speakers in the four provinces, if there were only Catholics in Northern Ireland, if Brussels had not been a predominantly French-speaking city within Flanders, then perhaps solutions might have been achieved more easily, one way or another. At the least, the issues might have been clearer. History and politics, however, are rarely so tidy.

This has been a general attempt to plot a way through the labyrinth, and we would hope that future studies using more detailed data would seek to test some of our typologies and hypotheses rigorously and systematically within a historical and comparative perspective. What is clear from this preliminary survey is that there is no simple centre-periphery polarity across culture, economics and politics. Peripheral predicaments and politicization emerge out of the incongruity between cultural, economic and political roles, an incongruity that has existed on the continent as long as there have been states. While this remains unresolved, the potential for territorial problems remains, irrespective of the waxing and waning of individual parties or movements.

Notes

CHAPTER 1
Peripheries and Centres

1. The study of French and Italian mayors by Tarrow (1977) provides some excellent illustrations of this point. It should be noted, however, that their influence is at the level of the historical units of the 'département': they have been reluctant to support the idea of new and wider regional institutions (Grémion, 1976).

2. Juillard and Nonn (1976), for example, have contrasted the concentrations in the secondary and those in the tertiary sector across Western Europe, and have pointed to several important differences: equal strength of the two sectors in Paris, London and Liverpool, Brussels and Rotterdam; clear secondary dominance in Birmingham and Manchester, the Ruhr 'megapolis', Barcelona, Turin and Milan; clear tertiary dominance in Amsterdam, Hamburg and Munich, Madrid, Rome and Naples.

3. The same, of course, is true of Austria, where the graph for 1890 shows the most startling indication of primacy. It should be remembered, however, that at this time Vienna was the capital of a vast territorial empire, and contained the manpower and resources for administering the same. In Figure 1.2 the size of Vienna in 1890 is compared only with the size of the next four largest urban centres in the area which after 1918 became the Austrian Republic.

4. A direct line between Bordeaux and Marseilles was eventually incorporated into the plan, but only reluctantly.

5. Two possible examples are the syncretism of the Catholic Church in Latin America, and the difficulties that Moscow has met in trying to maintain centralized control of the world communist movement.

6. Some more rigorous and detailed case studies have already been published in a longer companion volume (Rokkan and Urwin, 1982).

CHAPTER 2
The Territorial Structuring of Western Europe

1. This section reproduces a number of passages from an earlier text (Rokkan, 1973).

2. This, for instance, is a central theme of the macro-historical model developed by Moore (1966).

3. Similar defensive leagues established by cities along the Rhine and further north never succeeded in becoming sovereign territorial formations.

4. We might, perhaps, also mention the existence of a few enclave peripheries, such as the Sorbian and Lusatian territories in the Dresden and Cottbus areas of East Germany.

5. This section reproduces passages from an earlier text (Rokkan, 1973).

6. While it would clearly be possible to construct similar conceptual maps for other time periods, different criteria might well have to be applied; in addition, of course, the placement of territories would probably also be different.

7. In this, it is very similar to the underlying dimension of the analysis by Moore (1966) of alliance options and his contrast between two seaward powers, England and France, and two landward powers, Prussia and Russia.

8. For example, Belgrade and Serbia parallel Madrid and Castille; Ljubljana and Zagreb parallel Barcelona and Bilbao.

9. Holland tended to be content with autonomy for its own concerns rather than actively seeking to dominate the other provinces (Daalder, 1981). The same cannot perhaps be said of Berne, at least on several occasions in recent history.

10. The best collection of data for the early history of the European cities is Mols (1954-56).

11. Moreover, when you depart from administrative definitions of cities and identify multiple conurbations, you can run into trouble even for the first-ranked unit. For example, Hansen (1974: 9) treats the whole Ruhr as one conurbation, and arrives at a primacy score of 1.03 for West Germany. The problem is that in this cast the aggregate figure does not tell you that this is largely a concentration of industrial personnel with only limited decision-making or administrative functions for the whole federal territory.

12. Moreover, this accentuated contrast changed only marginally with the later arrival of the two new energy sources of hydroelectricity and oil.

13. The formula used was:

$$V_w = \frac{[i(y_i - \bar{y})]^2 (f_i/n)}{\bar{y}}$$

where y_i = income per capita of region i; $\bar{y}$ = national income per capital; f_i = population of region i; and n = national population.

14. However, to maximize the number of comparable variables, higher levels of aggregation were used in this exercise. The authors established, for 61 higher-level regions, a basic equation for the dependence of per capita income on distance from their European centre:

$$\ln y_i = 7.97387 - 0.00086 x_i$$
$$(\pm\ 0.00007)$$
$$R^2 = 0.71$$

where y_i = per capita income of region i; x_i = distance in kilometres from Düsseldorf.

15.

$$\ln y = 7.86149 - 0.00079\,x_i\,0.000192\,z_i$$
$$(\pm 0.00006) \quad (\pm 0.000003)$$
$$R^2 = 0.81$$

where z_i = population density of region i.

16. The problem facing any attempt at a detailed analysis at the continental level is one of sufficiently comparable data across countries. It is clear, for example, from Biehl, Hussman and Schnyder (1972), that there are considerable variations in estimates produced by different assumptions about benchmark years for prices and currency parities. One of the longer-term aims associated with this project was to encourage the collection of a series of time-series files for several countries that would conform to a common format. The ultimate objective, now endorsed by the International Federation of Data Organizations (Henrichsen, 1981), is to establish the consolidated data base for regional analyses proposed several years ago by Stein Rokkan (Lorentzen and Rokkan, 1976).

17. This is a much discussed irregularity. The French Midi remains economically backward, but still produces and attracts a higher-than-average number of doctors. Part of the explanation may be the historically strong position of the medical schools at the southern universities (Sussman, 1977). It may also be that the climate attracts a disproportionate number of doctors southwards, since their particular professional occupation does not necessarily demand proximity to Paris.

18. Using a factor analytic approach, Quellenec (1972) shows that the line from Saint-Malo to Geneva represented the best line of division in 1864, while the Caen-Marseilles line made for a more clear-cut difference in 1970. Other possible lines of division have also been suggested: cf. Chartier (1978); also Georgelin (1976); Le Roy Ladurie (1973).

19. This emphasis on continuity in the building of independent states parallels that by Seton-Watson (1977) on the continuities of nationhood. Seton-Watson distinguishes 'the old continuous nations' and the divided territories brought together under the pressure of movements for national unity. Interestingly, his list of continuous nations includes the Irish: in our typology this is an ethnically distinctive periphery characterized by a low level of administrative unification during the Middle Ages.

20. Clearly, the details of such statistical mapping of sources of diversity cannot be settled without better collections of regional time-series data. Reference has already been made to the current efforts to work towards a joint European data base. If the present discussion helps to structure priorities in such data development and analysis, it will have served its purpose.

CHAPTER 3
The Survival of Distinctiveness

1. This is perhaps a blind spot in those studies (Hechter, 1974; Nairn, 1977) that

tend to stress economics. These have been criticized by Orridge (1981) on the grounds of factual inadequacy, conceptual looseness and a general failure to account for some of the main aspects of contemporary peripheral political mobilization. See also the alternative hypothesis of Ragin (1979).

2. This has been a matter of some debate: see the comments in Gellner (1964); Hroch (1968); and Hobsbawm (1972).

3. There are now several overall reviews of the languages of Europe: Haarmann (1975); Stephens (1976); Heraud (1974); and, less satisfactorily, Straka (1970).

4. But there is considerable scholarly disagreement on how Portugal was able to obtain and maintain independence.

5. One key factor in this process of incorporation was the establishment of a university in Lund in 1672: this increased Scanian opportunity structures within Sweden.

6. The language of the Nederlands Bible of 1635 expressed the consensus of the educated bourgeoisie, but was much closer to the oral dialects of Holland than to the earlier Flemish standard.

7. Witness the demand of an unnamed revolutionary: 'The great number of dialects could have been useful in the tenth century and during the long reign of feudalism . . . but today . . . we are all Frenchmen and should have only one language, as we have only one heart.' Quoted in Schafer (1972).

8. For example, Dante's *Divina Commedia,* Petrarch's poetry and Boccacio's *Decamerone.*

9. While the current programme of autonomy is based upon such an equality, it was promulgated to indicate to the military and other centralists that no special privileges were being accorded to the Basques and Catalans.

10. The peasant grammarian, Ivar Aasen, developed a common norm for written communication from several rural dialects. His aim was to create continuity in the history of Norwegian culture by constructing a language built upon the traditions of the old Norse of the Middle Ages, yet reflecting the usage of the peasant communities least influenced by the centuries of Danish rule.

11. Haugen (1966) characterizes the Norwegian situation as one of 'schizoglossia', two alternative standards for a continuum of urban and rural dialects, and something distinct from 'diglossia' (Ferguson, 1959; 1962), which describes cases of a clear class split between standards.

12. This contrast between north and south has persisted since the Reformation. Indeed, the south wanted to join Berne after the collapse of the Napoleonic Empire, while the north did so only reluctantly (Gasser, 1978; also Campbell, 1978).

13. However, in the immigration of English speakers into South Wales in the late nineteenth century, more came from English-speaking Wales than from England (Thomas, 1930).

14. The province of Navarre had been a heartland of Carlism. In the Civil War it sided with Franco while the other Basque provinces fought for a status of autonomy within the Republic.

15. For example, the northern Scandinavian counties, Drenthe, Urschweiz, Valais, Appenzell, Basilicata, Calabria, Puglia, Sicily, the Vendée and other areas north of Occitania, Andalusia, Extremadura.

16. Indeed, the MacDonalds, as Lords of the Isles, had ruled the north-west virtually as a separate kingdom. They were defeated in the 1490s by the Scottish crown which, however, proved unwilling or incapable of filling the vacuum. If

anything, central influence in the Gaelic heartlands became even weaker.

17. The otherwise thorough linguist, Haarmann (1975), does not even list Cornish as an active language, though surprisingly he lists that other dying language, Manx, which could claim only one mother tongue speaker in 1969.

18. The standard proposed by the Félibrige was based on the Provencal of the Rhône valley, and did not take into account the broader range of variations within Occitan. It failed to mobilize much support beyond Provence, and other standards emerged in Limousin, Languedoc and Gascogne. This remained true of the first systematic presentation of the problems of standardization, the *Gramatica Occitana segon los parlars lengadocians* by L. Alibert (Bec, 1967). The most important recent contributions have been made by Robert Lafont in Toulouse, whose writings (1967; 1971a; 1971b; 1975) have had an impact in all the peripheries of France and have raised the debate to a high level of scholarship.

19. In this respect, this alliance overrode the economic contrast between the two Brittanies: larger 'seigneuries' and a more hierarchical society in the west, smaller peasant properties in the east (a division that is a major theme of the classic study by André Siegfried, 1913).

20. Furet and Ozouf (1977: 327-9) show graphically the consistently lower levels of schooling and literacy in the Basse Bretagne than in the Pays Gallo.

21. France reneged on its promise to maintain Savoy as a 'zone franche', an open trading area. The dispute lingered on until after World War I, to be an important element in whatever cultural distinctiveness remained in Savoy.

22. A count of newspapers published in Nice between 1848 and 1921 showed a distribution of 43 percent in French, 18 percent in Italian, 28 percent in some other European language (mainly English), and 11 percent in Nicois.

23. Indeed, not only peripheral languages have been challenged by the new electronic media and their content. Transmissions are no respecters of boundaries, and people in border areas can receive foreign television channels. More generally, the new media have reinforced the superiority of the European first division of languages, most especially English. With a much greater output of the written word and audio-visual productions, they have produced even greater strains on small European language communities with political independence, raising the possibilities of a new kind of linguistic centre-periphery dimension.

24. The *Encyclopedie,* for example, cites as 'nations' those of Normandy, Picardy, Brittany and Flanders. In Sweden the term 'nation' is still used in this sense in the universities (for example, 'Norrlands nation').

CHAPTER 4
The Politicization of Peripheral Predicaments

1. In 1948 the political elites agreed to remove linguistic questions from the agenda for a ten-year period. Apart from the royal issue, which almost inevitably divided Flanders from Wallonia, this agreement seems to have worked.

2. We prefer to use this terminology in this context rather than the somewhat similar dichotomy between the principle of territoriality and the principle of personality (MacRae, 1975). The former applies where the whole population within a territory is classified as belonging to a specific group; the latter, where individual

attributes determine the membership of the group. There is, we feel, some imprecision about this distinction, at least in some of the uses made of it, since it refers to both the act of self-identification and to treatment by others (especially governments).

3. A perfect example is the post-World War I arguments over where the boundaries of the new successor states would be drawn. Nearly all the fledgling states could find some historical experience of imperialism that could be used as the basis of a claim for a much larger territory (Urwin, 1980).

4. These points are discussed at length in Rogowski (1973).

5. Almost 50 percent of the Swedish Finns live in the metropolitan province of Uusimaa: by contrast, the monolingual Åland Islands hold only 7 percent of the total Swedish-speaking population (Miljan, 1976; Allardt and Miemois, 1982; Allardt, Miemois and Starck, 1979). The peaceful state of affairs has not always existed. Relationships between the language groups have gone through some stormy periods. The peculiarity of the case of the Swedish Finns is due in no small measure to the particular history of Finland and its location as an interface between the two expansive centres of Stockholm and St Petersburg (Alapuro, 1982).

6. Though in one instance — the Zonenrandgebeit of West Germany, shadowing the long border with East Germany and Czechoslovakia — strategic location has led to a decided reluctance to live there or to invest resources in the region.

7. Ecological analyses suggest that religion was important in the Jura dispute: given the clear religious divide between north and south, this is not altogether surprising. The survey analysis by Campbell (1982) shows that, while Catholics were united on the territorial issue, the Protestants were fairly evenly divided.

8. The study by Tarrow (1977), focusing on the role of local mayors in France and Italy, is an excellent review of this dilemma.

9. This interpretation seems to have at least as much validity as that which stresses the decreased importance of the European state as a result of decolonialization (Smith, 1979: 162-4; Esman, 1977: 260).

10. In some instances the catalyst can be dated most precisely. In the Jura the origins of the Rassemblement and its efforts can be dated to the 1947 refusal by the Bernese legislature to accept the nomination of a 'jurassien' for a public position. This was, as it were, the straw that broke the camel's back (Béguilin, 1972).

11. This parallels Weber's classical distinction between goal rationality (implying strategic calculation) and value rationality (unrestricted goal attainment).

12. Such as the recreation of the ancient state of Burgundy or the creation of a broader pan-Germanic state and nation.

13. In South Jutland this strategy proved to be short-lived. Even though both partners were in decline, they failed to reach an agreement in 1979, and consequently the German minority lost its parliamentary representation again.

14. In the Basque case violence is more the product of a fear of the consequences of a demographic decline and a weakening identity. In Ulster it may be the product of an attempt to sustain an identity among a group that lacks the most obvious stigma of identity.

15. Many of the smaller organizations are not as ambitious, settling for a series of ad hoc improvements in the use of the minority language.

16. We might also mention the Movimento per Trieste, founded as a protest against some provisions of the 1975 Treaty of Osimo, which envisaged an independent free zone on both sides of the border with Yugoslavia. In the 1979

election it was the strongest party (27 percent) in Trieste.

17. Apart from one result of 7 percent in a Corsican constituency, the 1978 electoral tally in Alsace, Brittany, the Basque area, Occitania and Roussillon was very few candidates who each polled 4 percent or less. Nor has the performance been much better in regional and local elections, although since 1977 the UDB has appeared on several urban councils.

18. To which we could add a fourth, that of the German minority. The Partei der deutschsprachigen Belger was formed in 1972, and in 1978 gained 7 of the 25 seats in the elections to the newly established German Cultural Council.

19. The progression of the Belgian territorial complex has been such that the statewide parties themselves have fragmented into what are de facto independent organizations. In a sense, therefore, all Belgian parties are now regional.

20. In Bavaria the BP had to contend with the strongly pro-region Christian Social Union. While the latter's hegemony in Bavaria may be attributed in part to its strong espousal of Bavarian interests, this hegemony has not been disturbed in the past two decades by the rapid economic change and large-scale in-migration experienced by the Land (Urwin, 1982a).

21. But at the height of the SNP boom, at least one survey indicated a high support for the SNP among young Catholics, and one that compared favourably with SNP levels among the young of other denominations (Brand, 1978).

22. The attitude data in Sani and Sartori (1983) show the moderate conservative identification of the Volksunie. The FDF has a strong pluralist base which it sees as an advantage in the competition for votes (Lefevre, 1980).

23. For the basis of selecting these parties, see the detailed discussion in Urwin (1983).

CHAPTER 5
The Central Response

1. Good examples can be found in the fate of established parties in the aftermath of the breakup of the Austro-Hungarian Empire. Witness also the problems of establishing traditional parties in the European Community.

2. The greater structural equilibrium of West Germany is stressed by OECD (1976); also Stöhr and Tödtling (1977).

3. Italy is typical. While apologists for the Mezzogiorno favoured a global strategy, the result was a series of special laws for delineated areas within the South (Mioni, 1976).

4. Regional plans or planning councils were introduced in 1956 in Britain, 1957 in the Netherlands and Italy, 1958 in Denmark and France, 1959 in Belgium, etc. (OECD, 1976).

5. France was the home of growth pole theory. It had some success in the Netherlands and Sweden, though its tentative beginnings were soon abandoned in Britain and Italy.

6. The studies are legion: see, among others, CECRSS (1968); Klaassen (1965); OECD (1970); Kalk (1971); Sant (1974); Hansen (1974).

7. 'The Community shall have as its task, by establishing a common market and progressively approximating the economic policies of Member States, to promote

throughout the Community a harmonious development of economic activities, a continued and balanced expansion, an increase in stability.'

8. The question of regional financial competence over economic development has arisen in all postwar discussions from the early Mezzogiorno debates onwards.

9. Violence occurred mainly in those communes with narrow referendum majorities, especially in the southern town of Moutier (Bassand and Fragnière, 1976: 48-54).

10. Allowing for some intermingling along the linguistic divide and for the small German minority in Wallonia.

11. Most combining solutions will be costly, and the question of the costs of safeguarding linguistic rights has been an important factor in the bitter debate over the fate of the Brussels suburbs.

12. Witness the comment in the 1973 (British) Royal Commission on the Constitution: 'A constitution which in its essentials has served us well for some hundreds of years.'

13. It is group accommodation because linguistic status of the communes is decided by a census question on self-reported main language. Thereafter, however, it is the territorial principle that is applied in administrative affairs: that is, if a commune has been declared monolingual, the rights of the minority language are more restricted than in bilingual communes.

14. Seiler (1978) claims such a change also for Fianna Fáil in Ireland. But this regarded itself as a genuinely Irish national party (Garvin, 1974; Mair, 1978).

References

Aarebrot, F.H. (1982). 'Norway: Centre and Periphery in a Peripheral State', in Rokkan and Urwin (1982).

Aarebrot, F.H. and Urwin, D.W. (1975). 'The Politics of Cultural Dissent: Religion, Language and Action in Norway in a European Context'. Paper presented at the ECPR Joint Sessions of Workshops, London.

Agostini, M.V. (1976). *Regioni Europee e scambio ineguale verso una politica regionale comunitaria?* Bologne: Mulino.

Agren, G. (ed.) (1974). *Hurrarna. En stridsskrift om finlandssvenskarnas nutid.* Vasa: Författarnas andelslag.

Ahnström, L. (1973). *Styrande och ledande verksamhet i Västeuropa: en ekonomisk-geografisk studie.* Stockholm: Almqvist & Wiksell.

Akenson, D.H. (1970). *The Irish Educational Experiment.* London: Routledge & Kegan Paul.

Alapuro, R. (1982). 'Finland: An Interface Periphery', in Rokkan and Urwin (1982).

Alcock, A.E. (1970). *The History of the South Tyrol Question.* London: Michael Joseph.

Allardt, E. (1979). *Implications of the Ethnic Revival in Modern Industrialized Society.* Helsinki: Societas Scientiarum Fennica. Commentationis Scientiarum Socialium 12.

Allardt, E. and Miemois, K.J. (1982). 'A Minority in Both Centre and Periphery: The Swedish-speaking Finns', *European Journal of Political Research,* 10: 265-292.

Allardt, E., Miemois, K.J. and Starck, C. (1979). *Multiple and Varying Criteria for Membership in a Linguistic Minority: The Case of the Swedish-speaking Minority in Metropolitan Finland.* Helsinki: Research Group for Comparative Sociology, Helsinki University, Report 21.

Andersen, L.B., Jensen, H.T., Plum, V. and Villadsen, S. (1974). *Samfundsanalyse og erhvervsstruktur.* Copenhagen: Paludans Forlag.

Anderson, P. (1974a). *Passages from Antiquity to Feudalism.* London: New Left Books.

Anderson, P. (1974b). *Lineages of the Absolutist State.* London: New Left Books.

Anderson, R.D. (1975). *Education in France, 1848-1870.* London: Oxford University Press.

Asheim, B.T. (1978). *Regionale ulikheter i levekar.* Oslo: NOU. no. 3.

Ashford, D.E. (1979). 'Territorial Politics and Equality: Decentralization and the Modern State', *Political Studies,* 27: 71-83.

Balsom, D. (1979). 'The Nature and Distribution of Support for Plaid Cymru'. Paper presented at the ECPR Joint Sessions of Workshops, Brussels.

Bassand, M. (1975). 'The Jura Problem', *Journal of Peace Research,* 12: 139-50.

Bassand, M. and Fragnière, J-P. (1976). *Les Ambiguités de la démocratie locale.* St Saphorin: Georgi.

Bec, P. (1967). *La Langue occitane.* Paris: Presses Universitaires de France.

Bechelloni, G. (1970). *Politica culturale e regioni.* Milan: Comunitá.

Beer, W.R. (1977). 'The Social Class of Ethnic Activists in Contemporary France', in Esman (1977: 143-58).

Béguilin, R. (1972). *Le Réveil du peuple jurassien 1947-1950.* Délémont: R. Béguilin.

Bergan, A. (1975). *Preliminary Paper on Restrictive Regional Policy Measures.* Paris: OECD.

Berry, B.J.L. and Horton, F. (1970). *Geographic Perspectives on Urban Systems.* Englewood Cliffs, NJ: Prentice-Hall.

Biehl, D., Hussmann, D. and Schnyder, S. (1972). 'Zur Regionalen Einkommenverteilung in der Europäische Wirtschaftsgemeinschaft', *Die Weltwirtschaft,* 64-8.

Brand, J. (1978). *The National Movement in Scotland.* London: Routledge & Kegan Paul.

Braud, P. (1978). 'Les Élections législatives de mars 1978 en Bretagne', *Revue Française de Science Politique,* 28: 1018-38.

Brenner, R. (1977). 'The Origins of Capitalist Development: a Critique of Neo-Smithian Marxism', *New Left Review,* 104: 25-92.

Brown, A.J. (1972). *The Framework of Regional Economics in the United Kingdom.* Cambridge: University Press.

Buch, H. (1979). 'Idéologie et politique dans les mouvements nationalistes en Belgique', *Revue Européenne des Sciences Sociales,* 46: 235-55.

Butler, D. and Kavanagh, D. (1974). *The British General Election of February 1974.* London: Macmillan.

Butler, D. and Pinto-Duschinsky, M. (1971) *The British General Election of 1970.* London: Macmillan.

Camilleri, G. and Galiay, C. (1980). 'Le Statut d'autonomie de la Catalogne', *Revue Française de Science Politique,* 30: 1012-47.

Campbell, D.B. (1978). 'Troubles in the Jura, 1815-1977: A Descriptive Essay'.

Paper presented to the ECPR Workshop on Nationalism, Glasgow.
Campbell, D.B. (1982). 'Nationalism, Religion and the Social Bases of Conflict in the Swiss Jura', in Rokkan and Urwin (1982).
CECRSS (1968). *Les Déséquilibres régionaux en Europe.* Brussels: Éditions de l'Institut de Sociologie.
Chartier, R. (1978). 'The Two Frances: The History of a Geographical Idea', *Social Science Information,* 17: 527-54.
Craig, F.W.S. (1972). *British Parliamentary Election Results, 1950-70.* Chichester: Political Reference Publications.
CREGE (1968). *Les Motivations de localisation des investissements internationaux dans l'Europe de Nord-Ouest.* Lille: CREGE.
Daalder, H. (1973). 'Building Consociational Nations', in Eisenstadt and Rokkan (1973: II 14-31).
Daalder, H. (1981). 'Consociationalism, Center and Periphery in the Netherlands', in P. Torsvik (ed.), *Mobilization, Center-Periphery Structures and Nation-Building.* Oslo: Universitetsforlaget.
Daalder, H. and Mair, P. (eds.) (1983). *Western European Party Systems: Continuity and Change.* London: Sage.
De Certeau, M., Julia, D. and Revel, J. (1975). *Une politique de la langue.* Paris: Gallimard.
Delaisi, R. (1929). *Les Deux Europes.* Paris: Payot.
Del Campo, S., Navarro, M. and Tezanos, J.F. (1977). *La Cuestion Regional Española.* Madrid: Cuaderno para el dialogo.
De Miguel, A. (1968). *Differencias regionales en España e Italia.* Madrid: Data S.A.
Díaz López, C. (1982). 'The Politicization of Galician Cleavages', in Rokkan and Urwin (1982).
Dierickx, G. (1978). 'Ideological Oppositions and Consociational Attitudes in the Belgian Parliament', *Legislative Studies Quarterly,* 3: 133-60.
Dulong, R. (1975). *La Question bretonne.* Paris: Colin.
Durand, P. (1974). *Industrie et régions. L'aménagement industriel du territoire.* Paris: DATAR.
EEC (1964). *La politique régionale dans la Communauté Economique Européenne.* Brussels: European Commission.
EEC (1969). *Note sur la politique régional dans la Communauté.* Brussels: European Commission.
EEC (1972). *Regional Statistics.* Luxemburg: Statistical Office of the European Commission.
Eisenstadt, S.N. and Rokkan, S. (eds.) (1973). *Building States and Nations* (2 vols). London/Beverly Hills: Sage.
Elklit, J. (1980). 'Centre-Periphery Structures in Denmark'. Arhus: Institut for Staskundskab, Aarhus University (mimeo).
Elklit, J., Noack, J.P., and Tonsgaard, O. (1978). *Nationalt tilhørsforhold i Nordslesvig.* Arhus: Det laerde selskab. Acta Jutlandica, Samfundsvidenskabelig serie 14.
Esman, M.J. (ed.) (1977). *Ethnic Conflict in the Western World.* Ithaca, NY: Cornell University Press.
Ferguson, C. (1959). *'Diglossia, Word,* 15: 325-40.
Ferguson, C. (1962). 'The Language Factor in National Development', *Anthropological Linguistics,* 4: 23-7.

Fleming, D.K. (1967). 'Coastal Steelworks in the Common Market Countries', *Geographical Review,* 57: 48-72.
Frognier, A-P. (1975). 'Vote, Classe Social et Religion/Pratique Religieuse', *Res Publica,* 17: 479-90.
Frognier, A-P. (1978). 'Parties and Cleavages in the Belgian Parliament', *Legislative Studies Quarterly,* 3: 109-31.
Frognier, A-P., Quevit, M. and Stenbock, M. (1982). 'Regional Imbalances and Centre-Periphery Relationships in Belgium', in Rokkan and Urwin (1982).
Furet, F. and Ozouf, J. (1977). *Lire et écrire. L'alphabétisation des français de Calvin à Jules Ferry.* Paris: Seuil.
Galtung, J. (1971). 'A Structural Theory of Imperialism', *Journal of Peace Research,* 2: 81-118.
Garvin, T. (1974). 'Political Cleavages, Party Politics and Urbanisation in Ireland: The Case of the Periphery-Dominated Centre', *European Journal of Political Research,* 2: 307-27.
Gasser, A. (1978). *Berne et le Jura 1815-1977.* Berne: Imprimerie fédérative.
Gaudard, G., Derron, J. and Repond, A. (1978). 'Coûts sociaux, équilibre de l'espace et federalisme'. Paper presented at the International Conference on Urbanization, Regional Development and Federalism, Lausanne.
Geertz, C. (1963). 'The Integrative Revolution: Primordial Sentiments and Civil Liberties in the New States', in C. Geertz (ed.), *Old Societies and New States.* New York: Free Press, 105-57.
Gellner, E. (1964). *Thought and Change.* London: Weidenfeld & Nicolson.
Georgelin, J. (1976). 'Des Disparités régionales en France (19è, 20è siècles)', *Anthinea,* 9-10: 27-31.
Gerth, H.H. and Mills, C.W. (1948). *From Max Weber: Essays in Sociology.* London: Routledge & Kegan Paul.
Gibbs, J.R. (ed.) (1961). *Urban Research Methods.* Princeton: Van Nostrand.
Glazer, N. and Moynihan, D.P. (1975). *Ethnicity: Theory and Experience.* Cambridge, Mass.: Harvard University Press.
Gonnet, P. (1977). 'Particularisme et patronage politique dans le Comté de Nice depuis 1870', in Gras and Livet (1977: 103-16).
Goody, J. (1977). *The Domestication of the Savage Mind.* Cambridge: University Press.
Gottmann, J. (1971). 'Pour une géographie des centres transactionals', *Bulletin de l'Association des Géographiens Français,* 385-6: 41-9.
Gottmann, J. (1975). 'The Evolution of the Concept of Territory', *Social Science Information,* 14: 29-47.
Gourevitch, P. (1978). 'Reforming the Napoleonic State: The Creation of Regional Governments in France and Italy', pp. 28-63 in S. Tarrow, P. Katzenstein and L. Graziano (eds.), *Territorial Politics in Industrial Nations.* New York: Praeger.
Gourevitch, P. (1981). *Paris and the Provinces: The Politics of Local Government Reform in France.* London: Allen & Unwin.
Gourvil, F. (1976). *Langue et littérature bretonnes.* Paris: Presses Universitaires de France.
Gras, C. and Livet G. (eds.) (1977). *Régions et régionalisme en France.* Paris: Presses Universitaires de France.
Gras, S. (1982). 'Regionalism and Autonomy in Alsace since 1918', in Rokkan and Urwin (1982).

Gravier, J.F. (1972). *Paris et le désert français en 1972.* Paris: Flammarion.

Greenwood, D. (1977). 'Continuity in Change: Spanish Basque Ethnicity as a Historical Process', in Esman (1977).

Gregori, J. (1970). *Nouvelle histoire de la Corse.* Paris: Marineau.

Grémion, P. (1976). *Le Pouvoir périphérique.* Paris: Seuil.

Haarmann, H. (1975). *Soziologie und Politik der Sprachen Europas.* Munich: Deutscher Taschenbuch Verlag.

Haas, H. and Stuhlpfarrer, K. (1977). *Österreich und seine Slovenen.* Vienna: Löcker & Wögenstein.

Habermas, J. (1976). *Zur Rekonstruktion des Historisches Materialismus.* Frankfurt: Suhrkamp.

Hagström, B. (1978). *1971 ars länsförvaltningsreform. En utvärdring.* Lund: Studentlitteratur.

Hansen, N.M. (1972). *Growth Centers in Regional Economic Development.* New York: Free Press.

Hansen, N.M. (ed.) (1974). *Public Policy and Regional Development.* Cambridge, Mass: Ballinger.

Haugen, E. (1966). *Language Conflict and Language Planning: The Case of Modern Norwegian.* Cambridge, Mass: Harvard University Press.

Hechter, M. (1974). *Internal Colonialism.* London: Allen & Unwin.

Heiberg, M. (1975). 'Insiders/Outsiders: Basque Nationalism', *Archives Européennes de Sociologie,* 16: 169-93.

Heiberg, M. (1982). 'Urban Politics and Rural Culture: Basque Nationalism', in Rokkan and Urwin (1982).

Heisler, M.O. (1974). 'Institutionalizing Societal Cleavages in a Cooptive Polity: The Growing Importance of the Output Side in Belgium', in M.O. Heisler (ed.), *Politics in Europe.* New York: McKay.

Heisler, M.O. and Peters, B.G. (1978). *The Implications of Scarcity for the Management of Conflict in Multicultural Societies.* Glasgow: Centre for the Study of Public Policy, Strathclyde University, Studies in Public Policy 19.

Henrichsen, B. (1981). 'Report on the IFDO Symposium on the Development of Joint Data Bases for Regional Analysis and Computer Cartography', *European Journal of Political Research,* 9: 113-18.

Heraud, G. (1974). *L'Europe des Ethnies.* Paris: Presses d'Europe.

Hill, T.K. (1974). 'Belgium: Political Change in a Segmented Society', in R. Rose (ed.), *Electoral Behaviour.* New York: Free Press, 29-107.

Hirschman, A.O. (1970). *Exit, Voice and Loyalty.* Cambridge, Mass: Harvard University Press.

Hobsbawm, E. (1972). 'Some Reflections on Nationalism', in T.J. Nossiter, A.H. Hanson and S. Rokkan (eds.), *Imagination and Precision in the Social Sciences.* London: Faber.

Hobsbawm, E. (1977). 'Reflection on the Break-up of Britain', *New Left Review,* 105: 3-23.

Hroch, M. (1968). *Die Vorkämpfer der nationalen Bewegung bei den kleinen Völkern Europas.* Prague: Acta Universitatis Carolinae, Philosophia et Historica. Monographia XXIV.

Innis, H. (1951). *The Bias of Communication.* Toronto: University Press.

Isaacs, H.R. (1975). *Idols of the Tribe: Group Identity and Political Change.* New York: Harper & Row.

Jaensch, D.H. (1976). 'The Scottish Vote 1974: A Re-aligning Party System?' *Political Studies,* 24: 306-19.

Janin, B. (1968). *Une région alpine originale, le Val d'Aosta.* Grenoble: Imprimerie Allier.

Juillard, E. and Nonn, H. (eds.) (1976). *Espaces et régions en Europe Occidentale.* Paris: Éditions CNRS.

Kalk, E. (ed.) (1971). *Regional Planning and Regional Government in Europe.* The Hague: International Union of Local Authorities.

Katzenstein, P.J. (1977). 'Ethnic Political Conflict in South Tyrol', in Esman (1977: 287-323).

Keating, M.J. (1978). 'Parliamentary Behaviour as a Test of Scottish Integration into the United Kingdom', *Legislative Studies Quarterly,* 3: 409-30.

Klaassen, L.H. (1965). *Aménagement économique et social du territoire.* Paris: OECD.

Krejci, J. (1978). 'Ethnic Problems in Europe', in S. Giner and M.S. Archer (eds.), *Contemporary Europe, Social Structure and Cultural Patterns.* London: Routledge & Kegan Paul, 124-71.

Lafont, R. (1967). *La Révolution régionaliste.* Paris: Gallimard.

Lafont, R. (1971a). *Clefs pour l'Occitanie.* Paris: Seghers.

Lafont, R. (1971b). *Décoloniser en France.* Paris Gallimard.

Lafont, R. (1975). *La Revendication occitane.* Paris: Flammarion.

LaPonce, J. (1960). *The Protection of Minorities.* Berkeley/Los Angeles: University of California Press.

Larsen, J., Rasmussen, O.B. and Villadsen, S. (1976). *Bliver Danmark skaevere? En undersøgelse af erhvervsstrukturens udvikling i det sydvestlige Danmark.* Copenhagen: Paludans Forlag.

Lefevre, P. (1977). 'Le Rassemblement Wallon au gouvernement: défi au gouvernement ou défi au parti', *Res Publica,* 19: 141-65.

Lefevre, P. (1980). 'Le FDF: seize ans d'expérience pluraliste', *Res Publica,* 22: 385-99.

Lerner, D. (1958). *The Passing of Traditional Society.* Glencoe, Ill.: Free Press.

Le Roy Ladurie, E. (1973). *Le Territoire de l'historien.* Paris: Gallimard.

Linz, J.J. (1973). 'Early State-Building and Late Peripheral Nationalisms against the State: The Case of Spain', in Eisenstadt and Rokkan (1973: II 32-116).

Linz, J.J. (1978). 'Spain: Party Systems in the Periphery'. Paper presented at the Colloquium on Recent Changes in European Party Systems, Florence.

Lipset, S.M. and Rokkan, S. (eds.) (1967). *Party Systems and Voter Alignments.* New York: Free Press.

Lorentzen, J. and Rokkan, S. (1976). 'A Multi-level Data Bank for Computer Mapping of Regional Variations in Western Europe', *European Political Data Newsletter,* No. 19.

Lovie, J. (1977). 'Essai sur la régionalisme Savoyard', in Gras and Livet (1977: 429-43).

MacRae, K.D. (1975). 'The Principle of Territoriality and the Principle of Personality in Multilingual States', *International Journal of the Sociology of Language,* 4: 33-54.

Magnago, S. (1974). 'The Situation of the German and Ladin Minorities in South Tyrol', *Europa Etynica,* 31: 146-65.

Mair, P. (1978). 'Ireland: The Politics of Predominance'. Paper presented at the

Colloquium on Recent Changes in European Party Systems, Florence.

Marcet, A. (1977). 'Le Roussillon, une province à la fin de l'Ancien Régime', in Gras and Livet (1977: 103-16).

Maugue, P. (1970). *Le Particularisme alsacien 1918-1967.* Paris: Presses d'Europe.

McAllister, I., Parry, R. and Rose, R. (1979). *United Kingdom Rankings: The Territorial Dimension in Social Indicators.* Glasgow: Centre for the Study of Public Policy, Strathclyde University. Studies in Public Policy 44.

McCrone, G. (1969). *Regional Policy in Britain.* London: Allen & Unwin.

McNeill, W. (1974). *The Shape of European History.* New York: Oxford University Press.

Meyn, H. (1965). *Die Deutsche Partei.* Düsseldorf: Droste.

Miljan, T. (1976). 'The Minority and Politics in a Bicultural Society: The Case of Finland'. Paper presented at the ECPR Joint Sessions of Workshops, Louvain-la-Neuve.

Mioni, A. (1976). *Le trasformazioni territoriali in Italia nella prima età industriale.* Venice: Marsilio Editori.

Mols, R. (1954-56). *Introduction à la démographie historique des villes d'Europe du XIVè au XVIIIè siècle* (3 vols). Louvain: Publications Universitaires.

Monod, J. and Castelbajac, P. (1971). *L'aménagement du territoire.* Paris: Presses Universitaires de France.

Moore, B. (1966). *Social Origins of Dictatorship and Democracy.* Boston: Beacon Press.

Moore, B. and Rhodes, J. (1974). 'The Effects of Regional Policy in the United Kingdom', in Sant (1974).

Nairn, T. (1977). *The Break-up of Britain.* London: New Left Books.

Noin, D. (1976). *L'espace français.* Paris: Colin.

Nordrefo (1978). *Nordisk forskning om regionalpolitik i omvandling.* Oslo: Nordiska Ministerradets Sekretariat.

O Ciuv, B. (ed.) (1969). *A View of the Irish Language.* Dublin: Stationery Office.

OECD (1968). *Multidisciplinary Aspects of Regional Development.* Paris: OECD.

OECD (1970). *Le Facteur régional dans le développement économique.* Paris: OECD.

OECD (1976). *Regional Problems and Policies in OECD Countries* (2 vols). Paris: OECD.

Orridge, A.W. (1981). 'Uneven Development and Nationalism', *Political Studies,* 29: 1-15, 181-90.

Payne, S.G. (1975). *Basque Nationalism.* Reno: University of Nevada Press.

Peacock, A.T. and Wiseman, J. (1967). *The Growth of Public Expenditure in the United Kingdom.* London: Allen & Unwin.

Perez-Alondon, J. (1979). 'Catalan: An Example of the Current Language Struggles in Spain: Sociopolitical and Pedagogical Implications', *International Journal of the Sociology of Language,* 21: 109-25.

Perroux, F. (1961). *L'économie du XXè siècle.* Paris: Presses Universitaires de France.

Petrella, R. (1971). *Le Développement régional en Europe.* Paris: Mouton.

Petrella, R. (1978a). *La Renaissance des cultures régionales en Europe.* Paris: Éditions Entente.

Petrella, R. (1978b). 'Les Politiques régionales d'égalisation et d'équilibre en Europe Occidentale'. Bergen: Institute of Sociology (mimeo).

Pintore, G. (1974). *Sardegna. Regione o colonia.* Milan: Mazzotti.

Prost, M-A. (1965). *La Hierarchie des villes en fonction de leurs activités de commerce et de services.* Paris: Gauthier-Villars.

Pumain, D. and Saint Julien, T. (1976). 'Fonctions et hierarchies des villes francaises. Étude du contenu des classifications réalisées en France entre 1960 et 1974', *Annales de Géographie,* 85: 385-440.

Quellenec, M. (1972). 'Analyse structurale de développement économique des régions francaises 1864-1970'. Paris: Thèse de doctorat, Université de Paris.

Ragin, C.C. (1979). 'Ethnic Political Mobilization: The Welsh Case', *American Sociological Review,* 44: 619-35.

Reece, J.E. (1977). *The Bretons Against France.* Chapel Hill, NC: University of North Carolina Press.

Renan, E. (1970). *Poetry of the Celtic Races and Other Studies.* London: Kenikat Press.

Rhodes, R.A.W. (1974). 'Regional Policy and a "Europe of Regions": A Critical Assessment', *Regional Studies,* 8: 105-14.

Rhys, J. and Brynmor-Jones, D. (1906). *The Welsh People.* London: Unwin.

Robinson, E.A.G. (ed.) (1969). *Backward Areas in Advanced Countries.* London: Macmillan.

Rogowski, R. (1973). *Rational Legitimacy.* Princeton: University Press.

Rokkan, S. (1967). 'Geography, Religion and Social Class: Cross-cutting Cleavages in Norwegian Politics', in Lipset and Rokkan (1967: 367-444).

Rokkan, S. (1973). 'Cities, States and Nations', in Eisenstadt and Rokkan (1973: I 73-97).

Rokkan, S. (1975). 'Dimensions of State Formation and Nation-Building: A Possible Paradigm for Research on Variations within Europe', in C. Tilly (ed.), *The Formation of National States in Western Europe.* Princeton: University Press, 562-600.

Rokkan, S. & Urwin, D.W. (eds.). *The Politics of Territorial Identity: Studies of Developments in the European Peripheries.* London/Beverly Hills: Sage.

Rokkan, S., Urwin, D.W., Aarebrot, F.H., Sande, T. and Adams, P. (1983). *Centre-Periphery Structures in Europe: A Data Workbook for Cross-National Analysis.* Frankfurt: Campus Verlag.

Rose, R. and Urwin, D.W. (1969). 'Social Cohesion, Political Parties and Strains in Regimes', *Comparative Political Studies,* 2: 7-67.

Rose, R. and Urwin, D.W. (1970). 'Persistence and Change in Western Party Systems since 1945', *Political Studies,* 18: 287-319.

Rose, R. and Urwin, D.W. (1975). *Territorial Differentiation and Political Unity in Western Nations.* London/Beverly Hills: Sage.

Rossingol, J. (1974). *Le Problème national catalan.* Paris: Mouton.

Ruffieux, R. and Prongué, B. (1978). 'Le Canton de Jura à travers les travaux de l'Assemblée Constituante', *Annuaire Suisse de Science Politique,* 18: 105-19.

Sani, G. and Sartori, G. (1983). 'Polarization, Fragmentation and Competition in European Party Systems', in Daalder and Mair (1983).

Sant, M.E.C. (ed.) (1974). *Regional Policy and Planning in Europe.* London: Saxon House.

Schafer, B.C. (1972). *Faces of Nationalism.* New York: Harcourt Brace.

Schermerhorn, R.A. (1970). *Comparative Ethnic Relations.* New York: Random House.

Seers, D. (1979). 'The Periphery of Europe', in D. Seers, B. Schaeffer and M.L. Kiljunen (eds.), *Underdeveloped Europe.* London: Harvester Press, 1-35.

Seiler, D. (1978). *Les Partis politiques en Europe.* Paris: Presses Universitaires de France.

Serant, P. (1965). *La France des minorités.* Paris: Laffont.

Serant, P. (1971). *La Bretagne et la France.* Paris: Fayard.

Serrani, D. (1972). *La via italiana alle regioni.* Milan: Comunitá.

Seton-Watson, H. (1977). *States and Nations.* London: Methuen.

Shoup, C.S. (ed.) (1967). *Fiscal Harmonization in Common Markets* (2 vols). New York: Columbia University Press.

Siegfried, A. (1913). *Tableau politique de la France de l'ouest sous la Troisième République.* Paris: Colin.

Silverman, D.P. (1972). *Reluctant Union.* University Park, PA.: Pennsylvania State University Press.

Smith, A.D. (1972). *Nationalism in the Twentieth Century.* Oxford: Martin Robertson.

Smout, T.C. (1972). *A History of the Scottish People, 1560-1830.* London: Collins.

Søfelde, J. (1977). *Regionale udvikling og offentlig planlaegning.* Copenhagen: Samfundsvidenskabeligt Forlag.

Statistisk Årbog (1976). Copenhagen: Det Statistiske Departement.

Statistisk Sentralbyrå (1977). *Sosialt utsyn 1977.* Oslo: Statistisk Sentralbyrå.

Steinberg, J. (1978). *Why Switzerland?* London: Cambridge University Press.

Stephens, M. (1976). *Linguistic Minorities in Western Europe.* Llandysul: Gomer Press.

Stöhr, W. and Tödtling, F. (1977). *Evaluation of Regional Policies: Experiences in Market and Mixed Economies.* Vienna: Interdisciplinäres Institut für Raumordnung.

Straka, M. (ed.) (1970). *Handbuch der Europäischen Volksgruppen.* Vienna/Stuttgart: Braumuller.

Strauss, A. (1969). *Mirrors and Masks: The Search for Identity.* Norwich: Robertson.

Sussman, G.D. (1977). 'The Glut of Doctors in Mid-Nineteenth Century France', *Comparative Studies in Society and History,* 19: 287-306.

Tarrow, S. (1977). *Between Center and Periphery: Grassroots Politicians in Italy and France.* New Haven, Conn.: Yale University Press.

Thomas, B. (1930). 'The Migration of Labour into the Glamorgan Coalfield, 1861-1911', *Economica,* 10: 275-94.

Thoss, R. (1977). *The Geographic Concentration in the Community Countries.* Brussels: European Commission.

Tudesq, A. (1977). 'Naissance et originalité des stations régionales de TSF', in Gras and Livet (1977: 545-61).

Urwin, D.W. (1978). *The Alchemy of Delayed Nationalism.* Bergen: INSS, Avdeling for Sammenliknende Politikk, Rapport 3.

Urwin, D.W. (1980). *From Ploughshare to Ballotbox: The Politics of Agrarian Defence in Europe.* Oslo: Universitetsforlaget.

Urwin, D.W. (1982a). 'Germany: From Geographical Expression to Regional Accommodation', in Rokkan and Urwin (1982).

Urwin, D.W. (1982b). 'Territorial Structures and Political Developments in the United Kingdom', in Rokkan and Urwin (1982).

Urwin, D.W. (1983). 'Harbinger, Fossil, or Fleabite?: "Regionalism" and the Western European Party Mosaic', in Daalder and Mair (1983).

Urwin, D.W. and Rose, R. (1970). 'Persistence and Disruption in Western Party Systems Between The Wars'. Paper presented at the World Congress of the International Sociological Association, Varna.

Wallerstein, I. (1974). *The Modern World System.* London: Academic Press.

Waterston, A. (1974). 'The Coming Surge in Regional Development', *Finance and Development,* 11, 2: 14-17.

Watson, M. (1978). 'A Critique of Development From Above: The Lessons of French and Dutch Experience of Nationally-Defined Regional Policy'. *Public Administration,* 56: 457-81.

Webber, R. and Craig, J. (1978). *Socio-economic Classification of Local Authority Areas.* London: HMSO.

Weber, E. (1976). *Peasants into Frenchmen: The Modernization of Rural France, 1870-1914.* Stanford: University Press.

Weber, M. (1968). *Economy and Society.* Totowa: Bedminster Press.

Wildavsky, A. (1975). *Budgeting.* Boston: Little Brown.

Williams, J.L. and Hughes, G.R. (eds.) (1978). *The History of Education in Wales.* Swansea: Christopher Davies.

Williamson, J.G. (1965). 'Regional Inequality and the Process of National Development: A Description of the Patterns', *Economic Development and Cultural Change,* 13: 3-45.

Wolff, F. (1974). *Effizienz und Erfolgs Kontroll in der regionale Wirtschaftsförderung: Ergebnisse einer Untersuchung in Hessen.* Wiesbaden: Hessische Landesentwicklung- und Treuhand Gesellschaft.

Wright, V. (1979). 'Regionalization under the French Fifth Republic: The Triumph of the Functional Approach', in L.J. Sharpe (ed.), *Decentralist Trends in Western Democracies.* London/Beverly Hills: Sage, 193-234.

Young, C. (1976). *The Politics of Cultural Pluralism.* Madison: University of Wisconsin Press.

Zipf, G.K. (1949). *Human Behaviour and the Principle of Least Effort.* Cambridge, Mass.: Addison-Wesley.

Zolberg, A.R. (1977). 'Splitting the Difference: Federalization without Federalism in Belgium', in Esman (1977: 103-42).

Subject Index

accommodation, policies of 4, 64, 70, 76–7, 81, 84, 91, 106, 111, 166–89
agriculture 20, 22, 25, 32, 49–56, 158–9, 172–3, 175
Åland Islands 62, 128, 188, 198
Albania 62
alphabets 24, 26, 30, 69, 70, 119
Alps 11, 13, 20, 24, 27, 29, 76, 103–4, 125–7
Alsace 13, 28, 53, 61, 84, 103, 105, 120, 126, 130, 134, 143, 146, 186, 199; economy 136; language 72, 87, 102–3; mobilization 121; parties 155
Alsace-Lorraine 34, 51, 53, 62
Alto Adige 29, 54–5, 61–2, 101, 127, 130, 136, 138, 143, 159, 184–5, 188; language 72, 104–5; parties 149; Proporzpaket 105, 144, 184, 188, 190
Amsterdam 39, 40, 193
Andalusia 54, 62, 143, 152–3, 196
Arabs: *see* Islam
aristocracy 5, 25–6, 33, 65, 99
Asia 20, 22
Asturias 42
Atlantic 22–3, 28, 38
Austria 10, 27, 29, 31, 34, 36–7, 41, 62, 65, 76, 101, 104–5, 130, 140, 150, 182, 184, 193, 199

Baltic 11, 44, 62, 66
banks 41, 56
Barcelona 37, 78, 156, 160, 193–4
Basle 28, 52, 103
Basque provinces 22–3, 34, 53–4, 56, 61–3, 67, 92, 127, 129, 131, 135, 139–40, 143, 150, 152–3, 158–9, 161, 181, 191, 196, 198–9; attitudes in 148, 152–4, 160; economy 93, 135–6; language 72, 87, 92–3, 108, 152, 156
Bavaria 12, 23, 28, 31, 49, 62, 121, 126, 143, 199
Bayernpartei 126, 155, 157, 163–4, 199
Belgium 10, 11, 31, 33–4, 36, 38, 40–1, 59, 62, 73, 76–7, 83–4, 111, 121–2, 127, 130, 135, 139–40, 143, 150, 152–3, 158–9, 161, 181, 191, 198–9; cities 10, 11, 39, 40; decentralization

185–6, 188; economy 46, 50; language 72, 77–8, 83, 106, 131; parties 136, 144, 149, 157, 168–9, 190, 199
Berlin 12, 38, 65
Berne 28, 83–4, 144, 183–4, 190–1, 194, 196, 198
Bernese Jura: *see* Jura
Bilbao 194
Birmingham 193
Bismarck 27
Blekinge 29, 62
Bohemia-Moravia 31, 62
Bordeaux 193
Bosnia 62
boundaries 4–6, 14, 17, 21, 25–6, 30, 42, 44, 48, 50–1, 59, 65, 76, 86, 106, 114, 134, 168–9, 179, 184, 198
bourgeoisie 15, 20, 90, 97, 100, 102, 128, 159–61
Brabant 50, 74
Brandenburg-Prussia: *see* Prussia
Britain: *see* United Kingdom, *also* England, Northern Ireland, Scotland, Wales
Brittany 23, 31, 34, 51, 53, 61–2, 126, 131, 143, 146, 186, 197, 199; economy 98–9; language 72, 85, 96, 98, 100; religion 98–9
Brussels 40–1, 48, 78, 84, 127, 131, 155, 185–6, 191, 193, 200
bureaucracy 5, 15, 20, 33, 83, 88, 98, 122, 178, 184
Burgenland 29, 62, 127
Burgundy 23, 27–8, 31, 34, 37, 41, 62, 73, 103, 198

Calvinism: *see* Protestantism
capitalism 20–1, 25, 27, 42, 59, 74–5, 137, 170
Carinthia 29, 127, 150
Castille 23, 34, 37, 63, 72–3, 78, 92, 106, 153, 194
Catalonia 23, 28, 31, 34, 37, 54, 56, 61–2, 78–9, 92, 97, 106, 127, 134, 143, 152–3, 159, 187, 196; attitudes in 148, 152–3, 160; economy 93, 135–6, 140; language 72, 78, 92–3, 108, 152, 156; parties 154, 156, 168
catalysts 17, 117, 124, 135–40
Catholic Conservative Party, Switzerland 168
Catholic Party, Belgium 149
Catholicism 31–4, 62, 75–6, 83–4, 87, 92, 94, 98–9, 126, 151–2, 157–8, 191, 193
Celts 22–3, 28, 85, 95–6
centrality 6–14, 41
centralization 8, 11–14, 16–17, 22, 30, 74, 110, 129, 178–9
Centre Democratic Party, Denmark 149, 169
Charlemagne 27
China 26
Christian Democratic parties 154; Italy 149
Christianity 22, 24, 113
Christian People's Party, Norway 190
Christian Social Party, Belgium 168–9
churches 14–15, 24, 26–7, 82, 113, 132 (*see also* religion)
cities 8, 11–15, 20, 24, 26–7, 30, 32, 35, 37–40, 80, 97, 119, 129, 194 (*see also* urbanization)
citizenship 25, 87, 97, 115–17
city leagues 24, 37, 194
city networks 10, 25–7, 31–2, 35, 38–9, 41, 63, 75–6
class 66, 90, 137, 156
clergy 5, 15, 26, 98
colonialism 2, 135
communications 2, 5, 7, 8, 11, 12, 14, 16, 24–6, 30, 65, 68–70, 75–6, 85–6, 113, 138
Communist Party, Belgium 167; Catalonia 160
confederation 27, 141, 143; Switzerland 27, 51, 77, 90–1, 145, 183–4
Congress of Vienna 38, 151
Conservative Party, United Kingdom 151, 159
consociationalism 24, 31–2, 36–7, 63, 75, 183–5, 187
Copenhagen 51, 81
Cornwall 23, 85, 96, 197
Corsica 23, 53, 61–2, 111, 126, 136, 143, 150, 187, 199; language 72, 100
Croatia 23, 62
Czechoslovakia 3, 40, 147

Dalmatia 62
Danube 27
decentralization 5, 132, 146, 153, 176–7, 179, 183, 185, 187 (*see also* devolution, regional autonomy)
Denmark 10, 11, 29–31, 36, 38, 41, 54, 62, 71, 74–5, 80, 82, 106, 125, 169, 182, 199; cities 10, 11; economy 50–1; language 72–3; parties 149, 169
dependence 2–4, 15–16, 39, 77, 129
Deutsche Partei 155, 157, 163–4, 190
devolution 144–5, 149, 151, 168, 177, 187 (*see also* decentralization, regional autonomy)
dialect 29, 34, 68–9, 71, 73, 75, 77, 79, 82–3, 86–7, 90–1, 97, 100, 103, 108–9, 111–13, 115, 117
distance 2, 3, 7, 8, 11, 14, 16, 35, 47–8, 54, 63, 69, 130
doctors, density of 49–51, 53–5, 60, 195

economic aid 17, 170–9
economic policy 58
economic sectors 7, 8, 25, 42, 171, 193
economies, core 20, 39, 41–2, 44–8, 50, 54, 58–60, 170–2
economy, subsistence 2; energy base 20, 39, 42, 44, 170; urban 20; world 20, 39, 42, 134
education 14, 15, 34, 50, 60, 67–8, 70, 73, 79, 82–8, 90–1, 93–5, 98–103, 106–8, 113, 118, 131, 138, 145, 184
Elbe 12, 20, 22
elections 128, 141, 144, 146, 150–1, 154–65, 199
electoral change 162–5
elites 3, 4, 7, 15, 21, 26, 30, 68–9, 71, 76–7, 79–81, 83, 89, 90, 94, 96–7, 103, 105, 107, 109–10, 130, 132, 135, 139, 147, 169, 172, 197
empires 11, 21–3, 27–8, 31–2, 34–7, 39, 51, 73, 75, 92, 97, 193, 199
England 27, 31, 39, 54, 57, 62, 71, 74–5, 96, 128, 139, 187, 194, 196; language 72
ethnicity 21–4, 66, 90, 95, 121–2, 152, 160
European Economic Community 46–8, 146, 174–5, 199
Extremadura 54, 56, 196

Faeroes 23, 62, 79–83, 125, 130, 143; language 72
federalism 17, 37, 70, 76, 78, 84, 87, 90–1, 141, 143, 153, 181–8
feudalism 25, 95
feudalization 25
Finland 10, 23, 29–31, 36, 38, 41, 44, 46, 62, 79–81, 125, 139, 160, 182, 188, 198; cities 10; economy 46, 58; language 72, 81, 145, 156
Flanders 27–8, 34, 61, 74, 79, 93, 96, 127, 143, 145, 155–6, 170, 185–6, 191, 197; economy 50, 74, 83, 135–6, 140; language 72, 83, 131; parties 149, 154; religion 83
France 5, 6, 8–13, 27–8, 31, 34, 36–7, 41, 44, 46, 48, 51, 59, 62–3, 67, 71, 75, 86, 92, 96–106, 110, 112, 120–1, 127, 143–4, 146, 148, 153–5, 161, 169, 175, 182, 186–7, 193–4, 197–9; cities 8–12; decentralization 122, 186–7; economy 46, 51, 53; education 68; language 68, 72, 74, 108, 112–13; parties 5, 122, 168; Third Republic 5, 74, 98–9
Franche Comté 53, 103
Frankfurt 13
French Revolution 5, 27, 33, 38–9, 74–5, 79, 96, 98, 102, 106, 111–12, 119–20
Friesland 23, 29, 50, 61–2, 74, 79, 125, 136, 143–4; language 72, 86
Friuli 29, 54–5, 61–2, 100, 127, 136, 143; language 72, 101
Front Démocratique des Francophones 127, 136, 155, 160, 163–4, 199
Frysk Nasjonale Partÿ 125, 144, 154

Gaelic 72, 89, 90, 95, 197
Gaelic League 88
Galicia 54, 56, 61–2, 64, 73, 92–3, 127, 136, 143, 151, 153; attitudes in 148, 152–3; language 72, 87, 92, 97
Geneva 52, 195

Genoa 100
geoeconomic location 8, 16, 19, 42–8, 63–4, 92, 129, 134
geopolitical location 7, 16, 17, 19, 28–30, 48, 61–5, 92, 124–30, 146
Germanic tribes 20, 22
Germany 12, 28–9, 31–2, 34, 51, 62, 65, 71, 86, 101–2, 106, 108, 155; Democratic Republic 36, 38, 44, 194, 198; Federal Republic 8–13, 36, 38, 40–1, 45, 47–8, 59, 65, 125, 146, 157, 159, 175, 182–3, 188, 190, 194, 198–9; economy 45–6, 49, 50, 171; language 72, 75–6; North German Federation 39; Second Reich 12, 38, 42, 155
Graubünden: *see* Grisons
Greek 26, 69, 87
Grisons 29, 51–2, 62, 77, 90–1, 126, 143
gross regional product 46–7, 171
Gutenberg 26, 33, 69

Habsburgs 27, 29, 37–9, 73–4, 101, 104
Halland 29, 62
Hamburg 47–9, 51, 193
Hochdeutsch 29, 72, 76, 86–7, 102
Holland 50, 74, 86, 194, 196
Holy Roman Empire 22, 28, 74
Hungary 23, 29, 31, 39, 62, 65, 199

Iceland 9, 23, 31, 36, 62, 79, 80, 125, 130, 182; language 72, 81–2
ideology 4, 15, 34, 38, 68, 74, 115, 141–2, 144
Île de France 8, 37, 74, 97, 112
imperialism 6, 12, 14, 198
income 40, 48, 50–1, 56, 171, 194
industrialization 42, 46, 83–5, 109, 111, 119, 137–8, 143, 152, 172, 174
Industrial Revolution 39, 42, 64, 69, 70, 74, 88, 90, 137, 152
industry 11, 49–53, 55–9, 99, 111, 159, 171, 174
infrastructures 12–14, 24, 65, 69, 81, 103, 112, 117, 129, 132, 148, 173–5
institutions, identity-maintaining 62, 87, 90, 117, 131–2, 134
integration 5, 14, 15, 18, 32, 74, 77, 90, 96, 118–19, 121, 141, 151, 175, 181, 188
investment 4, 12, 172–5
Ireland 23, 31, 33, 36, 62, 65, 74–5, 87, 90, 98, 111, 169, 182, 184, 195, 200; language 72, 75, 87–9, 97; religion 89
Irish nationalists 128, 155, 157, 163–4
irredentism 30, 105, 141, 143, 145
Islam 11, 22, 24, 35, 71, 78, 113
Italy 1–12, 23, 28–9, 31–2, 36–7, 41, 44–5, 54, 61, 71, 87, 91, 100–1, 104–5, 156, 172, 182, 184, 186, 188, 193, 198–9; cities 10, 11; decentralization 184–5; economy 46–7, 54–5; language 29, 72, 75–6, 100, 108

Jacobins 74, 96–7, 99, 120, 122
journalists 6, 133
Jura 28, 61–2, 79, 90, 93, 126, 140, 143, 148, 151–2, 156, 168, 183–4, 190–1, 198; economy 84, 136, 161; language 72, 83–4; religion 83–4, 151, 158
Jutland 51, 149, 159, 198

labour 4, 32, 84, 96, 100, 135, 175, 178
Labour Party, United Kingdom 138–9, 151, 159, 168–9
Ladins 72, 100
landlords: *see* aristocracy
landownership 25–6, 33, 89
languages 14, 21–2, 26, 28–9, 33, 67–117, 131, 138, 151, 155
langue d'Oc 28, 96, 98, 197
Languedoc-Roussillon 51, 53, 97
Lapps 62, 72, 94–5, 125, 143
Latin 21, 24, 26, 69, 75, 87
Latin America 193
Lazio 54–5
legitimacy 26, 68, 83, 87, 119, 122, 124, 166–7
Lia Rumantscha 91
Liberal Party, Belgium 168; Spain 92; United Kingdom 138, 151, 167
Limousin 51, 53, 197

Lisbon 73
literacy 69, 79, 88, 98–9, 197
Lithuania 23, 33, 62
Liverpool 128, 193
Loi Deixonne 98, 100, 106
Lombardy 23, 55, 62, 104
London 12, 13, 54, 57–8, 138–9, 150, 193
Lorraine 28, 53, 103
Low Countries 50, 73
Lower Saxony 29
Lutheranism: *see* Protestantism
Luxembourg 28, 34, 36, 79, 86–7, 103, 105; language 72, 86

Madrid 12, 37, 54, 56, 92, 139, 150–1, 193–4
marchlands, eastern 23, 28–9, 32–3, 37–8, 62–3, 76, 125
markets 2, 7, 15, 37, 42, 69, 88, 96, 114, 134; labour 69, 70, 74, 83–4, 88, 91, 93–6, 98–9, 108, 111, 117
Marseilles 51, 97, 193, 195
mass media 85–6, 91, 94, 102, 108, 110–11, 118, 137–8, 162, 177, 197
Mediterranean 11, 20, 23–4, 27, 35, 37, 51, 61–2, 97, 105, 127
Mezzogiorno 134, 199, 200
Middle Ages 11, 20–1, 23–4, 26, 33, 62–3, 65, 73–4, 82, 93, 104, 187, 195–6
middle classes: *see* bourgeoisie
Milan 193
mobilization 30, 37, 79, 82, 84, 87, 105, 107, 118, 120, 155, 159, 169, 189; aims and strategy 140–54; context 119–24; peripheral 15, 17, 61, 90, 116, 154–65, 167, 172, 176, 186, 191, 196
monarchy 24, 27, 29–30, 34, 38, 129
monetarization 5, 15, 32
monocephality 7, 35–41, 50, 129, 179, 186
Moscow 193
Movimento de Friuli 127, 154–5
Munich 12, 193
Muslims: *see* Islam
myths 4, 67

Naples 62, 193
Napoleon 27, 38
nationalism 33–4, 38–9, 67, 81–3, 91, 113, 120, 131, 140, 146–7, 159, 161, 186–7
nation-building 26, 30, 33–4, 37, 68, 112, 120, 123, 180–3, 188
nation-state 20, 36, 63, 74, 96, 113–14, 118–19, 136, 189
Navarre 62, 127, 196
Netherlands 10, 11, 27, 29, 31–2, 36–8, 41, 45, 48, 62, 71, 75, 86, 125, 182, 199; cities 10, 11, 39, 40, 73; economy 45–6, 50; language 72–4, 86; religion 73–4
networks 2, 5, 7, 11–13, 15, 16, 25, 37, 40, 42, 64, 68, 74, 99, 107, 114, 132, 134, 162
Nice 28, 104–5, 197
nomadism 20, 25, 94
Normandy 51, 122, 197
Northern Ireland 57, 61, 67, 88–9, 111, 114, 126, 130–1, 136, 143, 147, 150, 152, 155, 187, 191, 198
North-Rhine Westphalia 48
North Sea 11, 12, 22, 28, 39, 51, 139–40
Norway 10, 11, 13, 22, 31, 36, 38, 40–1, 44, 62, 79, 80, 86–7, 144, 169, 175, 182; cities 10, 11; economy 45–6, 58, 60; language 72, 81–2, 97, 108, 196

Occitania 23, 28, 34, 61–2, 97, 111, 126, 136, 143, 196–7, 199; language 72, 97–8
opportunity structures 3, 68, 70, 152
Orthodox Church 33
Oslo 13
Ostrobothnia 62, 81

Pacta Democratico de Catalunya 127, 154, 156, 160
Pacte d'Egmont 185
Paris 8, 9, 12, 13, 53, 103, 146, 186, 193, 195
Partido Nacionalista Vasco 127, 154, 156
parties 120, 122, 125, 128, 130, 138–9, 141, 144, 146, 148–9, 151, 154–65, 167–70, 189–91

Partito de Azione de Sardegna 126, 155
party systems 70, 119, 125, 130, 141, 151, 161, 163, 167–8, 191
peasants 82, 87–8, 97, 99, 102, 197
peripherality 2–6, 14, 16
peripheries, enclave 29, 51, 61; external 30, 32, 48, 51, 54, 61, 63–4, 77, 93–4, 99, 100, 129–30, 134, 145–6, 152; failed centre 28, 32, 61, 63, 97; geopolitical location 2, 3, 28–30, 48, 61–5; interface 28–30, 32, 48, 50–1, 54, 61–4, 71, 77, 97, 100–7, 111, 115, 125, 129–30, 134, 139, 145–6, 152, 168; typologies 6, 16, 28–30, 32, 48, 61
Picardy 53, 122, 197
Piedmont 27, 37, 62, 91, 104, 126
Plaid Cymru 125, 128, 145, 147, 151, 157–8, 161, 163–4, 168–9
planning 170–9
plebiscites 106–7
Poland 23, 29, 31, 35, 44, 62
policies, economic 134, 139, 170–9, 191
political violence 89, 92, 105, 142, 146, 150, 153, 184, 200
politicization 17, 70, 117–65
polycephality 7, 11, 35–41, 50, 75, 129, 179–80, 186
Portugal 23, 31, 36, 62, 71–3, 75, 93, 182, 196
primacy, first city 9–11, 39, 41, 193
printing, invention of 24, 26, 74, 111, 120
Protestantism 26, 31–4, 62, 69, 76, 83–5, 89, 95, 125, 151–2, 157–8, 187
Provence 27, 37, 62, 98
Prussia 12, 20, 23, 27, 29, 31, 34, 38–9, 62, 76, 106, 194

railways 12, 13, 104
rank-size step 8, 9, 39, 40
Rassemblement Jurassien 126, 144, 148, 156, 161, 198
Rassemblement Wallon 127, 136, 140, 159, 163–4
Reconquista 78
Reformation 20, 24, 26, 30, 33, 62, 73, 75, 82, 85–7, 95, 111, 127, 196
regional autonomy 91, 93, 101, 104–5, 131–2, 135, 141, 143–4, 153, 178, 184 (*see also* decentralization, devolution)
religion 15, 24, 67, 81, 83, 85, 89, 113, 130–1, 137, 156–7 (*see also* churches)
resources 2, 6, 12, 14, 24–5, 27, 32–3, 37, 40, 48, 94, 96, 124–35, 173, 177, 179, 183, 191
revolution 27, 96, 121, 136
Rhaeto-Romansch 23, 29, 72, 77, 87, 90–1, 100
Rhineland 12, 13, 27, 31, 38, 42, 48, 62, 194
Risorgimento 38, 75
Rome 20–1, 24–7, 33, 37, 101, 175, 184, 188, 193; empire 11, 21–3, 28, 73
Rotterdam 193
Roussillon 53, 61, 72, 96, 106, 126, 143, 199
Ruhr 12, 193–4
Russia 38, 44, 80, 136, 194

Saarland 106
Sardinia 23, 55, 61–2, 87, 91, 100, 126, 136, 143, 184; language 72, 91
Savoy 28, 53, 61–2, 104, 106, 143, 186, 197
Scandinavia 27, 61, 94, 160, 196
Scania 29, 62, 73, 196
Schleswig 29, 49–51, 62, 106–7, 121, 125, 136, 139, 143; language 72, 156
schools: *see* education
Scotland 23, 28, 31, 57–8, 61–2, 74, 78, 85, 87, 89, 90, 95, 109, 111, 117, 125, 131, 138–40, 143, 151, 153, 155, 157–60, 168, 187, 196; attitudes in 153, 160; economy 89, 90, 95, 135–6, 161; language 89, 90, 95; religion 158
Scottish National Party 125, 128, 140, 154–5, 157–61, 163–4, 168–9, 199
secularization 33, 65, 119
Serbia 23, 62, 194
Silesia 42

size, territorial 94, 123, 130
Slavs 20, 22, 29
Slesvig Parti 125, 136, 139, 147, 149, 156, 159–60, 163–4
Slovakia 62
Slovenia 23, 62, 101
Social Democrat Party, Denmark 169
socialism 159
Socialist Party, Belgium 168–9; Catalonia 160; France 186; Spain 156, 161
socialization 33, 67–8
South Tyrol: *see* Alto Adige
sovereignty 38, 80, 87, 119, 194
Spain 27, 31, 33–4, 36–7, 44–5, 54, 61–2, 76–7, 91–2, 97, 143, 148, 151–4, 160, 171, 175, 182, 188; decentralization 187, 196; economy 44, 54, 56; language 72, 77–8, 92–3, 108
standardization, cultural 3, 4, 14–16, 24, 30, 33, 35, 68, 132–3, 135, 138, 179, 186
state-building 25–8, 30, 32, 34–5, 40, 62–3, 68, 73, 93, 104, 120, 123, 136, 138, 179–83, 195
Stockholm 12, 58, 198
subsidies 4, 64, 91, 134, 174–5
Sudetenland 29, 62
Südschleswigscher Wahlerverband 125, 139, 156, 163–4
Südtiroler Volkspartei 127, 136, 139, 149, 154, 156, 163–4, 190
suffrage 70, 79, 138, 151
Svenska Folkparti 125, 128, 139, 151, 154–6, 159–60, 163–4, 189–90
Sweden 10, 11, 23, 27, 29–31, 36, 38, 41–2, 44–5, 54, 62, 71, 74–5, 80, 144, 175, 182, 196–7, 199; cities 10, 11; economy 45–6, 58–9; education 73; language 72–3, 115
Swedish Finns 81, 128, 151, 154–6, 160, 164, 198
Switzerland 8, 10, 11, 13, 27, 31–2, 34, 41, 51, 62, 75–8, 83–4, 87, 90, 104, 111, 145, 169, 183–4, 188; cities 8, 10, 11; economy 51–2; language 72, 76–7, 87, 108

Toulouse 28
trade 2, 5, 7, 11, 16, 21, 26–7, 30, 32–3, 35, 37, 42, 63, 70, 76, 78, 120, 129
transportation 7, 11–13
Trentino-Alto Adige: *see* Alto Adige
Trondheim 13, 58
Turin 91, 104, 193
Turkey 4

unemployment 56, 58
Union Democratico de Centro 151
Union Démocratique Bretonne 126, 154, 199
Union Valdôtaine 126, 156, 163–4
United Kingdom 9–11, 36, 41, 44–5, 48, 54, 78, 85, 96, 110, 151, 155, 172, 175, 182, 187–8, 199, 200; cities 10, 11; decentralization 187; economy 46, 54, 57–8; language 74, 85–6; parties 128, 138–9, 168
urbanization 30, 32, 48, 59, 70, 82, 98, 110, 119 (*see also* cities)

Val d'Aosta 28, 54–5, 61, 126, 136, 143, 149, 154, 184; language 72, 104
Valencia 97, 153
vernacularization 25–6, 30, 69, 75, 97, 120
Vienna 12, 37, 193
Vikings 22
Volksunie 127, 140, 145, 154–5, 160, 163–4, 199

Wales 23, 31, 57–8, 61–2, 74, 79, 86, 92, 96, 99, 111, 125, 131, 143, 151, 155, 158–9, 168, 187, 196; economy 136; language 72, 85–6, 151, 157–8
Wallonia 28, 34, 50, 61, 127, 143, 159, 168, 170, 185–6, 197, 200; economy 50, 136, 161
wars 4, 20, 38, 65, 82, 92, 106, 141
welfare state 137, 191
workers 69, 83, 97, 102, 160–1
World War I 29, 105–6, 121, 197–8
World War II 29, 44, 83–6, 95, 102

Yugoslavia 29, 36–7, 44–6, 101, 198

Zurich 52

About the Authors

Stein Rokkan was Professor of Political Sociology at the University of Bergen until his death in 1979. He had also served as President of the International Political Science Association, President of the International Social Science Council, and was the first Chairman of the European Consortium for Political Research. His many publications on European politics include *Party Systems and Voter Alignments* (with S.M. Lipset); *Quantitative Ecological Analysis* (with M. Dogan); *Mass Politics* (with E. Allardt); *Citizens, Elections, Parties*; and *Building States and Nations* (with S.N. Eisenstadt).

Derek Urwin is Professor of Politics at the University of Warwick. Until 1980 he was Associate Professor of Comparative Politics at the University of Bergen. He has been editor of *Scandinavian Political Studies,* and is currently co-editor of the *European Journal of Political Research.* His several publications on European politics include *Scottish Political Behaviour* (with I. Budge); *Western Europe Since 1945*; and *From Ploughshare to Ballotbox.*